19th Industrial Conference on Advances in Data Mining (ICDM 2019)

Poster Proceedings

New York, New York, USA
17-21 July 2019

Editors:

Petra Perner

ISBN: 978-1-5108-9518-8

Printed from e-media with permission by:

Curran Associates, Inc.
57 Morehouse Lane
Red Hook, NY 12571

CURRAN ASSOCIATES INC. proceedings.com

Some format issues inherent in the e-media version may also appear in this print version.

ibai-publishing
Arno-Nitzsche-Str. 45
04277 Leipzig, Germany

info@ibai-publishing.org

Additional copies of this publication are available from:

Curran Associates, Inc.
57 Morehouse Lane
Red Hook, NY 12571 USA
Phone: 845-758-0400
Fax: 845-758-2633
Email: curran@proceedings.com
Web: www.proceedings.com

Table of Content

Petra Perner (Ed.)

Advances in Data Mining

Applications and Theoretical Aspects

19th Industrial Conference on Data Mining, ICDM 2019
New York, USA, July 17 – July 21, 2019

Poster Proceedings

ibai Publishing
www.ibai-publishing.org

Petra Perner (Ed.)

Advances in Data Mining

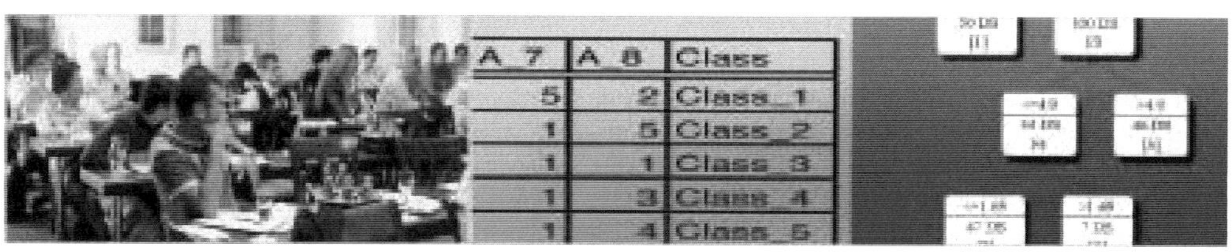

19th Industrial Conference, ICDM 2019
New York, USA, July 17-21 2019

Poster Proceedings

ibai - publishing

Preface

The nineteenth event of the Industrial Conference on Data Mining ICDM was held in New York (www.data-mining-forum.de) running under the umbrella of the World Congress on "The Frontiers in Intelligent Data and Signal Analysis, DSA 2019" (www.worldcongressdsa.com).

After the peer-review process, we accepted 39 high-quality papers for oral presentation, which are published in the ICDM Proceeding by ibai-publishing (www.ibai-publishing.org. The topics range from theoretical aspects of data mining to applications of data mining, such as in multimedia data, in marketing, in medicine, and in process control, industry, and society. Extended versions of selected papers will appear in the international journal *Transactions on Machine Learning and Data Mining* (www.ibai-publishing.org/journal/mldm).

In all, twenty one papers were selected for poster presentations, which are published in the ICDM Poster Proceeding by ibai-publishing (www.ibai-publishing.org.

A tutorial on Data Mining and a tutorial on Case-Based Reasoning were held after the conference.

The conference was running in an inspiring atmosphere. The presenters of the oral presentations gave excellent talks and the audience acknowledged each talk with excellent questions. The poster presenters presented well prepared posters and gave in front of their posters a summary of their work in five minutes for the audiences. Afterwards the audience could step to the poster that they were interested in. The audience had a lot of questions and they gave valuable comments and new directions for the work in progress. In all was the poster session a very successful session.

We would like to thank all reviewers for their highly professional work and their effort in reviewing the papers.

We also thank the members of the Institute of Applied Computer Sciences, Leipzig, Germany (www.ibai-institut.de), who handled the conference as secretariat. We appreciate the help and understanding of the ibai-publishing publishing house (www.ibai-publishing.org) that handled the papers and published the proceedings.

Last, but not least, we wish to thank all the speakers and participants who contributed to the success of the conference. We hope to see you in 2020 in New York at the next World Congress on "The Frontiers in Intelligent Data and Signal Analysis, DSA 2020" (www.worldcongressdsa.com), which combines under its roof the following three events: International Conferences Machine Learning and Data Mining MLDM (www.mldm.de) , the Industrial Conference on Data Mining ICDM (www.data-mining-forum.de), and the International Conference on Mass Data Analysis of Signals and Images in Artificial Intelligence and Pattern Recognition with Applications in Medicine, Biotechnology, Chemistry and Food Industry, MDA-AI&PR (www.mda-signals.de).

July 2019 Petra Perner

Volume Editor

Petra Perner
Institute of Computer Vision and Applied Computer Sciences, IBaI
PF 30 11 14
04251 Leipzig
E-mail: pperner@ibai-institut.de

19th Industrial Conference on Data Mining ICDM 2019

www.data-mining-forum.de
July 17 – 21, 2019, New York, USA

Chair

Prof. Dr. Petra Perner
Institute of Computer Vision and applied Computer Sciences, IBaI

Program Committee

Ajith Abraham	Machine Intelligence Research Labs (MIR Labs), USA
Mohamed, Bourguessa	Universite du Quebec a Montreal - UQAM, Canada
Bernard Chen	University of Central Arkansas, USA
Jeroen de Bruin	University of Applied Sciences JOANNEUM, Austria
Antonio Dourado	University of Coimbra, Portugal
Stefano Ferilli	University of Bari, Italy
Geert Gins	Glaxo Smith Kline, Belgium
Warwick Graco	Australian Tax Office ATO, Australia
Aleksandra Gruca	Silesian University of Technology, Poland
Pedro Isaias	The University of Queensland, Australia
Piotr Jedrzejowicz	Gdynia Maritime University, Poland
Martti Juhola	University of Tampere, Finland
Janusz Kacprzyk	Polish Academy of Sciences, Poland
Mehmed Kantardzic	University of Louisville, USA
Lui Xiaobing	Google Inc., USA
Eduardo F. Morales	National Institute of Astrophysics, Optics, and Electronics, Mexico
Samuel Noriega	Universitat de Barcelona, Spain
Wieslaw Paja	University of Rzeszow, Poland
Juliane Perner	Novartis Institutes for BioMedical Research (NIBR), Switzerland
Rainer Schmidt	University of Rostock, Germany
Moti Schneider	PCCW Global, Greece
Victor Sheng	University of Central Arkansas, USA
Kaoru Shimada	Fukuoka Dental College, Japan
Gero Szepannek	University of Applied Sciences Stralsund, Germany
Joao Miguel Costa Sousa	Technical University of Lisbon, Portugal
Markus Vattulainen	Tampere University, Finnland
Zhu Bing	Sichuan University, China

The LuNa Open Toolbox for the Luxembourgish Language

Joshgun Sirajzade and Christoph Schommer

University of Luxembourg
Dept of Computer Science and Communication, ILIAS Lab
Campus Belval, Maison du Nombre,
L-4365 Esch-sur-Alzette, Luxembourg

Abstract. Despite some recent work [17, p. 5], the ongoing research for the processing of Luxembourgish is still largely in its infancy. While a rich variety of linguistic processing tools exist, especially for English, these software tools offer little scope for the Luxembourgish language. LuNa (a Tool for Luxembourgish National Corpus) is an Open Toolbox that allows researchers to annotate a text corpus written in Luxembourgish language and to build/query an annotated corpus. The aim of the paper is to demonstrate the components of the system and its usage for Machine Learning applications like Topic Modelling and Sentiment Detection. Overall, LuNa bases on a XML-database to store the data and to define the *XML* scheme, it offers a Graphical User Interface (GUI) for a linguistic data preparation such as tokenization, Part-Of-Speech tagging, and morphological analysis – just to name a few.

1 Introduction

Luxembourgish is one of the youngest languages of Europe and is a native language for ca. half a million people [7]. Despite the fact that it has more written and digital sources in comparison to other languages of its size, its research is relatively sparse set by side to its neighboring languages like French or German. The same applies to the building of an universal annotated corpus of Luxembourgish, which can be used in research projects, as well as in NLP applications of various kinds. The aim of LuNa is to make a contribution to compiling a corpus for a language with lack of resources, which is also the case for Luxembourgish language.

LuNa's functionality is to tokenize and to standardize a text written in Luxembourgish, e.g., if orthographic variations for words appear. Additionally, LuNa foresees a tagging of words using a POS Tagger. To analyze a text, LuNa supports the search of word formation affixes as well as the annotation of them as such. In the context of the annotation process of word formation affixes, some other analysis can be carried out, for example the analysis of morphological productivity, or the search of the stems of the words with word formation suffixes in the entire corpus [18]. Also, LuNa offers a simple lemmatization for the Luxembourgish language. Several approaches have been investigated, and a hybrid (rule-based and statistical) lemmatizer is chosen because of its prominent performance for Luxembourgish language. Beside data processing components, first implementations in view of a sentiment analysis and topic modeling exist.

2 Implementation

The backbone of the system bases on a XML-Database eXist[1] (v4.6), which is run on an Ubuntu 14.4 Server. The corpus stored in this database is structured in *TEI-Format* (Text Encoding Initiative, vP5). The frontend consists of an application programmed in Java (v1.8). LuNa can act as a standalone application to process a XML-corpus or as a software client, which operates with the XML-Database.

2.1 Graphical User Interface

The following section describe parts of LuNa's components. A video about LuNa is available here[2].

2.2 TEI

The Text Encoding Initiative (*TEI*) is a kind of *XML* dialect for the organization and structurization of text data. The plain benefit of using *TEI* lies in the fact that it is standardized and well-documented. Thus, it is a format for exchanging data among project participants and external collaborators.

The downside of *TEI* is that *XML* takes more storage space than, e.g., *JSON*. *TEI* has guidelines for organizing metadata of the text and for structuring different kinds of text genres – in particular manuscripts, interviews, and transcription of speeches. This is useful, if a representative corpus of a language is to be build. Below, there is an extract of a header of the poem 'D'Lidd vum Jengsterdag' (English: *the song of yesterday* from Michel Rodange (1827-1876)):

```
<TEI>
 ...
 <titleStmt>
    <title type="main">D'Lidd vum Jengsterdag</title>
    <title type="sub"/>
     <title type="short">D'Lidd</title>
   <author>
    <forename>Michel</forename>
    <nameLink/>
    <surname>Rodange</surname>
    <addName type="pseudonym"/>
   </author>
   <editor>
```

[1] http://exist-db.org/exist/apps/homepage/index.html, last seen on July 17, 2019
[2] https://youtu.be/iLwz8DeJUoI

```
      <forename>Fernand</forename>
      <surname>Hoffmann</surname>
      </editor>
    </titleStmt>
  <publicationStmt>
    <publisher/>
    <pubPlace/>
    <date>1964</date>
  </publicationStmt>
  ...
</TEI>
```

2.3 XML-Database eXist

The XML-database *eXist* (v4.6) is used to manage the data. *eXist* has many in-build tools – such as the browser based IDE eXide (Figure 1) and the standalone Java Admin Client– and is open for public.

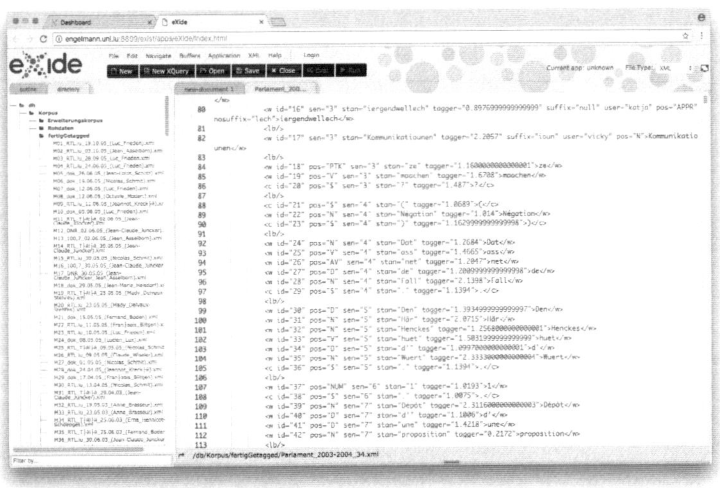

Fig. 1. eXide is a browser based editor provided by eXist. So, LuNa corpus can be viewed with this tool over the internet.

2.4 Tokenization

Luxembourgish texts have different kinds of spelling. Additionally, problems sometimes occur in preprocessing, because some writing applications or computers use different language settings. Thus, when the spelling seems to be correct, some characters are different according to their unicode encoding. As an example for the last case we name the Luxembourgish article, which can be joined to the following neutral and feminine nouns, like in *d'Wielerin* (English: voter) or *d'Opschwong (English: boost, boom, revival).* Different Applications from where our Luxembourgish texts are coming have different characters for apostrophes. Therefore, all versions of used apostrophes should be specified in the parameter for word delimiters (Figure 2). Low data quality can sometimes influence the research outcomes in a negative way.

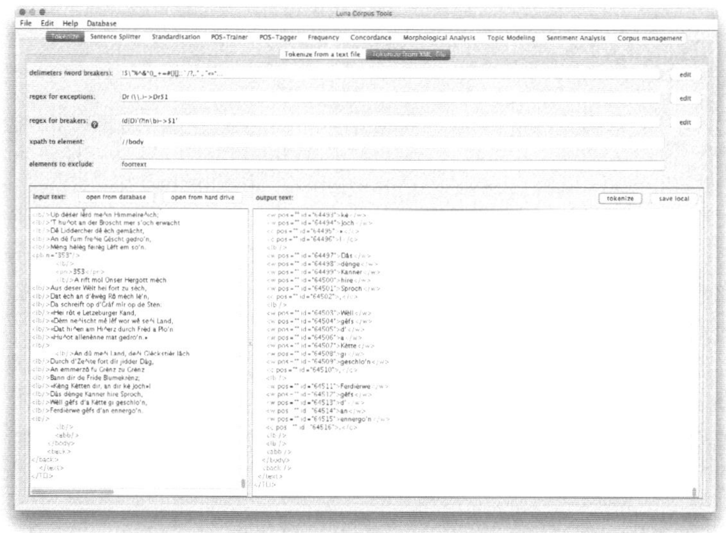

Fig. 2. XML-Tokenizer: Parameters like delimiters for tokenizing can be adjusted. Characters, which can be ambiguous, can be formulated as regular expression, in order to build exceptions.

2.5 Splitting the sentences

Similar to the question what a token is (at least formally) and accordingly how to tokenize a text, there are some debates about splitting the texts into the sentences [13, p. 166]. Without going into details of syntax research and asking for a definition of a sentence or a syntactical unit, it is crucial to point out the benefits of having this kind of information. LuNa uses sentence boundaries a lot, in building concordance lines, POS-tagging, morphological analysis, etc. The tools are delivering better results, if they are using sentence boundaries to carry out further processing, because it is a natural unit for syntactical relationships. The usage of sentence positions in POS-tagging will be discussed bellow. As

Figure 2.5 indicates, the parameter for sentence boundaries – a list of characters that divide sentences – can be specified in the GUI.

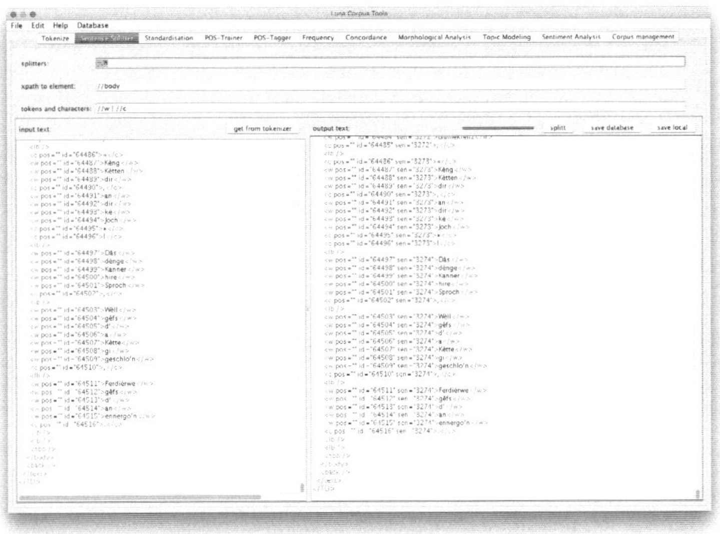

Fig. 3. Sentence splitter: Characters, which can denote sentence borders, can be adjusted. Each sentence gets an attribute, which signals its belonging to a certain sentence.

2.6 Normalization (Standardization)

Text normalization plays a crucial role in text mining, which is represented in the third tab in GUI of LuNa. Like the situation with English words *center* and *centre*, Luxembourgish also contains such variations for many words. However, comparing to English, it is particularly difficult in Luxembourgish text to deal with these variations. On the one hand there is no sufficient amount of text in Luxembourgish to support an automatic retrieval of these variations. On the other hand writing in Luxembourgish has not been fully standardized (also in comparison to German and French languages) for a long time. The official orthography of the Luxembourgish language is relatively young. The situation for the LuNa is peculiar for two reasons: First if one has literature or text in Luxembourgish language that are already older than lets say 50 years, you will already find many differences in spelling. Secondly, the aim of LuNa, is not only its usage in building big research corpora, but also to be used by others, like to be deployed behind language applications. And in such cases a good system for standardisation is very important. LuNa uses for that a table, which can hold regular expressions for normalizing the data (see Figure 4). The original text stays as always untouched in LuNa, and a new annotation is added with normalized versions for carrying out searches and other investigations. This is because some of the users might indeed be interested in spelling variations. By doing so, no information is lost. Searching *center* may reveal that in some texts *centre* occurs.

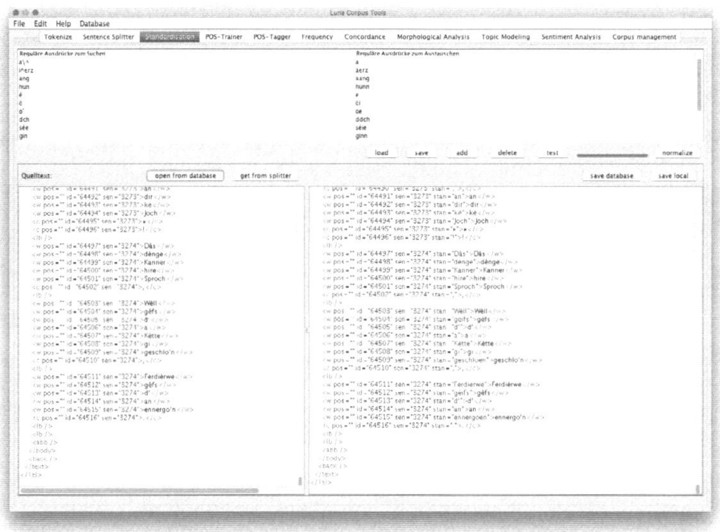

Fig. 4. Text Normalization in LuNa: A list of regular expressions can be specified, in order to normalize the text. The normalized forms are again added as attributes, so the original forms are not lost.

2.7 POS-tagging

Annotating a corpus with part of speeches is one of the most widely used methods in text mining, as well as in corpus linguistics. It is a crucial step for a wide range of tasks with various purposes. A vast amount of research has been carried out in this field and there are already many ready-to-use tools [13, p. 29]. Nevertheless the developers behind LuNa took the chance and the challenge to implement a new one. As there are many models available, it was easy to implement one. Mason[11] shows, how a tagger can be implemented in the programming language Java. Manning and Schütze[10, p. 341] discuss statistical backgrounds of taggers. The history of POS-Taggers began rule based with poor results. But they are performing better, since the machine learning algorithms are applied to them. Especially those like baayesian networks, decision trees and neuronal networks have been successfully applied in POS-tagging [14, 15]. And later on, the so called hybrid approach was introduced, which makes use of rules, where they are deterministic and classifying in all other cases. The developers of LuNa decided for baayesian statistics and decision trees, sine they are simple to implement and easy to understand. The intermediate results of a training process can be seen with the POS-Trainer component in LuNa (Figure 5). Such a functionality is beneficial for both research and application purposes. Users can repeat the calculations behind the algorithms to a certain point.

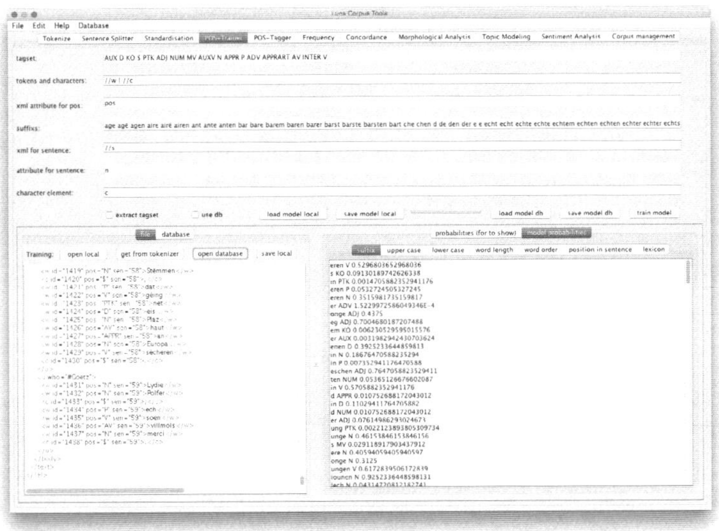

Fig. 5. POS Trainer: Here it is possible to choose training files and see the results of the training process. They are conditional probabilities for given feature. The model can be stored locally or into the database.

2.8 Other Features in POS Tagging

Approaching the problem from the linguistic point of view new features were added. LuNa uses not only the word order which is one of the most popular features used in POS-tagging, e.g. part of speeches like articles and adjectives are normally followed by a noun, but also uses the positions of the words in a sentence. This feature takes the information into account, which part of speeches are likely to occur in the first, second till the last position of the sentence. The reason of using positions is that for languages like Luxembourgish and German, the word order can be relatively flexible. These languages have more morphological means to express grammatical information than english such as declination of nouns. Because of the declination, one can change word order, but the subject and the object will still remain the same. Furthermore, in these Languages the positions for verbs can be at the end of a relatively long sentence. In this case,

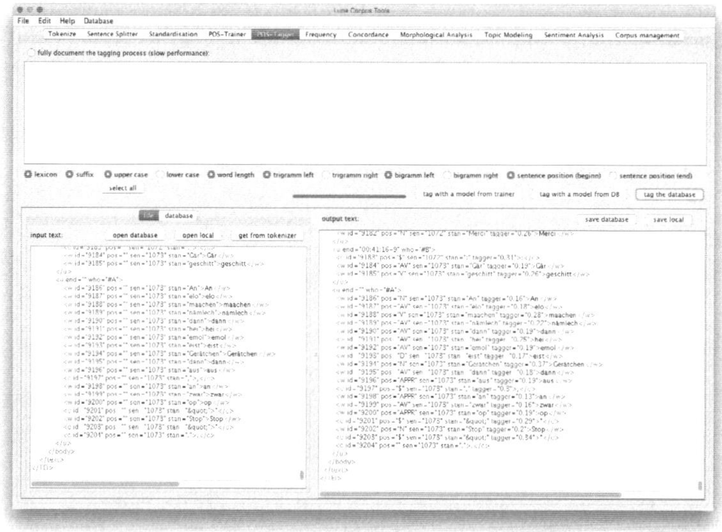

Fig. 6. POS-Tagger: The user can tag new texts with pre-trained models. It is also possible to choose between features to use.

the use of n-gramms is not always sufficient to capture such information. For this purpose, word positions in the sentence might be again very informative.

Another useful feature in Luxembourgish language is the so called 'upper case', because nouns are capitalized regardless of their positions in the sentence. Thus, this indicator is used to distinguish nouns from other word classes. (But this indicator is not useful for words appearing at the beginning of the sentence.) Besides, LuNa POS-Tagger uses rules, which are applied in two steps. 1) Before the tagging process, e.g. numbers are recognized as such or characters in a sentence. 2) After the tagging process. Here sometimes rules help to choose one candidate out of two possible ones. The features for the tagging can be selected in the GUI (Figure 6). After the tagging process the xml file has the following annotations.

```
<lb/>
<w pos="P" id="12" sen="3">Ech</w>
<w pos="V" id="13" sen="3">géing</w>
<w pos="D" id="14" sen="3">d'</w>
<w pos="N" id="15" sen="3">Regierung</w>
<w pos="V" id="16" sen="3">froen</w>
<c pos="$" id="17" sen="3">,</c>
<w pos="KO" id="18" sen="4">ob</w>
<w pos="P" id="19" sen="4">si</w>
<lb/>
<w pos="D" id="20" sen="4">iergendeng</w>
<w pos="N" id="21" sen="4">Kommunikatioun</w>
```

```
<w pos="APPR" id="22" sen="4">un</w>
<lb/>
<w pos="D" id="23" sen="4">d’</w>
<w pos="N" id="24" sen="4">Chamber</w>
<w pos="PTK" id="25" sen="4">ze</w>
<w pos="V" id="26" sen="4">maachen</w>
<w pos="V" id="27" sen="4">huet</w>
<c pos="$" id="28" sen="4">.</c>
<lb/>
```

2.9 Morphological Analysis

Morphological Analysis in LuNa concerns mainly the identifying and annotation of different affixes in the words. So far, the word formation affixes of Luxembourgish could be annotated successfully. Figure 2.9 shows how one can annotate the Luxembourgish prefix *on* in the words like *onbedéngt* (en. unconditionally), or *ongesond* (en. unhealthy). Annotating of morphological information can be useful for many reasons, especially in understanding of the structure of a language [18] or even in practical tasks like language generation etc.

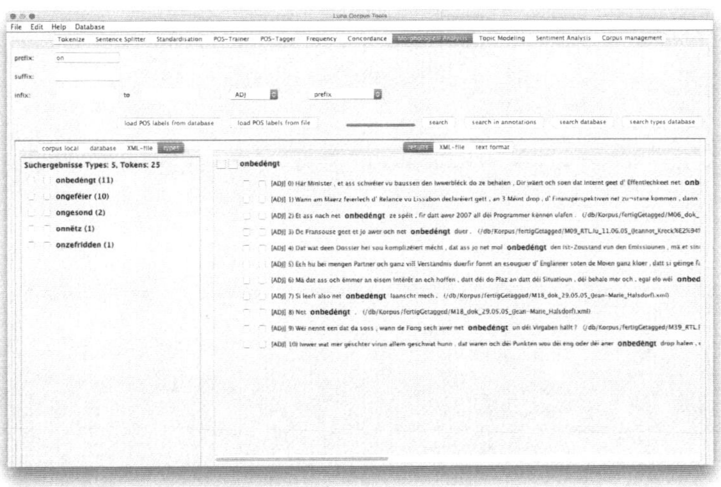

Fig. 7. Finding the tokens with the prefix *on* (en. *un* like in *uncertain*).

2.10 Exploring the Corpus

Under the tab Frequency an X-Path expression can be formulated, in order e.g. to see the frequent used words in the corpus. Because the corpus is well structured, it is possible to see the word counts per document or in the entire corpus, in order to carry out further analysis. The word counts can also be narrowed down to specific part-of-speeches, for example, it is possible to see the most used nouns or verbs. Figure 2.9 shows the extraction of frequent nouns from parliament speeches.

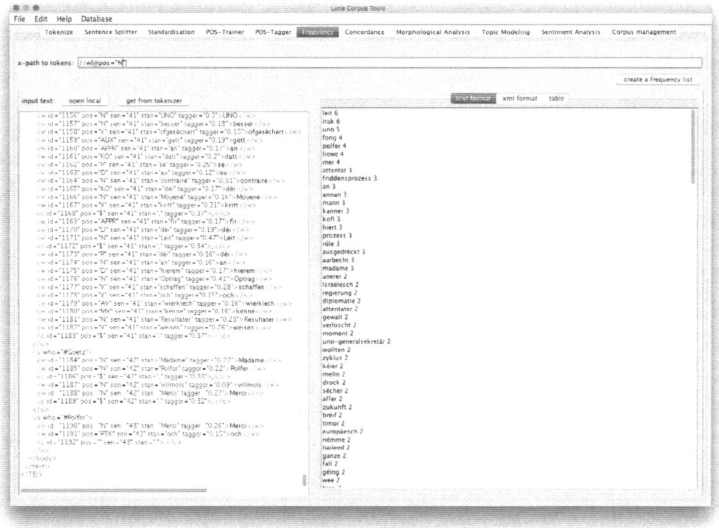

Fig. 8. Frequency analysis with x-path.

2.11 Topic Annotation

LuNa Corpus Tools integrates the ready to use java library MALLET (MAchine Learning for LanguagE Toolkit)[3], which has an implementation of various machine learning algorithms [12]. Luna uses MALLETs module for Topic Modeling, which is an implementation of Gibbs Sampling for Latent Drichlet Allocation [3, 19]. Topic Modeling has already been used successfully in many application cases, e.g. in financial news [16, 9]. [1] discusses the benefits of using topic annotation in corpus building. The obvious benefit of Topic Modeling for law resourced languages lies in its being a unsupervised technique. So, no labelled training set is needed. At the moment, LuNa is able to display the topics extracted from the corpus (Figure 9). The following xml file shows the first five topics with first five words in them extracted from parliament texts.

```
<topic>
```

[3] http://mallet.cs.umass.edu/, last seen on July 17, 2019

```
    <word rank="1" count="35.0">sécher</word>
    <word rank="2" count="16.0">verfassung</word>
    <word rank="3" count="12.0">géife</word>
    <word rank="4" count="12.0">eent</word>
    <word rank="5" count="12.0">hätten</word>
</topic>
<topic>
    <word rank="1" count="6.0">décidéiert</word>
    <word rank="2" count="2.0">fraktur</word>
    <word rank="3" count="2.0">statsfinanze</word>
    <word rank="4" count="2.0">wochen</word>
    <word rank="5" count="2.0">éischte</word>
</topic>
<topic>
    <word rank="1" count="13.0">weisen</word>
    <word rank="2" count="13.0">éischter</word>
    <word rank="3" count="10.0">bon</word>
    <word rank="4" count="8.0">ëffentlech</word>
    <word rank="5" count="8.0">hëllefen</word>
</topic>
<topic>
    <word rank="1" count="4.0">aféieren</word>
    <word rank="2" count="3.0">solle</word>
    <word rank="3" count="3.0">zil</word>
    <word rank="4" count="2.0">gesondheetspolitik</word>
    <word rank="5" count="2.0">populär</word>
</topic>
<topic>
    <word rank="1" count="3.0">schoulen</word>
    <word rank="2" count="3.0">suivi</word>
    <word rank="3" count="3.0">iwwerhaapt</word>
    <word rank="4" count="3.0">kéier</word>
    <word rank="5" count="2.0">iraneschen</word>
</topic>
```


2.12 Sentiment Detection

Some recent advances in sentiment analysis in various social platforms [6, 8] makes its application easy. There are attempts in building corpora with sentiment annotations and their linguistic description [20, 4, 5]. However, low resourced languages have special challenges, the accuracy may drop depending on the size of training data [2]. There is a tab with a functioning sentiment training and analysis in LuNa Corpus Tools. The concrete application case for sentiment analysis for Luxembourgish language emmerged from the collaboration with RTL. The RTL web presence began since the year 2008 allow readers to write commentaries on the news. After then more than half million commentaries are written on the RTL homepage for different news, articles and posts. Currently, LuNa uses the LibSVM[4] library, in order to classify the sentiments.


```
<sentence value="positive">
        <w id="97" pos="N" sen="7" tagger="0,2">Et</w>
        <w id="98" pos="AUX" sen="7" tagger="0,18">ginn</w>
        <w id="99" pos="PTK" sen="7" tagger="0,17">net</w>
        <w id="100" pos="AV" sen="7" tagger="0,15">nemmen</w>
        <w id="101" pos="N" sen="7" tagger="0,25">Jempi&apos;en</w>
        <w id="102" pos="AV" sen="7" tagger="0,23">hei</w>
        <w id="103" pos="APPRART" sen="7" tagger="0,16">am</w>
        <w id="104" pos="N" sen="7" tagger="0,56">Land</w>
        <c id="105" pos="$" sen="7" tagger="0,33">.</c>
</sentence>
<sentence value="positive">
        <w id="106" pos="P" sen="8" tagger="0,24">Et</w>
        <w id="107" pos="V" sen="8" tagger="0,26">gin</w>
        <w id="108" pos="AV" sen="8" tagger="0,15">och</w>
        <w id="109" pos="AV" sen="8" tagger="0,19">nach</w>
        <w id="110" pos="ADJ" sen="8" tagger="0,18" value="positive">gudd</w>
        <w id="111" pos="APPR" sen="8" tagger="0,12">an</w>
        <w id="112" pos="ADJ" sen="8" tagger="0,14" value="positive">diplômé&apos;ert</w>
        <w id="113" pos="N" sen="8" tagger="0,4">Studenten</w>
        <c id="114" pos="$" sen="8" tagger="0,31">.</c>
</sentence>
```


3 Tests

In the moment the corpus of Luxembourgish language is composed of two parts. The first part is the fully annotated part of the corpus. It provides rich meta data on the genre, date of origin, author(s) etc. The texts here are fully tokenized, normalized and POS-annotated. Currently this part has ca. 20 mio. running tokens. 10 mio. of these tokens belong to the transcriptions of speeches in the Luxembourgish Parliament (Chambre des Déptutés) from the year 2003 ongoing, divided in ca. 300 documents. Approximately 5 mio. tokens are gathered from the news from the web presence of RTL (Radio Télévision Luxembourg). These are mainly interviews. Furthermore, there is a part of corpus containing documents from Luxembourgish literature (literature in Luxembourgish language to be precise) with ca. 2.5 mio. running tokens. The rest is also interviews in the Luxembourgish language, but this time, carried out for research purposes at the university of Luxembourg. In the second part of the corpus there are some other 70 mio. token text data from the web presence of RTL, which are already digital and are going to be annotated. These data can be already used for several other purposes, fist of all for statistical analysis. Moreover, we are constantly provided

[4] https://www.csie.ntu.edu.tw/
cjlin/libsvm/, last seen on July 17, 2019

with new text data, which must be digitized in order to be used to enrich the corpus.

As mentioned before, using rules improves the performance of the tagger, especially in the case of low resourced languages. Trained with ca. 17 thousand pre-tagged tokens without the rules the tagger gives the accuracy of 87% with decision trees. Applying the mentioned rules improves the accuracy up to 92%, which is not good for languages like English or German, but seems to be sufficient considering the low resourced background of Luxembourgish language.

For Sentiment Analysis training the models with existing relative languages like German, does not help the performance much here. The same applies to the translation of existing English or German resources into Luxembourish, because due to lack of resources the translation in itself does not deliver good performance. That is why, the linguistic department of the university has decided to annotated sentiments manually. Currently, LuNa riches the accuracy of 67%, when trained with 2081 pre-labeled sentences. These sentences contain the classical notation for sentiments; *positive*, *neutral* and *negative*.

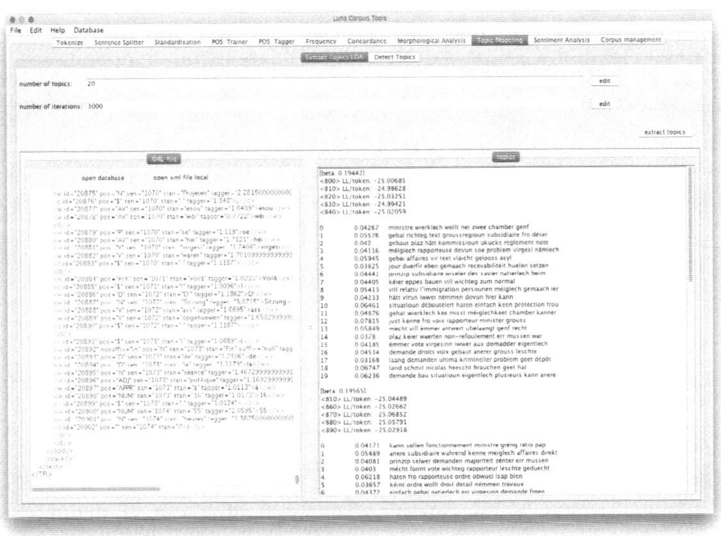

Fig. 9. Topic Modeling with Parliament text.

4 Conclusions and Future Work

LuNa has a strong decline to a corpus building. Many of the procedures like tokenization, normalization, POS-tagging, Lemmatization are a crucial steps in the processing of natural language. LuNa is currently applied in the processing of news messages (provided by RTL Luxembourg) as well as in the processing of users' comments. Working with such commentaries has its specific problems: firstly, the writing style is much more diverse than it is for the standard Luxembourgish language. Secondly, research fields like, e.g., Sentiment Analysis deliver consequently poor results in such low resourced languages. A training of the models with existing relative languages – like for example German – is not really supportative. The same applies to the translation of existing English or German resources into Luxembourgish, because due to lack of resources the translation in itself does not deliver good performance. Future work concern the support of research disciplines like Topic Modeling or Sentiment Analysis. It should be not only possible to extract Topics from the corpus, but also to store annotations for further usage.

References

1. Akira, M., Paul, T., Susan, H., Dominik, V.: 'what is this corpus about?': using topic modelling to explore a specialised corpus. Corpora **12**(2), 243–277 (2017)
2. Anh Le, T., Moeljadi, D., Miura, Y., Ohkuma, T.: Sentiment analysis for low resource languages: A study on informal indonesian tweets (12 2016)
3. Blei, D.M.: Probabilistic topic models. Commun. ACM **55**(4), 77–84 (Apr 2012)
4. Bolioli, A., Bosco, C., Patti, V.: Developing corpora for sentiment analysis: The case of irony and senti-tut. IEEE Intelligent Systems **28**, 55–63 (03 2013)
5. Bosco, C., Patti, V., Bolioli, A.: Developing corpora for sentiment analysis: The case of irony and senti-tut (extended abstract). In: Yang, Q., Wooldridge, M. (eds.) Proceedings of the Twenty-Fourth International Joint Conference on Artificial Intelligence, IJCAI 2015, Buenos Aires, Argentina, July 25-31, 2015. p. 4188. AAAI Press (2015), http://ijcai.org/Abstract/15/587
6. Feldman, R.: Techniques and applications for sentiment analysis. Commun. ACM **56**(4), 82–89 (Apr 2013)
7. Gilles, P.: Luxembourgish. In: Boas, H.C., Deumert, A., Louden, M. (eds.) Varieties of German Worldwide. Oxford University Press, Oxford (2018)
8. Guo, S., Höhn, S., Xu, F., Schommer, C.: Perseus: A personalization framework for sentiment categorization with recurrent neural network. In: International Conference on Agents and Artificial Intelligence, Funchal 16-18 January 2018. p. 9 (2018)
9. Kampas, D., Schommer, C., Sorger, U.: A hidden markov model to detect relevance in nancial documents based on on/off topics. In: European Conference on Data Analysis (2014)
10. Manning, C.D., Schütze, H.: Foundations of Statistical Natural Language Processing. MIT Press, Cambridge, MA, USA (1999)
11. Mason, O.: Programming for Corpus Linguistics. Edinburgh University Press (2001)
12. McCallum, A.K.: Mallet: A machine learning for language toolkit (2002), http://mallet.cs.umass.edu
13. McEnery, T., Hardie, A.: Corpus Linguistics : method, theory and practice. Cambridge Univ. Press, Cambridge (2011)
14. Schmid, H.: Part-of-speech tagging with neural networks. In: Proceedings of the 15th Conference on Computational Linguistics - Volume 1. pp. 172–176. COLING '94, Association for Computational Linguistics, Stroudsburg, PA, USA (1994). https://doi.org/10.3115/991886.991915, https://doi.org/10.3115/991886.991915

15. Schmid, H., Laws, F.: Estimation of conditional probabilities with decision trees and an application to fine-grained pos tagging. In: Proceedings of the 22Nd International Conference on Computational Linguistics - Volume 1. pp. 777–784. COLING '08, Association for Computational Linguistics, Stroudsburg, PA, USA (2008), http://dl.acm.org/citation.cfm?id=1599081.1599179
16. Schommer, C., Kampas, D., Bersan, R.: A prospect on how to find the polarity of a financial news by keeping an objective standpoint. Proceedings ICAART 2013 (2013)
17. Sirajzade, J.: Das luxemburgischsprachige Oeuvre von Michel Rodange (1827-1876). Editionsphilologische und korpuslinguistische Analyse. doctoralthesis, Universität Trier (2015)
18. Sirajzade, J.: Korpusbasierte Untersuchung der Wortbildungsaffixe im Luxemburgischen. Technische Herausforderungen und linguistische Analyse am Beispiel der Produktivität. Zeitschrift für Wortbildung = Journal of Word Formation **18**(1) (2018)
19. Steyvers, M., Griffiths, T.: Probabilistic topic models. In: Landauer, T., McNamara, S.D., Kintsch, W. (eds.) Latent Semantic Analysis: A Road to Meaning, chap. Probabilistic topic models. Laurence Erlbaum (2007)
20. Stuart, K., Botella, A., Ferri-Miralles, I.: A corpus-driven approach to sentiment analysis of patient narratives. In: Ortiz, A.M., P\'erez-Hern\'andez, C. (eds.) CILC2016. 8th International Conference on Corpus Linguistics. EPiC Series in Language and Linguistics, vol. 1, pp. 381–395. EasyChair (2016)

Text Classification Using Combinations of Different Versions of Input Files

Yaakov HaCohen-Kerner, Adir Prager, and Adiel Cohen

Dept. of Computer Science, Jerusalem College of Technology – Lev Academic Center
21 Havaad Haleumi St., P.O.B. 16031, 9116001 Jerusalem, Israel
kerner@jct.ac.il,
adir.prager@gmail.com, adielhod@walla.com

Abstract. Text classification (TC) is an important component in many research domains, such as information extraction, information retrieval, and text mining. Therefore, the question of whether and how TC can be generally improved is crucial. In this research, we implemented a method that partially resembles the multiplication method. An example of the multiplication method from an entirely new domain is the construction of a new high tower based on several adjacent towers of various heights (lower than the new tower). We tested our method on three benchmark text corpora. For each corpus, we applied TC, using three supervised machine learning methods, and combinations of 20 versions of the input files (e.g., the original input files and/or their first halves and/or their second halves and/or first thirds and/or second thirds and/or last thirds). Extensive experiments showed that TC using the first part (e.g., half or third) of the original input files yielded better results than TC using other partial parts of the original input files. Furthermore, the use of the original input files and their first thirds improved the accuracy results achieved by the original input files for the three tested corpora. The best results obtained by our model were significantly better than the state-of-the-art results in two corpora out of the three tested corpora.

Keywords: Benchmark Text Corpora, Input Files, Multiplication Method, Text Classification, Term Frequency, Supervised Machine Learning.

1 Introduction

Text classification (TC) is the supervised learning task that assigns natural language text documents to one (the typical case) or more predefined categories (Joachims [19]). Classification algorithms typically use at least one supervised machine learning (ML) algorithm (Sebastiani [35]). TC is being applied in an increasing number of fields, e.g., document indexing, information retrieval (IR), information extraction, stylometric analysis tasks, text filtering, text mining, and word sense disambiguation (Sebastiani [35]). In many domains, computerized TC often rivals human performance.

TC comprises two primary types: stylistic classification, and topic-based classification. Stylistic classification is typically performed using linguistic features such as quantitative features, orthographic features, part of speech tags, function words, and vocabulary richness features (e.g., [10, 11]), whereas topic-based classification is typically performed using bag-of-words (BOW) representation or word n-grams (for n > 1) (e.g., [12, 13]).

In this study, we develop creative ideas that will improve the accuracy of TC results. Boyd and Goldenberg [1] claimed that creative methods should be based on the world's experience ('inside the box'), i.e., creative ideas should be structured and based on existing templates. One of the methods suggested by Boyd and Goldenberg is the multiplication method. The multiplication method (or technique) is defined as copying an already existing element, but changing it in some counterintuitive way. Using the original element and/or the copied and changed element(s) might improve the original element, or might yield an innovative idea. Boyd and Goldenberg demonstrate how the construction of a tower with more than n floors is done using the multiplication method. Rather than building a single very high tower, which might be unstable because of winds or an earthquake(s), and therefore might be dangerous, it is recommended to build several adjacent towers of various heights (less than n+1 floors). At or near the middle of this set of towers, a tower with more than n floors could be built. The support of the various towers around the central tower allows it to be higher than n floors, and still be stable. Figure 1 presents the structure of the Sears Tower, now called the Willis Tower[1], which is where this idea was originally applied.

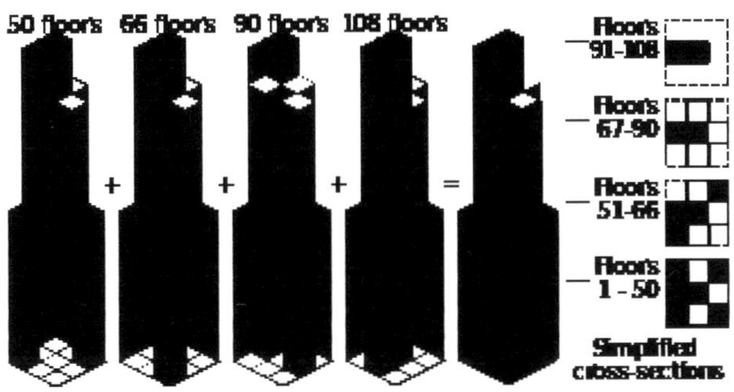

Fig. 1. Structure of the Sears Tower.

While Boyd and Goldenberg did not relate to TC, our motivation is to investigate whether TC based on BOW representation can be improved using an adapted multiplication method. In topic-based classification, various ML methods (e.g., support vector machines (SVMs, Cortes and Vapnik [7]) and Naive Bayes (NB, Heckerman [17])) have been reported to use BOW representation with accuracies of 90% and greater (Joachims [19]).

The idea of upweighting document zones for TC is not novel, and various variants of this idea have been tested (Section 2). However, in this study, we apply the weighting zones to TC in a manner that has not yet been attempted before, to the best of our

[1] https://en.wikipedia.org/wiki/Willis_Tower. By Cmglee - Own work, CC BY-SA 3.0, https://commons.wikimedia.org/w/index.php?curid=15436754. last accessed 11/MAR/2018.

knowledge, as follows. TC will be applied using 20 combinations of the original documents with/without different halves and thirds of the documents. In contrast to methods that were applied in various previous studies, our method is also applicable to documents that do not include any special parts such as title, keywords, headings, introduction, and conclusions. We validate the proposed model using three benchmark corpora to determine the best combinations for TC.

Let us define "ALL" as the set of all the original input files in the training sub-dataset (later, we will define "ALL" in a practical way as the normalized frequencies of the top 1000 occurring word unigrams for all files of the training sub-dataset). We hypothesize that (1) TC using a training sub-dataset consisting of the first parts (i.e., 1st half or 1st third) of ALL (i.e., using the 1st half or 1st third of each file of ALL) will yield better results than TC using a training sub-dataset consisting of other partial parts of ALL (e.g., 2nd half or 2nd or 3rd third) and (2) TC using ALL and 1st third (or 1st half) of ALL will yield better results than TC using ALL. We then validate these hypotheses by analyzing three benchmark corpora using three ML methods, feature filtering, and parameter tuning.

Thus, this study successfully and innovatively solves a well-studied TC problem from a different perspective using a solution (multiplication method) taken from a completely different area (general creativity).

The key contributions of this paper are (1) the implementation of an intensive set of experiments influenced by the multiplication method; (2) the primary findings of this study: TC using the first part (e.g., half or third) of the original input files yields better results than TC using other partial parts of the original input files, and TC using the original input files and their first thirds yields better results than TC using the original input files in three different benchmark text corpora (in two corpora, the improvements were statistically significant); (3) the conclusions of the study: the best results obtained by this model are significantly better than the state-of-the-art results for two of the three examined corpora.

The structure of the article is as follows. Section 2 introduces text classification, using upweighting document zones. Section 3 presents the examined datasets and the proposed model. Section 4 presents the experimental results of our model applied on the three examined benchmark datasets. Section 5 concludes and offers some suggestions for future research.

2 TC Using Upweighting Document Zones

As mentioned above, the idea of upweighting document zones for TC is not novel, and various variants have been tested (Manning et al. [27]). For example, upweighting title words was found to be effective for TC (Cohen and Singer [6], p. 163).

A widely used weighting method, is *term frequency - inverse document frequency* (TF-IDF) (Salton et al. [34]). This method assigns weights to terms based on their frequencies and inverse document frequencies. Various variants of the TF-IDF have been proposed to improve TC accuracy (e.g., Zhang et al. [40], Liu and Yang [25]).

Murata et al. [29] investigated IR in newspaper documents written in Japanese. Their system won the Japanese language IR contest held in 1999. The experiments confirmed the effectiveness of assigning high weighting to certain types of categories extracted from the document, such as the document's title, and the first sentence of the body of the document.

Lowe et al. [24] applied TC to full papers from the proceedings of ICED 1999. The papers were classified according to themes, using different document zones: title, keywords, snippet (the first 400 characters in a document), headings (the section headings), introduction and conclusions, and body text. The best results were shown to be achieved by the document keywords, title, and snippet. These findings confirm the expected hypothesis that important terms are featured in a paper's title, and are mentioned early in the document.

Ko et al. [22] applied TC based on the importance of sentences. They measured the importance of sentences using text summarization techniques. They represented each document by a vector of features, with different weights according to the importance of each sentence. The results of the experiments showed that their method achieved a significant improvement for all combinations of four classifiers (NB, Rocchio, k-nearest neighbors (k-NN), and SVM) and two data sets (one in English and one in Korean).

Ren and Sohrab [32] developed a class-indexing-based term-weighting scheme called TF-IDF-inverse class space-density frequency, giving a positive discrimination to both rare and frequent terms, thus enhancing the indexing process to generate more informative terms. The experimental results showed that their approach using SVMs and the centroid classifier outperformed six well-known baseline term-weighting approaches.

Escalantea et al. [8] presented a genetic algorithm that learned term-weighting schemes (TWSs) that represented documents under the vector space model. They reported experimental results in 16 well-known datasets comprising thematic TC, authorship attribution, and image classification tasks. The results demonstrated that their genetic TWS method outperformed the traditional schemes and the TWSs proposed in recent studies.

Jiang et al. [18] introduced a deep feature weighting method (DFW) for the NB ML method. The DFW method estimated the conditional probabilities of NB by deeply computing feature-weighted frequencies from the training data. The results on a collection of 36 benchmark datasets from the UCI repository showed that when compared to standard NB, NB with DFW significantly improved, in many cases, the TC performance.

3 Examined Datasets and Model

3.1 Examined datasets

The three examined datasets are benchmark datasets: mini 20 newsgroups (Mini20), WebKB, and R8. These datasets were constructed by Cardoso–Cachopo [4] for single-label TC to allow for an easier comparison of different studies and algorithms. Table 1 introduces general information about these three datasets; more details are given after

Table 1. General information about the three datasets.

Dataset	Mini20	Web4	R8
# of documents	2,000	4,199	7,674
# of classes	20	4	8

the table.

The Mini20 dataset [28] contains 2,000 documents evenly divided into 20 Usenet discussion groups. This dataset is a subset of the famous 20 newsgroups dataset, which contains approximately 20,000 documents.

The Web4 dataset (Cardoso–Cachopo [3]) - the four universities dataset - contains 4,199 documents. These documents are webpages that were manually classified into four classes: student, faculty, course, and project. The original WebKB dataset [37] contains webpages classified into seven classes. Three classes (department, staff, and other) were discarded according to Cardoso–Cachopo [3] because they either contain only a few pages from each university, or their pages are different from each other.

The R8 dataset [31] is a sub-corpus of the Reuters-21578 [33] dataset. R8 is distributed into 8 categories of the 10 most frequent classes. The collection contains 7,674 documents. The documents were classified by a human indexer. All datasets were downloaded from Cardoso–Cachopo [4].

3.2 The Model

Our model is language-independent, domain-independent, and text-structure-independent, in contrast to many systems, e.g., previous TC studies (Section 2) that assume special text zones (e.g., title, headlines, keywords, introduction, and conclusions).

In the model, we applied three supervised ML methods: sequential minimal optimization (SMO) (Platt [30], Keerthi et al. [21]), LibSVM [5], and simple logistics (SL) [23, 24] using the WEKA platform with their default parameters (Witten and Frank [38], Hall et al. [16]). For each TC task, we used the experimental mode in WEKA Version 3.9.1 with the following settings: train (67%) / test (33%) (data randomized) and the number of repetitions of the experiment set to 10.

A brief description of these three ML methods are as follows: SMO (Platt [30], Keerthi et al. [21]) is a variant of the SVM ML method (Cortes and Vapnik [7]). The SMO method is an iterative method created to solve the optimization problem frequently found in SVM methods. LibSVM is a programming library that facilitates researchers' SVM classification performance; it was developed by Chang and Lin [5]. It includes the typical kernels (linear, polynomial, radial basis function (RBF), and sigmoid) (Karatzoglou et al. [20]). SL is a variant of logistic regression (LR). LR (Le Cessie and Van Houwelingen [24]) is a variant of a probabilistic statistical classification model, which is used for predicting the outcome of a categorical-dependent variable (i.e., a class label) based on one or more features. SL is a variant of LR implemented in the WEKA platform (Landwehr et al. [23], Sumner et al. [36]).

The general TC algorithm is as follows (more details will be given afterwards):

For each dataset, the following steps were performed:

1. All instances of 421 known stopwords for English text (Fox [9]) were removed.
2. The frequencies of all word unigrams from the training dataset were computed.
3. The top 5000 frequent word unigram were chosen.
4. Three supervised ML methods (SMO, LibSVM, and SL) were applied to classify ALL using from 1000 to 5000 word unigrams (in steps of 1000) and determine a reasonable number of word unigrams for the BOW representation.
5. The accuracy results of these three supervised ML methods were defined using 1000 word unigrams as the baseline results (see explanation in the analysis of Table 2).
6. The three supervised ML methods were then applied on 19 additional combinations of the original documents with/without different halves and thirds of ALL.
7. For the best accuracy results, InfoGain (IG) (Yang and Pedersen [39]) was used for feature filtering and we also performed parameter tuning.
8. For improved accuracy results (step 7), additional measures were also computed including the precision, recall, and F-measures.

To determine the reasonable number of word unigrams to be applied to the BOW, we performed TC experiments for each pair of dataset and ML method, using five different sets, containing 1000-, 2000-, 3000-, 4000-, and 5000-word unigrams. Table 2 presents the TC accuracy results using 1000-, 2000-, 3000-, 4000-, and 5000-word unigrams for the three examined benchmark datasets and three applied supervised ML methods (SMO, LibSVM, and SL).

Tables 2-5 include various annotations as follows. The annotation "v" or "*" indicates that a specific result in a certain column is statistically better "v" or worse "*" than the baseline results (i.e., the results in the first row for each dataset).

To compare the different results, we performed statistical tests using a corrected paired two-sided t-test, with a confidence level of 95%. Underline represents the two best baseline accuracy results that were obtained for each dataset. *Italics* and "v" represent accuracy results that were significantly better than the baseline results for each ML method. *Italics* without "v" represent the accuracy results that were better than the baseline results (but not significantly better) for each ML method.

Table 2. TC accuracy results for various # of word unigrams for 3 datasets & 3 ML methods.

	Min20			**Web4**			**R8**		
# of uni-grams	SMO	Lib-SVM	SL	SMO	Lib-SVM	SL	SMO	Lib-SVM	SL
1000	80.80	90.17	93.03	89.66	91.22	91.01	95.74	96.47	95.84
2000	*81.61*	*90.48*	*93.21*	*90.03*	*91.65*	*91.79*	*95.95*	*96.79*	*96.00*
3000	*82.23 v*	*90.26*	*93.23*	*90.15*	*91.76*	*91.57*	*95.76*	*96.88*	*95.78*
4000	*82.77 v*	*90.30*	*93.30*	*90.01*	*91.77*	*91.39*	*95.62*	*96.96*	*95.92*
5000	*82.58*	*90.24*	*93.11*	*90.11*	*91.71*	*91.38*	*95.58*	*96.92*	*95.97*

For all three datasets and the two best ML methods (LibSVM and SL) according to their results, the best accuracy results were achieved using either 2000- or 4000-word unigrams. However, these results were not significantly better than the baseline accuracy results using 1000-word unigrams. Thus, owing to runtime considerations, we decided to continue our experiments using 1000-word unigrams.

We compared the accuracy of results obtained using ALL (the normalized frequencies of the top 1000 occurring word unigrams for all files of the training sub-dataset) to the accuracy of results achieved using the following combinations: the 1st halves of ALL (the normalized frequencies of the top 1000 occurring word unigrams for the training sub-dataset composed of the first half of each file of ALL), the 2nd halves of ALL, the 1st thirds of ALL, the 2nd thirds of ALL, the last thirds of ALL, the 1st and 2nd thirds of ALL, the 1st and 3rd thirds of ALL, and the 2nd and 3rd thirds of ALL.

Furthermore, we compared the accuracy results obtained using the additional combinations of ALL with different partial versions of ALL: ALL & 1st halves, ALL & 2nd halves, ALL & 1st thirds, ALL & 2nd thirds, ALL & 3rd thirds, ALL & 1st & 2nd thirds, ALL & 1st & 3rd thirds, ALL & 2nd & 3rd thirds, ALL & 1st halves & 1st thirds, ALL & 1st halves & 1st & 2nd thirds, and ALL & 1st halves & 1st & 3rd thirds. Owing to the large number of experiments (20 combinations for each ML method for each dataset) and time constraints, we did not implement our model with divisions smaller than a third.

It is noteworthy that the combination of ALL & 1st thirds of ALL does not mean that we can double the weight of each word in the first thirds of ALL and assign normal weights for all other words, because when we use the first thirds of ALL, we must obtain the top-1000 frequent word unigrams excluding the stopwords in the training dataset of the first thirds of ALL. These top-1000 frequent word unigrams will likely be different from the top-1000 frequent word unigrams derived from the training dataset of ALL.

4 Experimental Results

In subsections 4.1-4.3, we present the experimental results of our model, applied to the three examined benchmark datasets. Tables 3-5 display the TC accuracy results for the three datasets: Mini20, Web4, and R8. In addition to the annotations that were defined before Table 2, we use **bold** to note the highest result in each table. In subsection 4.4, we describe attempts to improve the results, such as feature filtering and parameter tuning. Finally, in subsection 4.5, we provide an analysis of the experimental results.

4.1 Experimental Results for the Mini20 Dataset

Table 3 presents the TC accuracy results for the Mini20 dataset.

Table 3. TC accuracy results for the Mini20 dataset.

Input file(s)	**SMO**	**LibSVM**	**SL**
ALL	80.80	90.17	93.03
1st half of ALL	*83.11*	*92.42 v*	*94.80 v*
2nd half of ALL	42.17 *	45.21 *	40.61 *
1st third of ALL	*83.77 v*	*92.44 v*	***95.11 v***
2nd third of ALL	37.47 *	39.18 *	36.77 *
3rd third of ALL	35.53 *	37.83 *	34.20 *
1st & 2nd thirds of ALL	*83.39*	*91.58 v*	*94.38*
1st & 3rd thirds of ALL	80.58	*90.42*	*94.36*
2nd & 3rd thirds of ALL	46.33 *	49.65 *	44.65 *
ALL & 1st half of ALL	*83.48 v*	*91.98 v*	*93.94*
ALL & 2nd half of ALL	77.23 *	84.80 *	91.29
ALL & 1st third of ALL	*83.62 v*	*92.35 v*	*94.64*
ALL & 2nd third of ALL	80.41	86.86 *	91.88
ALL & 3rd third of ALL	76.95 *	86.02 *	91.88
ALL & 1st & 2nd thirds	*83.50 v*	*91.47 v*	*93.23*
ALL & 1st & 3rd thirds	80.76	*90.79 v*	*94.06*
ALL & 2nd & 3rd thirds	76.21 *	83.44 *	90.95
ALL & 1st half & 1st third	*84.00 v*	*92.52 v*	*95.02 v*
ALL & 1st half & 1st & 2nd thirds	*83.94 v*	*91.95 v*	*94.08*
ALL & 1st half & 1st & 3rd thirds	*82.42*	*91.59 v*	*94.20*

The primary finding from the TC accuracy results for the Mini20 dataset indicated that the best accuracy result (95.11%) was achieved by the SL method using the 1st third of ALL. This result was significantly better than the best baseline accuracy result (93.03%) achieved by the SL method using ALL. Two more combinations using SL achieved significant improvements when compared to the baseline result: ALL & 1st half & 1st third (95.02%) and 1st half (94.80%). Ten combinations using LibSVM (the second best ML method) yielded significant improvements compared to the baseline accuracy result (90.17%). Among them were the following: ALL & 1st half & 1st third (92.52%), 1st third (92.44%), 1st half (92.42%), and ALL & 1st third (92.35%).

General conclusions on the TC accuracy results of the Mini20 dataset include (1) the 1st half results are significantly better than the 2nd half results for all the three ML methods; the 1st third results are significantly better than either the 2nd third or the 3rd third results for all the three ML methods; (2) the 2nd half, the 2nd third, the 3rd third, and the 2nd & 3rd thirds have significantly poorer results than ALL; (3) TC using ALL & (1st third or 1st half) yields better results than TC using ALL and other partial parts; some of these results are even significantly better than using ALL; (4) TC using ALL & (2nd half or 2nd third or 3rd third or 2nd & 3rd thirds) in most cases yields significantly poorer results than using ALL.

4.2 Experimental Results for the Web4 Dataset

Table 4 presents the TC accuracy results for the Web4 dataset.

Table 4. TC accuracy results for the Web4 dataset.

Input file(s)	SMO	LibSVM	SL
ALL	89.66	91.22	91.01
1st half of ALL	86.06 *	87.51 *	86.99 *
2nd half of ALL	77.57 *	78.04 *	77.99 *
1st third of ALL	83.80 *	84.79 *	84.17 *
2nd third of ALL	72.73 *	72.93 *	73.58 *
3rd third of ALL	72.75 *	72.83 *	73.06 *
1st & 2nd thirds of ALL	87.32 *	88.77 *	88.73 *
1st & 3rd thirds of ALL	87.82 *	89.20 *	88.06 *
2nd & 3rd thirds of ALL	80.82 *	82.17 *	82.23 *
ALL & 1st half of ALL	*90.55*	*91.98*	*91.71 v*
ALL & 2nd half of ALL	86.58 *	88.51 *	89.35 *
ALL & 1st third of ALL	*91.20 v*	***92.48 v***	*92.00 v*
ALL & 2nd third of ALL	86.82 *	88.94 *	89.71
ALL & 3rd third of ALL	87.58 *	89.08 *	89.96 *
ALL & 1st & 2nd thirds	*90.08*	*91.69*	*91.39*
ALL & 1st & 3rd thirds	*90.14*	*91.33*	*91.30*
ALL & 2nd & 3rd thirds	86.78 *	88.41 *	89.40 *
ALL & 1st half&1st third	*91.14 v*	*92.18*	*91.92*
ALL & 1st half &1st & 2nd thirds	*90.22*	*91.45*	*91.61*
ALL & 1st half & 1st &3rd thirds	*90.83 v*	*92.21*	*91.74 v*

The primary finding drawn from the Web4 dataset was that the best accuracy result (92.48%) was achieved by the ALL & 1st third combination using LibSVM. This result was significantly better than the best baseline accuracy result (91.22%) achieved by LibSVM using ALL. It is noteworthy that the best accuracy results were obtained using SL (92.00%) and SMO (91.20%) by the same combination, ALL & 1st third. Furthermore, these two results are significantly better than their relevant baseline accuracy results (91.01% and 89.66%, respectively).

General conclusions on the TC accuracy results of the Web4 dataset include (1) using the first part (e.g., 1st half or 1st third) of the text files with ALL leads to better results than using ALL & the remaining parts of the text files; (2) in general, the first parts (1st halves or 1st thirds) of the files lead to better results than other partial parts of the files, but still poorer than the results obtained by ALL; (3) similar to Table 3, the 1st half results are significantly better than the 2nd half results for all three ML methods; the 1st third results are significantly better than either the 2nd third or the 3rd third results for all three ML methods.

4.3 Experimental Results for the R8 Dataset

Table 5 presents the accuracy results for the R8 dataset.

Table 5. TC accuracy results for the R8 dataset.

Input file(s)	SMO	LibSVM	SL
ALL	95.74	96.47	95.84
1st half of ALL	93.46 *	94.10 *	93.87 *
2nd half of ALL	89.59 *	90.02 *	89.07 *
1st third of ALL	91.77 *	92.07 *	91.84 *
2nd third of ALL	87.71 *	87.98 *	87.96 *
3rd third of ALL	85.64 *	85.52 *	85.02 *
1st & 2nd thirds of ALL	94.30 *	95.25 *	94.37 *
1st & 3rd thirds of ALL	94.85 *	95.43 *	94.63 *
2nd & 3rd thirds of ALL	92.07 *	92.99 *	91.99 *
ALL & 1st half of ALL	95.98	*96.57*	*96.05*
ALL & 2nd half of ALL	94.50 *	95.54 *	94.84 *
ALL & 1st third of ALL	*96.08*	***96.74***	*96.11*
ALL & 2nd third of ALL	95.03 *	96.07 *	95.38
ALL & 3rd third of ALL	94.44 *	95.54 *	94.84 *
ALL & 1st & 2nd thirds	*95.89*	*96.56*	*95.88*
ALL & 1st & 3rd thirds	*95.66*	96.46	95.64
ALL & 2nd & 3rd thirds	94.62 *	95.72 *	94.89 *
ALL & 1st half & 1st third	*95.97*	*96.54*	95.84
ALL & 1st half & 1st & 2nd thirds	*95.90*	96.43	*95.94*
ALL & 1st half & 1st & 3rd thirds	*96.05*	*96.68*	*95.84*

The primary finding from Table 5 for the R8 dataset is that the best accuracy result (96.74%) was achieved by LibSVM using the ALL & 1st third combination. This result was better (but not significantly better) than the best baseline accuracy result (96.47%) achieved by LibSVM using ALL. Furthermore, the best accuracy results achieved by SL and SMO (96.11% and 96.08%, respectively) were using the ALL & 1st third combination. These results are better (but not significantly better) than their relevant baseline results (95.84% and 95.74%, respectively).

General conclusions on the TC accuracy results of the R8 dataset include (1) similar to Tables 3 and 4, in general, the first part (i.e., 1st half or 1st third) of the text files contributes to better results than the remaining parts. In other words, this means that the 1st half results are better than the 2nd half results, the 1st third results are better than the 2nd third results, and the 2nd third results are slightly better than the 3rd third results; (2) for the two best ML methods (LibSVM and SL) TC using ALL & 1st third (or 1st half) yields better results than TC using ALL; (3) TC using ALL & 2nd half or 3rd third or 2nd & 3rd thirds yields results that are significantly poorer than the results using ALL for all three ML methods.

4.4 Feature Filtering and Parameter Tuning

Various improvement attempts, such as feature filtering using IG (particularly selection of features with nonzero weights), and parameter tuning trials, were applied to the best result for each dataset. Table 6 presents (1) the state-of-the-art accuracy results, (2) the best accuracy result before and after feature filtering and parameter tuning, (3) the number of features after IG filtering, (4) the best ML method that yielded the best result, (5) the value of the tuned parameter, and (6) the results of various additional measures (precision, recall, and F-measure) after filtering and tuning for each dataset.

The state-of-the-art accuracy results known to us prior to the study are as follows. An accuracy of 82.74% was obtained for Mini20 by Cardoso–Cachopo and Oliveira [2], who applied LibSVM using the 2500 most informative terms (words or tokens) according to IG. An accuracy of 85.82% was obtained for Web4 by Cardoso–Cachopo [3], who applied LibSVM using an unknown number of terms. An accuracy of 96.98% was determined for R8 by Cardoso–Cachopo [3], who applied LibSVM using unknown number of terms. For all three datasets, LibSVM was applied with a linear kernel with five-fold cross-validation. No specific information was provided about the application of any feature filtering and parameter tuning.

Table 6. Our TC results compared to the state-of-the-art results.

State	Measure	Dataset			
		Mini20	**Web4**	**R8**	
State-of-the-art results	Accuracy & study	82.74 Cardoso-Cachopo & Oliveira [2]	85.82 Cardoso-Cachopo [3]	96.98 Cardoso-Cachopo [3]	
	Best ML method & # of features	LibSVM 2500 most informative terms according to IG	LibSVM using an unknown number of terms	LibSVM using an unknown number of terms	
Our system before IG and parameter tuning	Accuracy	95.11	92.48	96.74	
	Best ML method method & # of features	SL using 1000 top word unigrams of 1st third of ALL	LibSVM using 1000 top word unigrams of ALL & 1st third of ALL	LibSVM using 1000 top word unigrams of ALL & 1st third of ALL	
Our systemter IG and parameter tuning	accuracy	96.06	92.79	96.96	97.16
	# of features	183	975	950	5000
	Best ML method	SL	LibSVM	LibSVM	
	Tuned parameter	numBoostIngIterations=15	Kernel type: li-near & cost: 200	Kernel type: linear & cost: 200	
	Precision	96.4	92.7	97.0	97.2
	Recall	96.1	92.8	97.0	97.2
	F-M	96.25	92.75	97.0	97.2

According to Table 6, our best accuracy results after performing IG and parameter tuning were better than the state-of-the-art accuracy results in all three corpora, and significantly better in two of them (Mini20 and Web4).

4.5 Analysis of the Experimental Results

We have fully confirmed the validity of our first hypothesis, that claimed TC using the first part (i.e., 1st half or 1st third) of ALL (the original input files) yields better results than TC using other partial parts (e.g., 2nd half, 2nd third, and 3rd third) of ALL. The experimental results for all three datasets and three ML methods show that the 1st half results are significantly better than the 2nd half results, and that the 1st third results are significantly better than the 2nd third or the 3rd third results.

TC using the first part (i.e., 1st half or 1st third) of ALL yields better results than TC using ALL only for the Mini20 dataset (significantly better for 5 out of 6 results for all 3 ML methods). However, for the two other datasets, TC using the first part (i.e., 1st half or 1st third) of ALL yields results that are significantly poorer than the results using ALL for all three ML methods. That is to say, we cannot discard the whole file for the best TC performance; however, it is clear that the first parts of ALL contribute more to TC than using other partial parts of ALL.

We have also almost fully confirmed the validity of our second hypothesis, that TC using ALL & 1st third (or 1st half) of ALL yields better results than TC using ALL. The experimental results show that for three datasets and three ML methods, in all 9 cases, TC using ALL & 1st third of ALL yields better results than TC using ALL; in 5 cases (out of these 9 cases), the results are significantly better. Furthermore, TC using ALL & 1st half of ALL yields better results than TC using ALL in all 9 cases, but only 3 of them are significantly better.

These findings suggest that in future TC experiments, all data should be considered with the possibility to assign higher weights to word unigrams that are located at the first halves/thirds of the original input files.

5 Conclusions and Proposals for Future Work

We herein presented a novel method that resembles the multiplication method, illustrated by the construction of a high tower, for the TC domain. The primary findings were as follows: (1) TC using the original input files and their first thirds improved the accuracy results in three benchmark text corpora for all three ML methods (with significant improvements in two corpora); (2) TC using the first parts (1st halves or 1st thirds) of the original files led to better results than TC using other partial parts of the files. However, TC using the first parts of the original files was poorer in most cases than TC using the original files. This implied that we could not discard the whole file; however, it was clear that the first parts contributed more to TC than the other partial parts; (3) the best results obtained by our model were significantly better than the state-of-the-art results in all three corpora and significantly better in two of them (Mini20 and Web4). It is noteworthy that the first two phenomena were not claimed to be relevant to all corpora worldwide. However, in our opinion, they could be relevant to corpora where the first part is more informative, such as the three corpora examined in this study.

Possible future research proposals include (1) exploring the size of the first section of the document: which would be the best for each tested dataset (including parts smaller than a third) for various domains and languages? (2) extracting a summary (e.g. [14])_and keyphrases (e.g., [15]) from each document, and then applying TC using these new elements, with or without different parts of the original documents, (3) applying TC using the combinations based on the multiplication method on TF-IDF values; (4) applying deep-learning methods, and (5) conducting experiments on larger benchmark corpora.

Acknowledgements.

The authors thank two anonymous reviewers for their reviews and fruitful comments. Thanks also to Shalom Mashbaum for his English editing

References

1. Boyd, D., Goldenberg, J.: Inside the box: A proven system of creativity for break-through results. Simon and Schuster (2013).
2. Cardoso-Cachopo, A., Oliveira, A. L.: An empirical comparison of text categorization methods. In International Symposium on String Processing and Information Retrieval (pp. 183-196). Springer, Berlin, Heidelberg (2003).
3. Cardoso-Cachopo, A.: Improving Methods for Single-label Text Categorization. Ph.D. thesis, Instituto Superior Técnico, Universidade de Lisboa, Lisbon, Portugal (2007).
4. Cardoso-Cachopo, A.: HomePage. http://ana.cachopo.org/datasets-for-single-label-text-categorization. last accessed 2018/MAR/11 (2018).
5. Chang, C. C., Lin, C. J.: LIBSVM: a library for support vector machines. ACM transactions on intelligent systems and technology (TIST), 2(3), 27 (2011) https://www.csie.ntu.edu.tw/~cjlin/libsvm/. last accessed 2018/MAR/11.
6. Cohen, W. W., Singer, Y.: Context-sensitive learning methods for text categorization. ACM Transactions on Information Systems (TOIS), 17(2), 141-173 (1999).
7. Cortes, C., Vapnik, V.: Support-vector networks. Machine Learning, 20 (3), 273–297 (1995).
8. Escalante, H. J., García-Limón, M. A., Morales-Reyes, A., Graff, M., Montes-y-Gómez, M., Morales, E. F., Martínez-Carranza, J.: Term-weighting learning via genetic programming for text classification. Knowledge-Based Systems, 83, 176-189 (2015).
9. Fox, C.: A stop list for general text. ACM SIGIR Forum, 24, 1-2, 19-35 (1989).
10. HaCohen-Kerner, Y., Beck, H. Yehudai, E., Mughaz, D.: Stylistic feature sets as classifiers of documents according to their historical period and ethnic origin. Applied Artificial Intelligence, 24(9), 847-862 (2010).
11. HaCohen-Kerner, Y., Rosenfeld, A., Tzidkani, M., Cohen, D. N.: Classifying papers from different computer science conferences. In Proceedings of the International Conference on Advanced Data Mining and Applications (pp. 529-541). Springer, Berlin, Heidelberg, (2013).
12. HaCohen-Kerner, Y., Mughaz, D., Beck, H., Yehudai, E.: Words as classifiers of documents according to their historical period and the ethnic origin of their authors. Cybernetics and Systems: An International Journal, 39(3), 213-228 (2008).
13. HaCohen-Kerner, Y., Dilmon, R., Friedlich, S., Cohen, D. N.: Classifying true and false Hebrew stories using word n-grams. Cybernetics and Systems, 47(8), 629-649 (2016).
14. HaCohen-Kerner, Y., Malin, E., Chasson, I: Summarization of Jewish law articles in Hebrew. In CAINE (pp. 172-177) (2003).

15. HaCohen-Kerner, Y., Gross, Z., Masa, A.: Automatic extraction and learning of keyphrases from scientific articles. In International Conference on Intelligent Text Processing and Computational Linguistics (pp. 657-669), Springer, Berlin, Heidelberg (2005).
16. Hall, M., Frank, E., Holmes, G., Pfahringer, B., Reutemann, P., Witten, I. H.: The WEKA data mining software: an update. ACM SIGKDD explorations newsletter, 11(1), 10-18 (2009).
17. Heckerman, D.: Bayesian networks for data mining. Data Mining and Knowledge Discovery, 1(1), 79-119, (1997).
18. Jiang, L., Li, C., Wang, S., Zhang, L.: Deep feature weighting for naive Bayes and its application to text classification. Engineering Applications of Artificial Intelligence, 52, 26-39 (2016).
19. Joachims, T.: Text categorization with support vector machines: Learning with many relevant features. In Proceedings of the European Conference on Machine Learning (ECML). 137–142 (1998).
20. Karatzoglou, A., Meyer, D., Hornik, K.: Support vector machines in R (2005).
21. Keerthi, S. S., Shevade, S. K., Bhattacharyya, C., Murthy, K. R. K.: Improvements to Platt's SMO algorithm for SVM classifier design. Neural Computation, 13(3), 637–649 (2001).
22. Ko, Y., Park, J., Seo, J.: Improving text categorization using the importance of sentences. Information Processing & Management, 40(1), 65-79 (2004).
23. Landwehr, N., Hall, M., Frank, E. Logistic model trees. Machine Learning, 59(1-2), 161–205 (2005). http://doi.org/10.1007/s10994-005-0466-3
24. Le Cessie, S., Van Houwelingen, J. C.: Ridge estimators in logistic regression. Applied Statistics, 191-201 (1992).
25. Liu, M., Yang, J.: An improvement of TFIDF weighting in text categorization. In Proceedings of Computer Science and Information Technology, 44-47 (2012).
26. Lowe, A., McMahon, C. A., Shah, T., Culley, S. J.: The application of an automatic document classification system to aid the organizers of ICED 2001. Design Management: Process and Information Issues, 2, pp. 179-186 (2001).
27. Manning, C. D., Raghavan, P., Schütze, H.: Introduction to information retrieval. Cambridge University Press, 2008. Ch, 20, 405-416 (2008).
28. Mini 20 newsgroups. 2014. The mini 20 newsgroups dataset. http://ana.cachopo.org/datasets-for-single-label-text-categorization. last accessed 2018/MAR/11.
29. Murata, M., Ma, Q., Uchimoto, K., Ozaku, H., Utiyama, M., Isahara, H.: Japanese probabilistic information retrieval using location and category information. In Proc. of the Fifth Int. Workshop on Information Retrieval with Asian languages, pp. 81-88 (2000). ACM.
30. Platt, J. C.: Sequential minimal optimization: a fast algorithm for training support vector machines. Technical Report MSR-TR-98-14, Microsoft Research, pp. 1–21 (1998).
31. R8. https://www.cs.umb.edu/~smimarog/textmining/datasets/. last accessed 2018/MAR/15. (2007).
32. Ren, F., Sohrab, M. G.: Class-indexing-based term weighting for automatic text classification. Information Sciences, 236, 109-125 (2013).
33. Reuters-21578. http://www.daviddlewis.com/resources/testcollections/reuters21578/. last accessed 2018/MAR/11. (1997).
34. Salton, G., Wong, A., Yang, C. S.: A vector space model for automatic indexing. Communications of the ACM, 18(11), 613-620 (1975).
35. Sebastiani, F.: Machine learning in automated text categorization. ACM Computing Surveys. 34. 1, 1-47 (2002).
36. Sumner, M., Frank, E., Hall, M.: Speeding up logistic model tree induction. In Proceedings of Knowledge Discovery in Databases: PKDD 2005 (Vol. 3721, pp. 675–683). Springer.

37. WebKB. The 4 Universities Data Set. last accessed 2018/MAR/11. http://www.cs.cmu.edu/afs/cs/prject/theo20/www/data/. (1998).
38. Witten, I. H., Frank, E.: Data Mining: Practical machine learning tools and techniques. Morgan Kaufmann (2005).
39. Yang, Y., Pedersen, J. O.: A comparative study on feature selection in text categorization. In Proc. of the 14th International Conference on Machine Learning (ICML), 412-420 (1997).
40. Zhang, W., Yoshida, T., Tang, X.: A comparative study of TF* IDF, LSI and multi-words for text classification. Expert Systems with Applications, 38(3), 2758-2765 (2011).

Use of Big Data for Disaster Management

Gijoo Yang[1], Kangwoo Lee[2], and Dongho Kim[3]

[1]Department of Information and Communication Engineering
[2]Department of Computer Science and Engineering
[3]Convergence Software Institute
Dongguk University, Seoul 04620, South Korea
gjyang@dgu.edu

Abstract. Predicting and responding to disastrous events properly is critical. We propose a new machine learning based decision support system which recognizes disasters from examining news articles and social media posts. Once the news article or the social media post is recognized as a notification of a disaster event, our model extracts attribute information about the disaster. Then, it infers possible afterward situations that can be triggered by the extracted information. To handle real-world situations, we didn't just use the extracted facts for reasoning but also used the facts that can be inferred from a commonsense knowledge base. Our machine reasoning system uses fully differentiable neural network so that deep learning method can be deployed.

Keywords: Disaster Management, Reasoning, Hierarchical recurrent neural network.

1 Introduction

Nowadays, bigger and more complicated disasters that haven't been seen previously occur more often. Predicting and responding properly to such disasters became more important. In this work, we propose a machine learning based decision support system which recognizes disasters from examining news articles and social media posts. First, by using the big data of news articles and social media posts, disasters are recognized based on our supervised deep learning system. Once the occurrence of a disaster is recognized, we extract attribute information about the disaster from the news and the social media posts to figure out the location, scale, and situation of the disaster. The information obtained about the disaster is then used to predict the possible afterward situation which can be triggered by the situation at that time. Prediction is accomplished by a reasoning system which can carry out multi-step reasoning process in an end-to-end fashion.

The Korean government maintains the manuals prepared for national disasters. Such manuals can be seen as the set of a priori responsive actions to various disasters at different levels. The knowledge in such manuals can be represented as <event, probability, action> 3-tuple. This type of knowledge can be converted into probabilistic logical knowledge and it can be used to automatically provide the appropriate actions under a certain circumstance of a disaster. Albeit such a knowledge base can be implemented under many experienced conditions, not all cases about various disasters can be well prepared because previously unseen disasters occur nowadays. Thus, in order to respond properly to unexperienced disasters, we need a reasoning process that can predict the possible afterward situation which can be triggered by the identified factors of the disaster.

For reasoning, various approaches have been proposed, including logic program, rule engines, deductive classifiers, machine learning systems, and etc. In addition, probabilistic methods have been added to handle the reasoning under uncertainty. Typically, reasoning is done by matching facts against theories in a probabilistic deductive knowledge base. Let's suppose that someone's status is *tired* is true if he/she has an infant child, Then, for example, if Peter has an infant child, his status can be reasoned to be *tired*. The problem with probabilistic deductive knowledge base is that it might take non-linear time (thus, not possible to do the reasoning process in real time).

Another problem with probabilistic deductive knowledge base is that it is not clear how to integrate this reasoning process into gradient-based learning systems. To handle these problems, we borrow a method called MAC network[6] in which reasoning uses a differentiable process. Its belief propagation is linearly proportional to the size of knowledge base with a slope of smaller than 1. To reason about real-world situations, we also perform reasoning based on commonsense knowledge in addition to the extracted information about the disaster. In the following sections, we will describe our model for disaster recognition, attribute information extraction, and reasoning. We then discuss our experiment done with government disaster management manuals and news articles and social media posts between 2008 and 2017.

2 Proposed Work

2.1 Machine Learning based Disaster Recognition

Since we know the time when news articles and social media posts were written as well as the time of disasters for the past, it is like we have labeled datasets which can be used for supervised learning. In addition, since there are so many news articles and social media posts, it is sufficient to employ a deep learning method to model the news articles and social media posts so that we can determine whether they indicate disasters or not.

In the research area of deep learning, Recurrent Neural Network (RNN) has been widely used for sequential inputs such as sentences. Among various variants of RNN, LSTM (Long Short Term Memory) and GRU (Gated Recurrent Unit) are the top two choices that alleviate the vanilla RNN's "vanishing gradient" problem which occurs when the input sequence becomes long (more than 7 units long). We choose GRU for our work because the architecture of LSTM is more complicated and hence it is computationally expensive[4].

To process a news article or a social media post, we need to segment it into sentences first. Then each sentence is fed to GRU, word by word. For each word representation, we use pre-trained Word2vec word embedding. The final hidden state of GRU can be considered as the representation of the sentence meaning.

To encode the meaning of the article or the post as a whole, we employ a hierarchical GRU[7] that takes each sentence representation as input as shown in Fig. 1. Thus, the representation of each sentence is fed to another GRU. The final hidden state of this GRU can then be considered as the representation of the meaning of the news article or the social media post. This final representation is fed to a softmax layer which classifies the news articles and social media posts into disaster classes, indicating whether this article or post belongs to a certain type of disaster or not.

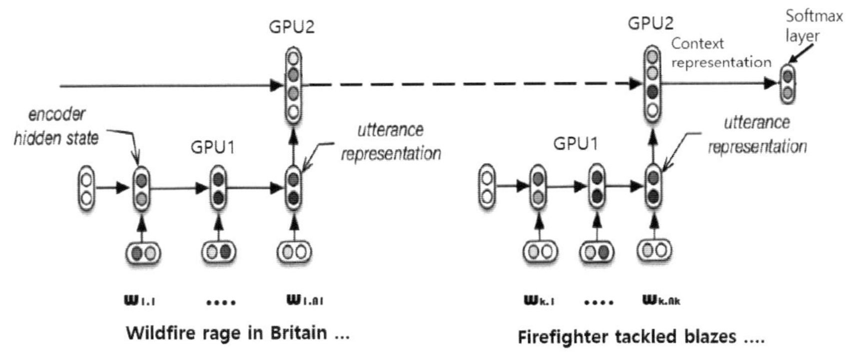

Fig. 1. The architecture of our model. Adapted and modified from [7]

2.2 Event Attribute Information Extraction based on Parsing and FrameNet

Once an article or post is classified as a certain type of disaster, sentences in the article or post are then parsed to identify the attribute information of the disaster. Since the parse tree of each sentence now specifies the thematic roles of each component of the parse tree, we can extract attribute information about the disaster. For example, from the news articles saying "wildfire arose 10 hours ago, and 3 hectares are lost", we can conclude that the duration of the fire is 10 hours long, and it damaged 3 hectares of forests.

To parse a sentence, we use our neural dependency parser previously developed. Our parser takes a sentence as input and produces heads and their dependents with the relations between them. From the semantic point of view, parsing is the process that determines primary elements of the sentence such as agent, theme, beneficiary, and etc. It is common and easy to find primary elements from the parsed tree. However, to identify extra-thematic elements, we need a more detailed description of headwords. Since FrameNet[1] provides a thorough explanation about thematic roles according to headwords, we use the concepts (such as relations, phrase type, frame elements, and etc.) that can be found in the frames of FrameNet to figure out attribute information of disasters.

2.3 Reasoning

The reasoning is the ability to manipulate previously acquired knowledge to draw a novel inference or answer the query. Human seems to do this kind of knowledge analysis and gain supreme intelligence effectively[2]. However, building a large scale knowledge base using such networks is not easy because the transformation of concepts is computationally expensive and the amount of transformation is tremendous.

[5] introduced fully differentiable neural network called TensorLog. It uses a probabilistic deductive database and factor graph for reasoning and it can perform reasoning linear in database size. [6] introduced a novel neural network called MAC which facilitates reasoning. It also has a fully differentiable neural network so that deep learning can be deployed, and it approaches problems by decomposing them into a series of reasoning steps so that reasoning can be done effectively in an end-to-end fashion. In addition, it has an attention module that maintains a separation between control and memory. MAC seems to be better than TensorLog because attention module keeps the related knowledge to be focused.

We borrow the MAC model for reasoning the situation of disasters, however, we augment it with a commonsense knowledge base in order to handle the real-world situation. Several commonsense knowledge bases such as SenticNet[3] and ConceptNet[9] have been developed during the last decades. Such a kind of knowledge representation gives a foundation to reason about real-world events. With this type of knowledge base, typically it can be seen as a semantic network where concepts are nodes and relations are edges in the graph shown in Fig. 2. Then, <concept, relation, concept> tuple forms a fact. For example, from Fig. 2, <oven, UsedFor, cook> is a fact which can be formed from the knowledge base.

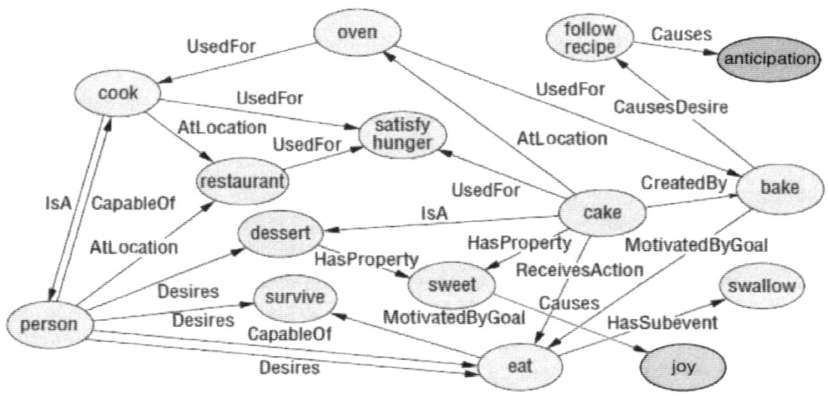

Fig. 2: A sketch of SenticNet semantic network. Adapted from [10].

3 Experiments

We use news articles and social media posts from 2008 to 2017. As shown in Table 1, during that time South Korea had various damage from many natural disasters including flood, typhoon, earthquake, tsunami, wildfire, abnormally high temperature, extreme cold wave, and etc.

Table 1. Damage by Natural Disaster in South Korea (2008 – 2017).

Year	Casualties (Number of people)	Property Damage (100 million Korean Won)
2008	11	637
2009	13	2,988
2010	14	4,268
2011	78	7,942
2012	16	10,892
2013	4	1,721
2014	2	1,800
2015	0	318
2016	7	2,883
2017	7	1,873

We gathered the news articles and social media posts between 2008 and 2017 and it turned that only less than 2% of them are about disasters. We applied our hierarchical recurrent neural network model to them and successfully classified them into proper types of disasters.

Once the news article or the social media post is classified as a disaster, it is parsed and the attribute information about the disaster is extracted. For this information extraction, the extra-thematic information from the corresponding frame of FrameNet is used to identify more detailed attribute information about the disaster.

After attribute information about the disaster is extracted, facts are formed as knowledge. Our reasoning model infers possible deployment from this knowledge. In addition, we also use relevant commonsense knowledge to infer the real-world situations. Then the inferred facts are compared with the disaster management manuals from the government to verify whether the manuals are well prepared. It turned out that 6.8% of the manuals are not sufficient enough for the various factors of the disaster which can be inferred from the given situation. Based on this automatic reasoning, our system can be used to support the decisions that have to be made at the disaster scene.

4 Conclusions

We propose a deep learning model which can recognize disasters by examining news articles and social media posts. Then we propose a method to extract attribute information about the disaster and predict the possible future of the identified situation. For reasoning, we suggest an end-to-end reasoning model augmented with a commonsense knowledge base.

We applied our model to news articles and social media posts for 2008 – 2017. Disaster situations were successfully recognized and from the identified disaster information, we infer possible afterward situations by reasoning based on the extracted facts and the commonsense knowledge base. We verified the disaster management manuals from the government by comparing the derived facts with the manuals. From this comparison, the supplement of the manuals could be automatically provided..

References

1. Baker C., Charles, F., Fillmore, J., Lowe, J.: The Berkley FrameNet Project. In Proceedings of COLING/ACL, 86-90, Montreal (1998)
2. Cambria, E., Hussain, A.: Sentic Computing. Springer (2015)
3. Cambria, E., Poria, S., Bajpai, R., Schuller, B.: SenticNet 4: A semantic resource for sentiment analysis based on conceptual primitives. In COLING, 2666-2677. (2016)
4. Cho, K., Bahdanau, D., Bougares, F., Schwenk, H., Bengio, Y.: Learning Phrase Representation using RNN Encoder-Decoder for Statistical Machine Translation. In Conference on Empirical Methods in Natural Language Processing, 1724-1734 (2016).
5. Cohen, W.: TensorLog: A Differentiable Deductive Database. arXiv preprint arXiv:1605.06523 (2016)
6. Hudson, D., Manning C.: Compositional Attention Networks for Machine Reasoning. arXiv preprint arXiv:1803.03067 (2018).
7. Searban, I., Sordoni, A., Bengio, Y., Courville, A.: Building End-to-End Dialogue Systems Using Generative Hierarchical Neural Network Models. arXiv preprint arXiv:1507.04808 (2016).
8. Sordoni, A., Bengio, Y., Vahabi, H., Lioma, C., Simonsen, J., Nie, J.: A hierarchical recurrent encoder-decoder for generative context-aware query suggestions. In Proceedings of the ACM International Conference on Information and Knowledge Management. 553-562 (2015)
9. Speer, R., Havasi, C.: ConceptNet 5: A large semantic network for relational knowledge. In Hovy, E., Johnson, M., Hirst, G. (eds.) Theory and Applications of Natural Language Processing. Springer. Chapter 6. (2012)
10. Young, T., Cambria, E., Chaturvedi, I., Zhou, H., Biswas, S., Huang, M.: Augmenting End-to-End Dialogue Systems with Commonsense Knowledge. In 32nd AAAI Conference on Artificial Intelligence (AAAI-18), 4970-4977 (2018)

Does Ambient Intelligence for Mobile User Assistance dissolve in Privacy Oriented Policies?

Denys Proux and Frederic Roulland

Abstract. We are developing and testing concepts for an Ambient Intelligence Experiment evaluating embedded mobility analytics to support mobile users within a strong data privacy paradigm. The first part of the project discussed in the paper addresses user profiling based on stay area detection and point of interest disambiguation to feed an on-the-fly recommendation system.

Keywords: Privacy, Ambient Intelligence, Mobility, Point of Interest, Profiling.

1 Introduction

1.1 Context

User data analytics for improving Search and Recommendation has been intensively developed over the past decades with one key driver: selling products or services that best fit users' needs at the time they need it. This objective has been built around one paradigm which is collecting, aggregating, and analyzing as much data as possible on every user piling up a growing number of contextual features. Internet companies which have popularized their search and recommendation engines are the best example of the success of this paradigm. They provided efficient, convenient and free tools to users in exchange of their private data.

However, recent affairs related to the access of user data by third parties for commercial or political reasons have generated a growing trend for privacy protection such as the General Data Protection Regulation (GDPR) put in place in the European Union. This trend implies a paradigm shift both economic and technical. Data should remain a user property which means they may no longer be available for centralized analysis. Prediction models may be compelled to be built and to run locally on users' devices without the benefit of big data analytics (e.g. context sharing, similarity calculus, collaborative filtering).

In this paper we discuss some challenges related to this new paradigm, and the architecture and concepts developed in an experiment to deliver ambient recommendation services for wandering people in a privacy protective environment.

1.2 About Ambient Intelligence

Traditionally search and recommendation (S&R) systems aim at being as seamless as possible, making use of user behavior (e.g. navigation history) and context (e.g. social connections) to support the decision making process. Whereas previously confined to web navigation the current trend is to move this monitoring to the physical world including instant localization. A whole set of sensors now embedded on smartphones give access to satellite based positioning, acceleration, rotation, magnetic environment, wireless connectivity, temperature, pressure, light intensity, providing valuable direct and indirect information to perform user profiling based on mobility analytics. Our goal is to experiment Ambient Intelligence [1] to achieve context awareness and deliver user centered services through the use of pervasive and ubiquitous computing. Recent smartphone enhancements in terms CPU, GPU and storage capability open the door for such profiling and recommendation without relying that much on externalized resources.

1.3 About the user privacy protection paradigm

Data Protection Regulations give more rights to users. They must now be informed about what sort of personal data is collected and should be able to access, redact and even delete it which raises some issues for S&R systems making use of data aggregation and matrix factorization for instance.

Popular techniques such as collaborative filtering methods [2] now add similarity among users to existing data models taking into account similarities upon user's history and targeted objects [3]. Whatever specific method is used in this domain (memory-based [4], model-based [5], dimensionality-reduction [6], generative-model [7], spreading-activation [8] or link-analysis [9]) it intensively relies on data aggregation and cross-references. This as a consequence creates some cold start issues [10]. In a paradigm where users are anonymized and history or preference data is not kept server side this is a major technical problem. New deep learning approaches [11] which demonstrated huge improvements in result relevance are even more data greedy to support multi-layered architectures.

To increase privacy protection still preserving data aggregation, new techniques explore obfuscation of private data to support ranged queries [12]. But even though users' data still need to be collected and compared, which ends-up in being a question of trust.

In our experiment we are testing concepts and methods to provided user centric, customized services, taking into account history, taste, constraints and context still preserving privacy. Our proposal is to make use of ambient monitoring and decentralized S&R to achieve this objective.

1.4 The Ambient Wanderer Experiment

The Ambient Wanderer project (AW) aims at developing and experimenting a recommendation system for people unfamiliar with their environment (e.g. travelers in a new city) willing to spent some time exploring and discovering interesting places. One noticeable aspect is that it is not a search engine. People do not request the system for a place, but rather, depending on their availability, are suggested near-by points of interests (POI). It means that AW must know, depending on the context (e.g. time, place, availability) with limited user interaction, what suggestion best fits current tastes or interest. This particular aspect of the project relates to the ambient intelligence concept introduced earlier in this paper as it means that AW should discover through mobility data analytics both user's profile and on-the-fly opportunities. Suggested activities can cover permanent POI (such as restaurants) and temporary events in permanent POI.

User profile can off-course be defined manually but our assumption is that it generally does not support or adapt smoothly to contextual changes. In AW, user profiling makes use of trajectory analytics to discover significant places and time constraints. However, an additional dimension is required to explicit the meaning of these places: a data warehouse of point of interest (POI). The role of this database is twofold: for the profiling part to provide structured and standardized information about visited POI then for the recommendation part to provide a list of nearby POI along with contextual information. For our experiment we mapped information from 4 different Geographic databases (HERE, FourSquare, Grand-Lyon, IGN), and 9 different social and cultural events databases (PreditHQ, International Sowtime, Evenbrite, Songkick, Allevents.in, Meetup, Sportradar, 10times).

With respect to the privacy protection aspect, our proposal is to run the profiling part on the device (which means no centralized processing). However, some data need to be exchanged with the data warehouse (i.e. position and POI details) but as no recommendation or ranking as to be performed by the data warehouse, no user identification is required. To a larger extent, for increased privacy protection intermediate network routers our virtual private networks can be used without impacting query results.

This paper discuss experiments made to test the concept of local profiling thanks to user mobility analytics.

2 Mining trajectories for profile inference

2.1 Knowledge Acquisition through Trajectory Analysis and POI Discovery

Trajectories contain a wealth of information about users, about their favorite places, habits, schedules, constraints, transportation modes and to some extent their tastes. But inferring such meta information requires to process raw data. Trajectories are typically sets of way points $WP_i = \{ \varphi, \lambda, \sigma, \tau \}$ where φ is a latitude , λ a longitude, σ the altitude and τ a time stamp. This information may come from direct sources of data such as Satellite based Navigation Systems (SNS). But other sources of data are also available such as semi-direct (Wi-Fi, Bluetooth, Internet of Thing beacons) via radio maps or indirect ones (e.g. linear acceleration, rotational acceleration, magnetic field, light, pressure, sound environment).

Direct sources are almost unavoidable in terms of precision but they come with 2 major drawbacks. The first one is energy consumption. However, new SNS chips combined with the use of multiple satellite constellations and more powerful batteries should proportionally reduce the relative impact of such computation with respect to other components (such as screen display) consumption within smartphones [13].

The second concern is related to a loss of precision while entering an indoor location. A lot of researches are now focusing on using semi-direct and/or indirect sources to overcome this issue ([14], [15], [16]).

Semi-direct sources are a good alternative to SNS in term of energy consumption but the main limitation is to get access to radio maps. Wi-Fi hot spots are interesting as they offer more accuracy typically for indoor localization and can, in some cases, provide additional information thanks to broadcasted network identification.

Indirect sources of data only provide physical measures [17] with respect to a local referential (i.e. a smartphone). Such information is generally very noisy and un-calibrated but might provide some clues about move patterns typically for indoor locations [18].

As a first implementation of AW we started with SNS positioning. Sampling intervals can be optimized to preserve energy consumption taking into account motion characteristics for indoor and outdoor location such as those detailed in table 1.

Table 1. Selected NSS sampling intervals

Outdoor	Speed (m/sec)	Time Interval (sec)
	$0 < s < 0.5$	10
	$0.5 < s < 2$	5
	$2 < s < 15$	20
	$s > 15$	30
Indoor	-	60

Such settings prioritize precision for walking phases. AW is not a navigation system per se. One salient aspect of the profiling part is to detect to which POI a user walks to.

2.2 Stay Area versus POI: definitions

One key concepts tested in AW is to build user profiles making use of visited POI. Our assumption is to consider user navigation in the real world similar to navigation on the world wide web. A visited POI is similar to a selected hyperlink. Therefore, we use POI metadata (type, price, ambience, etc) as well as time series and event sequences for content based modeling and recommendation. However, before going further in the analysis, we need to define some concepts first.

A stay area (SA) is a place where a user spent "some" time. It is different from a stay point, where no move is recorded for a given amount of time. To illustrate this, we can consider a stop at a gas station where a user moves around a car, stay still when filling the tank then go to pay and comes back to the car. In AW it is considered as a Stay Area. Shapes, borders, centroids and methods to build SA are discussed in the next section.

A point of interest (POI) at least in its basic definition as implemented by POI databases is a place (a location) associated with a description (e.g. type, price, …). POI share with SA similar questions about size, shape and centroid definition. Typically, is a particular place (such as a bench or a fountain) within a park a POI in itself or should it be the park as a whole. Where the centroid should be located? In databases POI are generally registered as a point (the centroid is typically positioned at the center of the POI surface).

One aspect of user profiling in AW is performed thanks to matching overlap between SA and POI. We use primarily the Harversine distance (Hd) among centroids (1) complemented by vertical distance (2) if available. Haversine formulae is a less accurate than Vincenty's formulae [19] but deliver enough accuracy for short distance considered in SA to POI comparison.

$$Hd = 2\,R \arcsin\left(\sqrt{\sin^2\left(\frac{\varphi 2 - \varphi 1}{2}\right) + \cos(\varphi 1)\cos(\varphi 2)\sin^2\left(\frac{\lambda 2 - \lambda 1}{2}\right)\ \sin 2\left(\frac{\varphi 2 - \varphi 1}{2}\right)}\right) \tag{1}$$

$$Vd = |\ \sigma_1 - \sigma_1\ | \tag{2}$$

where φ is the latitude, λ the longitude, σ the altitude and R is earth's radius (mean radius = 6,371km)

2.3 Stay Area detection method

Standard methods are based on Stay Point detection [20]. A distance comparison is made between an anchor point and its successors to check if it stays below a predefined distance threshold. In such case a second test is performed to measures the time span between the anchor point and the last successor that is within the distance threshold. If the time span is larger than a given threshold, a stay point is detected. This may give partial results so improved methods [21] apply density clustering as post processing to aggregate close candidates.

In our experiments we realized that it was insufficient to address every cases such as "cloaked areas". It typically occurs when a user enters a place where localization information is lost. For various reasons such as to reduce energy consumption the tracking application may stop recording. We end-up in having a gap (or a significant difference) in time intervals between recorded way points. Therefore, depending on selected thresholds there might not be enough way points to activate Stay Point creation. We developed an adaptation to the standard stay points detection algorithm to detect such disappearance and reappearance within the same vicinity. It makes use of trend analytics. The trend computes the mean time θ over *m* previous way points. Therefore, for 3 consecutive way points (W_{i-1}, W_i, W_{i+1}) a "cloaked" Stay Area is created if:

$$(\ t_{i+1} > \alpha\,.\,\theta)\ \ AND\ \ \left(d_{i+1} < \beta\left(\frac{d_i}{t_i} \times t_{i+1}\right)\right) \tag{3}$$

where t_i and d_i are respectively the time and distance intervals between W_{i-1}, and W_i, and t_{i+1} and d_{i+1} the time and distance intervals between W_i, and W_{i+1}. The size m of the trend window depends on the default sampling interval used for data collection. In our experiments, considering 5 way points with a 10 seconds sampling interval and a walking speed of 1.5 m/sec it allows computing a mean values over 60 meters which is enough to build the trend. α can be set either dynamically or statically depending on the targeted goals. In our experiments we create as Stay Area if the disappearance is longer than 10 times the mean time interval ($\alpha = 10$). As for setting the maximal radius allowed from W_i, the idea is to keep the reappearance position (W_{i+1}) close enough from the disappearance position (W_i) and therefore much below the distance that could have been made in the meantime keeping the same mean speed). In our experiment we used the following setting: $\beta = 0.2$.

Also, as a stay area is a sequence of way points, for convenience when computing a distance with respect to another location (such as a POI), we define the centroid as a temporal barycenter where each way point W_i gets as weight the value of the time interval t_i between W_i and W_{i+1}.

$$G_j = \frac{\sum_{i=1}^{n} t_i W_i}{\sum_{i=1}^{n} t_i} \quad (4)$$

As for the shape of a SA we use the convex hull [22] which provides a closer fit to the covered surface.

3 Experiments

3.1 Dataset

In order to test our hypothesis, we performed several data collection campaigns monitoring users moves around cities such as Lyon and Grenoble in France. We developed a data recording application deployed on Android phones to capture various direct (SNS), semi-direct (Wi-Fi) and indirect (acceleration, gyroscopic rotation, magnetic field, footsteps) sources of information.

We collected 30 days of data that have been annotated to build a ground truth. This annotation focused on identifying "significant events" (SE) which have a minimal duration of at least 5 minutes. We used 10 days of data for our developments, then 20 days for our evaluation. The size is limited to test cold start profiling starting with small amount of observations. The ground truth is a set of labeled events characterized as $E=\{C_E, T_E, D_E, P_E\}$ where C_E is the event centroid, T_E the starting time stamp of the event, D_E a duration and P_E the event type (which may be related to a registered POI). As a convention in our ground truth the centroid C_E has been positioned at the entrance of the event area. In comparison, $POI=\{C_P, P_P\}$ reflects a registered point of interest within our data warehouse where C_P is the centroid location as defined in the database and P_P the name of the POI. $A=\{C_A, T_A, D_A, P_A\}$ is a detected area where $P_A \leftarrow P_P$ if $C_A \approx C_P$.

Therefore, from this dataset two different evaluations are performed: the SA detection method and the sematic disambiguation. For the first task (Table 2) a match between A and E is validated if: the Haversine distance between C_A and C_E is below 30 meters and $(T_A - T_E) < 5$ minutes. For the second task (Table 3) a match is validated if : $P_A \approx P_E$.

Table 2. Evaluation of Detected Stay Areas

Labelled events above 5 min (E)	152
Detected Stay Area Candidates (A)	143
Correct Stay Area ($C_A \approx C_E$)	121
False positive	22
Missed events	9
Recall	0.796
Precision	0.8461
F1-mesure	0.8202

Table 3. Evaluation of POI match

Labelled events above 5 min (E)	152
Labelled POI registered in our database	89
Valid match ($P_A \approx P_E$)	49
Candidates not in database	63
Incorrect candidates	9
Missed events	40

3.2 Results analysis

For the first task (table 2), the lack of way point precision within trajectories is the main source of false positive. Computed temporal barycenters are located too far from real event centroids for match validation. Then noise in trajectory data (artificial leaps in way point sequences) also impacts stay points (and therefore Stay area) detection. Exact WP positioning is really critical to increase recall and precision for SA detection.

Exact localization of centroids for detected SA, labelled events and registered POI is also a major issue for the second task as it cumulates two problems. The first one is a lack of overlap between centroids. If, due to a lack of a precision, C_A and C_P are not close enough then no alignment is made between A and P. Furthermore, even if a match is granted it may happen that C_P and C_E are not close enough. In such case it is not possible to match P_A and P_E and therefore to miss some events. To overcome this problem one option could be to increase the distance threshold for matching centroids but this has side effects.

Indeed, the second issue involves the lack of completeness of POI databases. If a user visits a friend in his apartment, this place generally is not registered ("candidates not in database") in our database, but if there is a near-by POI (e.g. a doctor or business office in the next apartment) then flexibility over centroid distances ends-up in allowing a match between the stay area and the POI. Ruling out these cases is very challenging and may involve comparing SA surfaces with registered POI surfaces (if available), or possibly to consider additional information such as broadcasted Wi-Fi identification.

4 Discussion and Next Steps

4.1 Conclusion

We presented in this paper the first phase of an on-going experimental project aiming to test ambient intelligence to support mobile users in a context of strong data privacy protection. Users' profile and preferences are computed locally, in isolation from the crowd. This is a paradigm shift facing several challenges such as exact user localization (typically when entering to indoor or covered areas) and semantic disambiguation of significant places taking into account a lack of completeness in existing POI databases. The next development phase will address indoor POI detection and the disambiguation of detected stay areas based on the context. Then we plan to compare these results with non-privacy oriented POI detection methods as those performed by central servers to evaluate the loss depending on selected paradigm. The last phase will be to test the usefulness of inferred user's profiles for on-the-fly POI recommendation in the Ambient Wanderer experiment.

References

1. Cook D., Augusto J., Jakkula V.: Ambient Intelligence: Technologies, applications, and opportunities. In Pervasive and Mobile Computing. Vol. 5, Issue 4, pp. 277-298, (2009). https://doi.org/10.1016/j.pmcj.2009.04.001
2. Goldberg, D., Nichols, D., Oki, B. M. and Terry, D.: Using collaborative filtering to weave an information tapestry. Communication. ACM 35, pp. 61–70, (1992)
3. Salton, G., Wong, A. and Yang, C. S.: A Vector Space Model for Automatic Indexing. Communication ACM 18, pp.613–620, (1975).
4. Levinas C.: An Analysis of Memory Based Collaborative Filtering Recommender Systems with Improvement Proposals. In master thesis. Universitat Politecnica de Catalunya, (2014).
5. Pennock D., Horovitz E., Lawrence S., Giles L.: Collaborative filtering by personality diagnosis: a hybrid memory- and model-based approach. In Proceedings of the Sixteenth conference on Uncertainty in artificial intelligence (UAI'00), pp. 473-480 Stanford, California, (2000)

6. Sarwar B., Karypis G., Konstan J. and Riedl J.: Item-Based Collaborative Filtering Recommendation Algorithms. In Proceedings of the 10th World Wide Web Conference (WWW10), Hong Kong. ACM 1-58113-348-0/01/0005, (2000).
7. Li B., Yang Q., Xue X.: Transfer Learning for Collaborative Filtering via a Rating-Matrix Generative Model. Proceedings of the 26th International Conference on Machine Learning, Montreal, Canada, (2009).
8. Griffith J, O'Riordan C., Sorensen H.: A Constrained Spreading Activation Approach to Collaborative Filtering. In Proceedings of the 10th International Conference on Knowledge-Based & Intelligent Information & Engineering Systems (KES06), Bournemouth, (2006). DOI:10.1007/11893011_97
9. Kubica J., Moore A., Cohn D., Schneider J.: Finding Underlying Connections: A Fast Graph-Based Method for Link Analysis and Collaboration Queries. In Proceedings of the Twentieth International Conference on Machine Learning, Washington DC, USA, (2003).
10. Lee J, Sun M., Lebanon G..: A Comparative Study of Collaborative Filtering Algorithms. Arxiv 2012. https://arxiv.org/pdf/1205.3193.pdf
11. Hidasi B., Karatzoglou A., Baltrunas L., Tikk D.: Session- based Recommendations with Recurrent Neural Networks. In Proceedings of the 6th International Conference on Learning Representations (ICLR 2016), Vancouver, Canada, (2016).
12. Fanaeepour M., Rubinstein B.: Beyond Points and paths: Counting Private Bodies. In Proceeding of the 16th Conference on Data Mining (ICDM 2016), Barcelona, Spain, pp. 131-140, (2016).
13. Sumitkumar K. ,Sheetal G., Debajyoti M.: User Profiling Trends, Techniques and Applications. In International Journal of Advance Foundation and Research in Computer (IJAFRC) Volume 1, Issue 1, (2014)
14. Carroll A., Heiser G.: An Analysis of Power Consumption in a Smartphone. In Proceedings of the 2010 USENIX conference, Boston, USA, (2010).
15. Li F., Zhao C., Ding G, Gong J., Liu C, Zhao F.: A Reliable and Accurate Indoor Localization Method Using Phone Inertial Sensors. In Proceedings of 14th International Conference on Ubiquitous Computing (UbiComp 2012), Pittsburgh, USA, (2012).
16. Hoflinger F., Zhang R., Reindl L., Muller J., Burgard W.: A Wireless Micro Inertial Measurement Unit (IMU). In Proceedings of the IEEE International Instrumentation and Measurement Technology Conference (I2MTC), Graz, Austria, (2012).
17. Guo S., Xiong H., Zheng X. and Zhou Y.: Activity Recognition and Semantic Description for Indoor Mobile Localization. In Journal Sensors (Basel), Mar; 17(3): 649., (2017), doi: 10.3390/s17030649
18. Radu V., Katsikouli P., Sarkar R. and Marina M.: Semi-Supervised Learning Approach for Robust Indoor-Outdoor Detection with Smartphones. In Proceedings of 12th ACM Conference on Embedded Networked Sensor Systems (SenSys 2014), Memphis, USA. ACM 978-1-4503-3143-2/14/11, (2014). http://dx.doi.org/10.1145/2668332.2668347
19. Vincenty, T.: Direct and Inverse Solutions of Geodesics on the Ellipsoid with application of nested equations. Survey Review. XXIII (176): pp. 88–93 (1975)
20. Li Q., Zheng Y., Xie X., Chen Y., Liu W., and Ma W.-Y.: Mining user similarity based on location history. In Proceedings of the 16th ACM SIGSPATIAL international conference on Advances in geographic information systems, Irvine, California, (2008)
21. Yuan N., Zheng Y., Zhang L., and Xie X.: T-Finder: A recommender system for finding passengers and vacant taxis. Published in IEEE Transaction on Knowledge and Data Engineering, Vol. 25, Issue 10, pp. 2390–2403, (2013).
22. Andrew A.: Another Efficient Algorithm for Convex Hulls in Two Dimensions, Info. Proc. Letters 9, pp. 216-219 (1979). DOI:10.1016/0020-0190(79)90072-3

Machine Learning-Assisted Prediction of Surgical Mortality of Lung Cancer Patients

Sidra Xu

The Harker School, San Jose, CA 95130, USA

Abstract. Operative mortality rates are currently not predictable; there are no tools to help health professionals determine prognoses and assist patients in making informed decisions. To address these issues, a machine learning algorithm was developed to accurately predict operative mortality using lung cancer patients as an example, which provides quick and accurate information as to whether or not a lung-cancer patient should undergo surgery based on a mortality prediction. We implemented a comparison of five different computational models: Naive Bayes, Support Vector Machine, Random Forest, Adaptive Boost, and Extreme Gradient Boost (XGBoost). Of the five algorithms we tested, XGBoost, a powerful yet relatively new algorithm that is just beginning to make its presence in the field of medical research, produced the best results, giving a testing-accuracy over 97%, a 10% increase over previous research. A broader goal of this project is to help redefine decision-making procedures for hospitals, healthcare professionals, and patients by providing an intelligent system capable of data analysis and optimization. Although our current example utilizes only data on thoracic surgery for lung cancer, this concept of machine learning-assisted decision-making can be expanded to incorporate more types of diseases, hospitals, and patients in the future.

Keywords: Surgical mortality · Operative mortality · Lung cancer · Machine learning · Algorithms · Extreme Gradient Boost.

1 Introduction

Operative mortality rates are currently not predictable; there is no data available in a systematic format to help health professionals predict prognoses and help patients make informed decisions. Postoperative complications are the main reason for increased costs in surgery, and patients who develop complications use a disproportionately larger share of available resources for a hospital. According to the US National Library of Medicine, between 1992 and 2003, the average cost of operative death on lung cancer patient was $38,088 [1]. Moreover, a study conducted by the British Medical Journal found that doctors were only able to predict life expectancies accurately 19.7% of the time [6]. As a result, many patients are uncertain if surgery is a viable option for them. To address this issue, we aim to develop machine learning algorithms that accurately predict operative mortality of patients, with lung cancer patients as an example, to use in an intelligent system that allows for data analysis and optimization. The application of such systems is expected to redefine decision-making procedures for patients, hospitals, and healthcare professionals in the near future.

2 Methods

Five different machine learning models (Naive Bayes, Support Vector Machine, Random Forest, Adaptive Boosting, and Extreme Gradient Boost) from the Python scikit-learn library were evaluated on the dataset and compared using 10-fold cross validation under two data pre-processing procedures, data balancing and feature engineering.

2.1 Data

Publicly available data from the UC Irvine Machine Learning Repository was used to train and test the machine learning algorithms. The database is part of the National Lung Cancer Registry and contains data compiled by researchers Marek Lubicz, Konrad Pawelczyk, Adam Rzechonek, and Jerzy Kolodziej at Polands Wroclaw Thoracic Surgery Centre [7]. It is collected from patients that underwent major lung resection surgery for primary lung cancer between 2007 and 2011. The data is represented as follows: each of the 470 rows represents one patient and each of the 17 columns represents one feature. One of the 17 features is a true/false label, indicating whether the given patient lived or died within a year after surgery. The 17 features include both class data, such as the presence of pain or cough before surgery, as well as continuous data, such as a patients forced vital capacity, size of the original tumor, and age.

The main challenge of this study is the highly imbalanced data: only 70 out of 470 instances, i.e. 14.9% of the data, are associated with the positive label (death within one year). This problem is resolved with a bootstrapping algorithm, ROS (Random Over Sampler). Other sampling techniques are also experimented with, including SMOTE (Synthetic Minority Over-sampling Technique). Another challenge lies with the features that are available for in-depth analysis of the data by machine learning. It was shown in previous study that there was much difficulty in drawing correlations between the various features. This issue is dealt with feature engineering. A number of new features are created in this study for the purpose of better representing the underlying relationships amongst various features of the dataset and thus improved model accuracy [8].

2.2 Data Balancing

Data balancing algorithms, ROS and SMOTE, are implemented to compare with the base case without data balancing. ROS algorithm generates new samples in the under-represented class by randomly sampling with replacement the current available samples until the classes are balanced [4]. SMOTE, on the other hand, generates new samples through interpolation of nearby samples [3].

2.3 Feature Engineering

To derive the important features that could be used for creating new features, a feature ranking model is conducted on the original dataset. Subsequently the top three most relevant features, FVC, FEV, and Age (Figure 1) are used to create nine new features in total, by performing various mathematical operations, including addition, subtraction, multiplication, division, and exponential calculations.

3 Results and Discussions

Shown in Table 1 is a summary of prediction accuracy data obtained in this study. Among five different predictive models examined, XGBoost has provided the highest accuracy, with an improvement of nearly 8% than the next best algorithm, namely adaptive boosting. Both boosting models are more robust than Random Forest and Support Vector Machine, with close matches between training accuracy and test accuracy. Results with Random Forest and Support Vector Machine are also decent except over-fitting could be an issue. In contrast, the performance of Naive Bayes is only slightly better than random guess.

The success of gradient boosting algorithms in this study contrasts with the previous study, where Support Vector Machine was used [2]. Similarly to what has been found in this work with Support Vector Machine, the researchers noted that their models also struggled with over-fitting, with their testing accuracy at 87% but training accuracy at 99% [2]. This difference in performance between the two types of algorithms suggests that gradient boosting models may be good choices of predictive models for datasets similar to what is used in this study as they implement gradient boosted decision trees, where new models are created that predict the residuals or errors of prior models and subsequently added together to produce the final prediction [5]. In comparison to other algorithms, these models are still very new to the field of medical research.

Table 1. Training and testing accuracy of various algorithms with data balancing (ROS) and feature engineering

Model	Training Accuracy	Testing Accuracy
Naive Bayes	0.5563	0.5521
Support Vector Machine	0.9969	0.8629
Random Forest	0.8723	0.8436
Adaptive Boosting	0.9000	0.8943
Extreme Gradient Boost	0.9997	0.9731

In addition to algorithm selection, data balancing and feature engineering have also played important roles in model performance, as demonstrated in Table 2 using the best algorithm XGBoost as an example. The testing accuracy of XGBoost is improved by more than 10% after data balancing and then by another 2% after feature engineering, reaching a final testing accuracy of 97.3%. For data balancing, ROS, in comparison with SMOTE, has produced better results (over 5%) across all five algorithms tested.

Table 2. Testing accuracy of XGBoost under various pre-processing procedures

Pre-processing Procedure	Testing Accuracy
Base Case	0.8553
Data Balancing (ROS)	0.9588
Data Balancing (ROS) and Feature Engineering	0.9731

Although an improvement of only 2% has been obtained with feature engineering, this procedure has shown to be capable of identifying of both features that are important and that are negligible. Such information is very useful for providing better directions to data collection and analysis and thus help with health care cost savings. Particularly for this study, the feature ranking model before and after feature engineering, as displayed in Figures 1 and 2, reveal that many of the newly engineered features are of significant relevance to the prediction results.

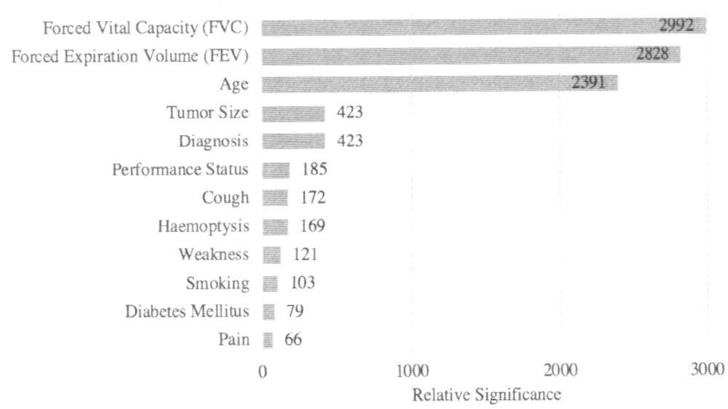

Fig. 1. Feature importance ranking (top 12) - base case

In summary, a robust and accurate machine learning model based on XGBoost for prediction of surgical mortality of lung cancer patients is developed in this study. Combining with data balancing and feature engineering, this model is capable of providing a prediction accuracy up to 97%, an improvement of 10% compared with previous studies [2]. In light of the lack of tools nationwide for doctors and patients to make informed decisions about surgery, this research is an important step to fill the gap. Although the algorithm focuses on only one disease at the moment, it can be applied to incorporate more hospitals and diseases in the future to benefit more people.

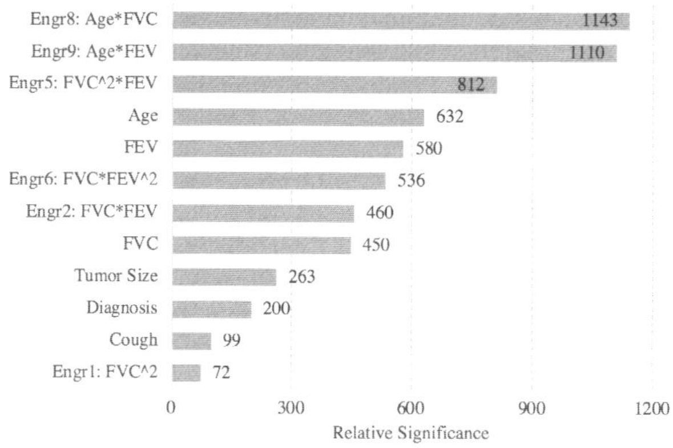

Fig. 2. Feature importance ranking (top 12) - with feature engineering

On the other hand, the output of a machine-learning algorithm, such as what we propose here, should be interpreted with extreme caution, especially when the life a patient is on the line. The prediction result should only be used in a supportive role in assisting doctors and patients when a surgical decision is made. To make this research and others alike practically applicable, it is thus proposed that further research should look into the possibility of re-framing surgical mortality problems into multi-class or multi-label classification, or even regression (e.g. the number of years that a patient survives after a surgery) projects, where more specific and relevant information can be provided, instead of just binary classification. This will be possible with more and more data is becoming available. Additionally, depending on the algorithm used, it would be more informative to provide doctors and patients with detailed information on how the algorithm makes its decision (e.g. the decision tree used in XGBoost) than to provide just a black-box output.

References

1. Cipriano, L.: Lung cancer treatment costs, including patient responsibility, by stage of disease and treatment modality, 19922003. Value Health **14**(1), 41–52 (2011)
2. Abdulhamid, A.: Life Expectancy Post Thoracic Surgery. Stanford University - CS 229 (2014)
3. Chawla, N.: SMOTE: Synthetic Minority Over-sampling Technique. Journal of Artificial Intelligence Research **16**, 321–357 (2002)
4. Lemaitre, G.: Imbalanced-learn: A Python Toolbox to Tackle the Curse of Imbalanced Datasets in Machine Learning. Journal of Machine Learning Research **7**, 1–5 (2016)
5. Chen, T.: XGBoost: A Scalable Tree Boosting System. Proceedings of the 22nd ACM SIGKDD International Conference on Knowledge Discovery and Data Mining, 785–794 (2016)

6. Christakis, N.: Extent and determinants of error in doctors' prognoses in terminally ill patients: prospective cohort study. British Medical Journal **320**(7233), 469–473 (2000)
7. UCI Machine Learning Repository - Thoracic Surgery Data Data Set, https://archive.ics.uci.edu/ml/datasets/Thoracic+Surgery+Data. Last accessed 18 Mar 2019
8. Zheng, A., Casari, A.: Feature Engineering for Machine Learning: Principles and Techniques for Data Scientists. 1st edn. O'Reilly, Sebastopol (2018)

The Impact of Preprocessing on the Classification of Mental Disorders

Yaakov HaCohen-Kerner, Yair Yigal, and Daniel Miller

Dept. of Computer Science, Jerusalem College of Technology – Lev Academic Center
21 Havaad Haleumi St., P.O.B. 16031, 9116001 Jerusalem, Israel
kerner@jct.ac.il,
yigalyairn@gmail.com, danielmiller20@gmail.com

Abstract. Hundreds of millions of people worldwide suffer from various mental disorders. Recent studies have shown that using text classification models, some of the disorders can be identified by intelligent analysis of the texts written by these people. Another related domain is the automatic classification of documents according to their authors' mental state, using supervised mental medical datasets. It is well known that many text classification applications perform various types of preprocessing, e.g., conversion of uppercase letters into lowercase letters, HTML object removal, stopword removal, punctuation mark removal, lemmatization, correction of commonly misspelled words, and reduction of replicated characters. We hypothesize that the application of several specific combinations of preprocessing methods can improve TC results. In this study, we explore the impact of all possible combinations of six basic preprocessing types on text classification of mental disorders. We tested these combinations over three supervised mental medical datasets. In the larger dataset, the best result showed a significant improvement of about 28% over the baseline result using all the six preprocessing methods. In the two other datasets, several combinations of preprocessing methods showed minimal improvement rates over the baseline result. Possible explanations for the small improvements in the two other datasets might be that they are too small to enable significant learning and that the larger dataset includes a much higher number of spelling mistakes, which increases the success of the preprocessing method that deals with correction of commonly misspelled words.

Keywords: Bag of Words, Mental Medical Datasets, Supervised Machine Learning, Text Classification, Text Normalization, Text Preprocessing, Word Unigrams.

1 Introduction

According to the official website of the World Health Organization[1], there are many types of mental disorders. A mental disorder (also called a mental illness), is a behav-

[1] https://www.who.int/en/news-room/fact-sheets/detail/mental-disorders. Last access date: 18-MAR-19.

ioral or mental pattern that causes significant distress or impairment of personal functioning (Bolton [6]). Estimates for common mental disorders for all the world's residents are as follows: depression - about 300 million, bipolar affective disorder - about 60 million people, dementia - about 50 million people, and schizophrenia - about 23 million people. In high-income countries, between 35% and 50%, and in low- and middle-income countries, between 76% and 85%, of people with mental disorders do not receive any treatment for their disorder. Many of these people are not even officially identified.

A mental disorder should be diagnosed by a mental health professional. However, initial identification (or at least suspicion of mental disorder) of many mental disorders can be provided by an intelligent supervised machine learning (ML) system based on a person's social texts such as tweets and blog posts. Such a system would be able to detect suspicion of various mental disorders among people participating in social networks. These data can be presented to professional experts, to whom the suspects can be referred.

Bloom et al. [5] claimed that treating mental disorders generates the single largest health cost, with global costs increasing to $6 trillion annually by 2030. It is known that mental health increases the risk of chronic, non-communicable disorders. Thus, the importance of mental health has driven the attention for new and innovative methods for obtaining reliable information and evidence about mental disorders.

The research domain of text classification (TC) can make a significant contribution to achieving the goal of automatic identification and classification of documents according to the mental state of their authors. TC is a supervised learning task that assigns natural language text documents to one (the typical case) or more predefined categories (Joachims [26]). Classification algorithms typically use a supervised machine learning (ML) algorithm or a combination of several ML algorithms (Sebastiani [41]).

TC is an important component in many research domains including text indexing, information extraction, information retrieval, text mining, and word sense disambiguation (Knight [30]). There are two main types of TC: topic-based classification and stylistic classification. An example of a topic-based classification application is classifying news articles as Business-Finance, Lifestyle-Leisure, Science-Technology, and Sports (Liparas et al. [33]). An example of a stylistic classification application is the classification of literary genres, e.g., action, comedy, crime, fantasy, historical, political, saga, and science fiction (Kessler et al. [28]). Whereas stylistic classification is typically performed using linguistic features such as quantitative features, orthographic features, part of speech (POS) tags, function words, and vocabulary richness features ([18, 19, 21]), topic-based classification is typically performed using word unigrams and/or word n-grams (for $n > 2$) ([22, 23]).

The traditional model for topic-based TC is based on the bag-of-words (BOW) representation, which associates a text with a vector indicating the number of occurrences of each chosen word in the training corpus (Sebastiani [41]). In topic-based classification, various ML methods (e.g., Maximum Entropy (ME, Jaynes [25]), support vector machines (SVMs, Cortes and Vapnik [9]), Naive Bayes (NB, Heckerman [17]), and C4.5 decision tree [36, 37]) have been reported to use the BOW representation to achieve accuracies of 90% and greater (e.g., Joachims [26]).

This study addresses topic-based classification based on the BOW representation. We hypothesize that the application of a selection of preprocessing types can improve the accuracy results of different TC tasks in general. In particular, we investigate the impact of all possible combinations of six basic preprocessing types on TC of mental disorders. We validate the proposed model on three mental medical datasets to determine what preprocessing combination(s) is (are) best suited to classification tasks.

The key contributions of this study are (1) systematic application of all possible combinations of six basic preprocessing types on three mental medical datasets using five ML methods and training and test sets; and (2) presenting the findings that demonstrate what preprocessing combinations for what datasets improve the classification results when using a BOW representation.

The article structure is as follows: Section 2 introduces the issue of identification of mental disorders. Section 3 provides a general background regarding preprocessing for TC. Section 4 introduces the three mental medical examined datasets and several previous classification studies performed on these datasets. Section 5 presents the model and preliminary classification results. Section 6 presents the experimental results and analysis. Finally, Section 7 summarizes, concludes, and suggests ideas for future research.

2 Identification of Mental Disorders

During the last five years, research on mental health has turned to web data sources, with a focus on social media, e.g., Twitter, Facebook and blog entries (Coppersmith et al. [9]; Milne et al. [35]). Previous mental health work has largely focused on several specific mental disorders such as depression (De Choudhury et al. [12]), post-traumatic stress disorder (PTSD) (Coppersmith et al. [8]), and suicide (Jashinsky et al. [24]). According to Coppersmith et al. [10], at least 10 mental conditions can be detected in social media by using NLP methods. These mental conditions are (1) Attention Deficit Hyperactivity Disorder (ADHD), (2) Generalized Anxiety Disorder (Anx), (3) Bipolar Disorder, (4) Borderline Personality Disorder (Border), (5) Depression (Dep), (6) Eating Disorders (Eating; includes anorexia, bulimia, and eating disorders not otherwise specified [EDNOS]), (7) obsessive-compulsive disorder (OCD), (8) post-traumatic stress disorder (PTSD), (9) schizophrenia (Schizo; to include schizophrenia, schizotypal, schizophreniform), and (10) seasonal affective disorder (Seasonal).

In this study, we plan to work on three existing supervised datasets containing texts written by different people with mental disorders of various types. The planned study will deal with automatic TC, with an emphasis on the use of preprocessing methods to test their impact on TC quality. The metric that we use is the accuracy measure.

3 Preprocessing for Text Classification

Preprocessing is common to many information retrieval and text mining tasks in general, and TC tasks in particular. There is a wide variety of text preprocessing types. Examples of basic types are conversion of uppercase letters into lowercase letters,

HTML object removal, stopword removal, punctuation mark removal, reduction of different sets of emoticon labels to a reduced set of wildcard characters, replacement of HTTP links to wildcard characters, word stemming, correction of common misspelled words, and reduction of replicated characters. Examples of more complex preprocessing types are word lemmatization, translation of common slang words into phrases that express the same ideas without using slang, and expansion of abbreviations.

A small number of simple preprocessing types (e.g., conversion of all the uppercase letters into lowercase letters and stopword removal) are performed by many TC systems. Nevertheless, not all of the preprocessing types are always performed. Furthermore, not all of the preprocessing types are considered effective by all TC researchers. For instance, Forman [13], in his study on feature selection metrics for TC, claimed that stopwords are ambiguous and occur sufficiently frequently as to not be discriminating for any particular class. However, HaCohen-Kerner et al. [22] demonstrated that the use of word unigrams including stopwords in the domain of Jewish law documents written in Hebrew-Aramaic lead to improved classification results compared to the results obtained using word unigrams excluding stopwords.

A limited number of studies have analyzed the influence of preprocessing types on TC. A brief summary of some of these studies follows. Song et al. [42] examined 32 combinations of five preprocessing types: stopword removal, word stemming, indexing with term frequency (TF), weighting with inverse document frequency (IDF), and normalization of each document feature vector to unit length. These combinations were applied to two benchmark datasets: Reuters-21578 and 20 Newsgroups using a linear SVM and different lengths of a BOW representation. Their experimental results demonstrated that normalization to unit length can always significantly improve the effectiveness of text classifiers. Conversely, the impact of the other factors, e.g., stopword removal, word stemming, indexing, and weighting are rather minimal.

Lemmatization, stemming, and stopword removal were examined by Toman et al. [45] using the multinomial NB classifier on two datasets: 8000 documents in English selected from Reuters Corpus Volume 1 divided into six categories, and 8000 Czech documents provided by Czech News Agency divided into five categories. They concluded that the best preprocessing method for TC is to apply only stopword removal. Their experiments indicated that stopword removal improved the classification accuracy in most of the cases, although the results were not statistically significant. Further, lemmatization and stemming were more negative than positive for both languages.

Srividhya and Anitha [43] evaluated four preprocessing types: stopword removal, stemming, TF-IDF weighting (Salton [40]), and document frequency on the Reuters 21578 dataset. Their main conclusions were as follows: (1) stopword removal can expand words and enhance the discrimination degree between documents and improve the classification performance, and (2) TF-IDF is required to create the index file from the resulting terms.

Ayedh et al. [2] investigated the effect of three preprocessing types (stopword removal, word stemming, and normalization of certain Arabic letters that have different forms in the same word to one form) on TC for an in-house corpus containing 32,620 news documents divided into ten categories, downloaded from different Arabic news websites. Three ML methods were applied: NB, kNN, and SVM. Experimental analysis revealed that preprocessing has a significant impact on the classification accuracy, especially with the complicated morphological structure of the Arabic language. Choosing appropriate combinations of preprocessing tasks provides a significant improvement in the accuracy of TC depending on the feature size and the ML methods. The best result (a 96.74% micro-F1 value) was achieved by the SVM method using the combination of normalization and stemming.

To summarize the studies that have been presented above, there are no uniformity in the examined datasets, languages, preprocessing types, ML methods, results, or conclusions. Most of the studies use a relatively small number of the following components: datasets, ML methods, preprocessing methods, and combinations of them. Moreover, portions of the conclusions of these studies seemingly contradict each other (e.g., stopword removal improves (Song et al. [42]; Gonçalves et al. [15]) or does not improve classification accuracy (HaCohen-Kerner et al. [22]; Toman et al. [45]). However, the conclusions are not contradictory, because they were derived from experiments on different datasets, different languages, different stopword lists, and different sizes of BOW representation.

Thus, we decided in this research (in contrast to many of the previous studies) to explore the influence of all possible combinations of six basic preprocessing types (more than the number of preprocessing types that were tested in each of the studies mentioned above) on TC for three mental medical datasets, to determine what preprocessing combination(s) is (are) best suited to TC, if any. Our experiments were applied using training and test sets.

4 The Examined Mental Medical Datasets and Several Previous Classification Studies Performed on These Datasets

The three examined mental medical datasets are presented below. Table 1 presents the general statistics of each dataset.

Table 1. Statistics about the three datasets.

Dataset	CLPsych 2015	CLPsych 2016	CLPsych 2017
# of words in the dataset	30,655,951	140, 678	234,490
# of char. In the dataset	208,178,868	1,772,235	3,016,516
avg. # of words per doc.	26,773.75	148.55	147.66
avg. # of char. per doc.	181,815.60	1,871.42	1,899.56
median # of words per doc.	29,926	111	113
median # of char. per doc.	198,217	1628	1,690
std. # of words per doc.	14,954.15	114.97	107.41
std. # of char. per doc.	103,424.93	803.14	743.01

CLPsych 2015[2]

The 2015 dataset was constructed as part of the 2015 CLPsych shared task (Coppersmith et al. [9]). The dataset consists of public tweets collected using the Twitter API, and is divided into training and testing categories. The training portion consists of 327 users with depression, and 246 users with posttraumatic stress disorder (PSTD). For each user, an age-and gender-matched control user is included, resulting in a total of 1,146 users. The test data contained 150 users with depression, 150 users with PTSD, and an age- and gender-matched control for each, making a total of 600 users. For each user, their most recent public tweets – up to 3,000 tweets – were included in the dataset. Due to resource and time limitations, we used only the 500 most recent tweets. The exact procedure and the specific details of how the data were collected and labeled are described in Coppersmith et al. [8].

Coppersmith et al. [9] summarized the results of the 47 systems that took part in three binary classification experiments on the 2015 dataset: (1) depression versus control, (2) PTSD versus control, and (3) depression versus PTSD. The results were presented in precision and ROC curve values. The most successful systems use topic modeling approaches, which provide strong signals relevant to mental health, and some interpretable groupings of words without significant manual intervention. Simple linguistic features, without the use of advanced machine learning methods, also provide reasonable classification results for these tasks. No information was provided about the application of any preprocessing method.

CLPsych 2016[3]

The 2016 CLPsych Shared Task dataset is centered on the automatic triage of posts from a mental health forum, ReachOut.com, which is an online youth mental health service that provides information, tools, and support to young people aged 14-25. This forum enables people to communicate with each other about issues anonymously, as well as a trained team of moderators who offer support and guidance to users. This dataset contains 65,025 ReachOut.com forum posts, of which 1,277 posts are annotated with four triage labels (*crisis, red, amber,* and *green*, which serve as control cases). The database is split into 977 training posts and 250 testing posts, while the remaining 63,797 posts are unlabeled.

Milne et al. [32] summarized the results of 60 submissions from 15 different teams, which classified triage posts into one of the four labels: green, amber, red or crisis of the 2016 dataset. The official metric for the shared task was macro-averaged F-score. However, the authors note that ordering results by accuracy produces a fairly similar ordering. The top systems achieved similar performance via very different approaches with a (crisis, red and amber) macro-averaged F-score of 0.42 and accuracy value of 0.85 for the three following labels: crisis, red, and amber. Kim et al. [29] applied a SGD classifier with a small feature space including only TF-IDF weighted unigrams, and post embeddings. They applied the following preprocessing methods: HTML object

[2] http://www.cs.jhu.edu/~mdredze/datasets/clpsych_shared_task_2015/ Last access date: 19-MAR-19.

[3] http://www.aclweb.org/anthology/W16-0312 Last access date: 19-MAR-19.

removal, non-ASCII characters removal, converting uppercase letters into lowercase letters, and stopword removal. Brew [7] applied a baseline RBF-kernel SVM using TF-IDF weighted unigrams and bigrams, author type, post kudos, and whether a post is the first in its thread. No information was provided about the application of any preprocessing method.

CLPsych 2017[4]

The CLPsych 2017 dataset contains data from the same source as the CLPsych 2016 dataset. The 2017 version contains 65,756 forum posts (compared with 65,025 forum posts from 2016), of which 1,188 posts are annotated with triage labels (crisis, red, amber or green) – compared to the 1,277 annotated posts in 2016. The data collection and the annotation process were similar to that of the CLPsych 2016 dataset. Although there is a large overlap in data between the data sets CLPsych 2016 and 2017, we decided to also experiment on the CLPsych 2017 dataset in order to have more experiments.

Altszyler et al. [1] obtained the first place for several of the subtasks of the CLPsych 2017 Shared Task. They applied various versions of SVMs with linear kernels and Radial Basis Function (RBF) kernels using 2,799 features belong to seven feature sets, four of them were content based features: (Word2vec, word unigrams and bigrams, Metadata, and Body), and the remaining are context-based ones (Interaction features, Adjacent features, and Author features). They applied HTML object removal, and conversion of uppercase letters into lowercase letters in addition to word tokenization and conversion of ReachOut links, other webpage links, author mentions, and forum's emoticons to tokens such as #reachout link, #ref link, and #reference.

5 The Model and Preliminary Results

Our approach is to compare the accuracy results obtained using the original files without any preprocessing, to the results achieved using all possible combinations of the following six basic preprocessing types: **C** – spelling correction, **H** – HTML object removal, **L** – converting uppercase letters into lowercase letters, **P** – punctuation mark removal, **R** – reduction of repeated characters, and **S** – stopword removal. We consider all 63 ($2^6 - 1$) non-empty combinations of these six basic preprocessing types. The spelling correction is performed using an autocorrect library, written by McCallum [34][5]. The application of the S preprocessing type deletes all instances of 423 stopwords for English text (421 stopwords from Fox [14] plus the letters 'x' and 'z' that are not found in Fox [14], yet are included in many other stopword lists).

In the model, we applied five supervised ML methods: (1) Bayes networks (BN) (Pourret et al. [38]), (2) simple logistics (SL) (Landwehr et al. [31], Sumner et al. [44]), (3) sequential minimal optimization (SMO) (Platt [39], Keerthi et al. [27]), (4) J48

[4] http://clpsych.org/shared-task-2017/ Last access date: 19-MAR-19.

[5] https://github.com/phatpiglet/autocorrect/ Last access date: 19-MAR-19.

(Quinlan [36, 37]), and (5) Random Forest (RF) (Breiman [3,4]) using the WEKA platform with their default parameters (Witten and Frank [46], Hall et al. [16]). For each TC task, we used the experimental mode in WEKA Version 3.9.1 with the following settings: train (67%) / test (33%) (data randomized) and the number of repetitions of the experiment set to 10. As mentioned before, we use the accuracy measure as our metric.

A brief description of these five ML methods is as follows: BN is a variant of a probabilistic statistical classification model that represents a set of random variables and their conditional dependencies via a directed acyclic graph (Pourret et al. [38]). SL is a WEKA implementation of a multinomial logistic regression (LR) model with a ridge estimator. SMO (Platt [39], Keerthi et al. [27]) is a variant of the SVM ML method (Cortes and Vapnik [11]). The SMO method is an iterative method created to solve the optimization problem frequently found in SVM methods. J48 is a JAVA implementation of Quinlan's C4.5 (version 8) algorithm (Quinlan [36, 37]). J48 uses greedy techniques, determines the most predictive attribute at each step, and splits a node based on this attribute. RF is an ensemble learning method for classification and regression (Liaw and Wiener [32]). Ensemble methods use multiple learning algorithms to obtain better predictive performance than that which can be obtained from any of the constituent learning algorithms. RF operates by constructing a multitude of decision trees at training time, and outputting classification for the case at hand by averaging the results of all the decision trees.

The general TC algorithm is as follows:
For each dataset, perform the following steps:

1. Compute the frequencies of all word unigrams included in the training dataset
2. Sort these words in descending order according to their frequencies.
3. The top 5,000 frequent word unigrams are selected.
4. Apply five supervised ML methods (BN, SL, SMO, J48, and RF) to classify, using from 1,000 to 5,000 word-unigrams (in steps of 1,000).
5. Determine 1,000 as the number of word unigrams for the BOW representation (see explanations after this algorithm).
6. The accuracy results of each of these five supervised ML methods, using 1,000 word-unigrams, are defined as the baseline results.
7. For each combination of the six preprocessing methods (there are 63 possible combinations), perform:
   - 7.1. Apply the chosen preprocessing combination on the training dataset.
   - 7.2. Compute the frequencies of all word unigrams.
   - 7.3. Sort these words in descending order according to their frequencies.
   - 7.4. Select the top 1,000 frequent word unigrams.
   - 7.5. Apply each ML method on the selected 1,000 word-unigrams.

To determine the number of word unigrams for the BOW representation, we performed TC experiments for each pair of dataset and ML method, using five different sets, containing 1000-, 2000-, 3000-, 4000-, and 5000-word unigrams. Tables 2-4 present the TC accuracy results using 1000-, 2000-, 3000-, 4000-, and 5000-word unigrams for the three examined benchmark datasets and five applied supervised ML methods.

The best accuracy result in each table is highlighted in **bold**. The annotation "v" or "*" indicates that a specific result in a certain column is statistically better (v) or worse (*) than the results using 1000 word unigrams (i.e., the first row in each dataset). To compare the different results, we performed statistical tests using a corrected paired two-sided t-test with a confidence level of 95%.

Table 2. TC accuracy results for various feature set sizes & 5 ML methods on CLPsych 2015.

# of word unigrams	ML methods				
	BN	**SL**	**SMO**	**J48**	**RF**
1000	52.61	62.13	57.55	49.3	58.9
2000	53.13	59.59	58.32	48.48	58.69
3000	53.37	61.68	58.29	47.95	56.97
4000	54.27	**62.39**	60.67	49.17	58.27
5000	54.46	60.94	61.33	49.62	57.21

Table 3. TC accuracy results for various feature set sizes & 5 ML methods on CLPsych 2016.

# of word unigrams	ML methods				
	BN	**SL**	**SMO**	**J48**	**RF**
1000	61.04	65.81	65.66	61.34	**67.06**
2000	61.09	64.56	63.82	61.22	65.58
3000	61.09	64.69	65.09	61.24	64.97
4000	61.09	66.06	66.06	61.24	64.12
5000	61.09	65.55	66.7	61.24*	63.36*

Table 4. TC accuracy results for various feature set sizes & 5 ML methods on CLPsych 2017.

# of word unigrams	ML methods				
	BN	**SL**	**SMO**	**J48**	**RF**
1000	57.33	66.6	**66.89**	60.9	66.24
2000	57.4	65.23	64.37	61.09	65.17
3000	57.4	65.4	64.22*	61.07	64.22*
4000	57.4	65.55	64.22*	61.07	63.49*
5000	57.4	65.11	65.04	61.07	63.09*

In Tables 3 and 4, the best accuracy result was obtained using 1,000 word uni-grams. Only in Table2, the best result was obtained using more than 1,000 word unigrams. However, the difference between the best result (62.39%) and the 2nd best result (62.13%) is minimal and insignificant. Due to runtime considerations, we decided to use 1,000 word unigrams as our baseline feature set in the next experiments.

6 Experimental Results

It is imoptnat to note that we are not competing with the teams that won the competitions on the above mentioned databases. We use only 1,000 word n-grams, and our goal is to check which combinations of preprocessing methods can improve TC results.

Table 5 presents the comparisons between the baseline accuracy results, obtained using the normalized frequencies of the top 1,000 occurring word unigrams, to the accuracy results achieved using every single preprocessing type. The best accuracy result in each column (i.e., ML method) is highlighted in **bold**, and the best accuracy result for each dataset is highlighted in **bold** and underscore.

Table 5. TC accuracy results using each single preprocessing type for the three datasets.

Dataset	Preprocessing type	BN	SL	SMO	J48	RF
CLPsych 2015	None	52.61	62.13	57.55	49.3	58.9
	C	**85.53v**	**83.79v**	**81.54v**	**78.23v**	**84.63v**
	H	52.61	62.13	57.55	49.3	58.9
	L	51.55	62.26	58.45	46.81	57.97
	P	52.76	62.52	57.53	50.2	57.08
	R	52.47	62.68	58.11	48.16	58.72
	S	52.1	65.22	58.82	51.6	59.11
CLPsych 2016	None	61.04	65.81	**65.66**	61.34	67.06
	C	60.66	65.83	65.5	61.27	67.03
	H	60.5	61.47*	59.18*	59.66	61.30*
	L	61.93	**66.01**	65.53	**62.34**	67.47
	P	**62.57**	64.97	63.79	60.96	66.57
	R	61.29	65.68	65.45	61.29	67.11
	S	41.05*	62.65	64.74	62.32	**67.59**
CLPsych 2017	None	57.33	**66.6**	66.89	60.9	**66.24**
	C	56.98	66.47	67.21	60.63	65.63
	H	59.41	60.11*	57.04*	58.76	59.83*
	L	57.42	65.88	**67.27**	60.84	66.03
	P	**63.11v**	65.36	66.54	61.28	65.17
	R	57.08	66.34	67.12	61.05	66.05
	S	42.63*	62.63*	63.64	**62.84**	65.94

The main findings shown in Table 5 are as follows. Regarding the CLPsych 2015 dataset, only the C preprocessing method significantly improved the baseline results for all ML methods, while the other preprocessing methods also improved the results but not significantly. This finding is probably due to the fact that tweets, in general, contain many spelling mistakes and in particular, this is true for the CLPsych 2015 dataset, which is much larger than the other datasets. The best result (85.53%) was achieved by BN, presenting a substantial improvement of 23.4% over the best baseline result (62.13%) among the five baseline results (one baseline for each ML method).

Regarding the CLPsych 2016 and 2017 datasets, no preprocessing method significantly improved the baseline results. The best result for the CLPsych 2016 dataset (67.59%) was achieved by RF using the S preprocessing method, presenting a minimal improvement of 0.53% over the best baseline result (67.06%). The best result for the CLPsych 2017 dataset (67.27%) was achieved by SMO using the L preprocessing method, presenting a minimal improvement of 0.38% over the best baseline result (66.89%).

Interestingly, for all three datasets, some of the combinations of the preprocessing methods not only did not improve the baseline results, but some of them even reduced accuracy results.

As mentioned in Section 4, for each pair of dataset and ML methods, we consider all 63 non-empty possible combinations of the six preprocessing types. Due to space limitations, we cannot present the results of all combinations for all pairs of one dataset and one ML method. In Table 6, we present the three best results for each dataset. The C and L preprocessing methods are included in the best combination for each dataset; therefore, we also present the result of the CL combination for the 2015 dataset, even though the CL combination was not among the three best combinations for this dataset. For each dataset, the best accuracy result and the combination that achieved this result are highlighted in **bold**.

Table 6. TC accuracy results for the three datasets.

Dataset	Rank	Preprocess-ing combination	Best results (BR)	Method yielding best result	Best base-line result (BBR)	Improve. rate = BR - BBR
CLPsych 2015	1st best	**CHLPRS**	**90.32v**	RF	62.13	28.19
	2nd best	CHLPRS	89.84v	SL		27.71
	3rd best	CHLPRS	89.61v	SMO		27.48
		CL	85.24v	BN		23.09
CLPsych 2016	1st best	**CLS**	**67.95**	RF	67.06	0.89
	2nd best	CL, LS	67.77	RF		0.71
	3rd best	S	67.59	RF		0.53
CLPsych 2017	1st best	**CL**	**67.63**	SMO	66.89	0.74
	2nd best	LR	67.33	SMO		0.44
	3rd best	L	67.27	SMO		0.38

The main findings of CLPsych 2015 are as follows. The best result (90.32%) was achieved by RF using all the six preprocessing methods (CHLPRS), presenting a significant improvement of 28.19% over the best baseline result (62.13%). This result is another significant improvement beyond the result (85.53%) that was achieved by BN using the C preprocessing method.

The main findings of CLPsych 2016 are as follows. The best result (67.95%) was achieved by RF using CLS, presenting a minimal improvement of 0.89% over the best baseline result (67.06%). Unlike the findings for CLPsych 2015, no combination of preprocessing methods significantly improved the baseline result. It is interesting to note that the best system on the 2016 CLPsych Shared Task dataset, Kim et al. (2016)

also applied the LS preprocessing methods in addition to HTML object removal and non-ASCII characters removal.

The main findings of CLPsych 2017 are similar to those achieved for CLPsych 2016. This phenomenon is not surprising, because the 2017 dataset is very similar to the 2016 dataset. The best result (67.63%) was achieved by SMO using CL, presenting a minimal improvement of 0.74% over the best baseline result (66.89%). Altszyler et al. [1] that obtained the first place for several of the subtasks of the CLPsych 2017 Shared Task also applied the L preprocessing method in addition to HTML object removal as well as other preprocessing methods.

For the the 2017 dataset as well, unlike the findings for CLPsych 2015, no combination of preprocessing methods significantly improved the baseline result. This phenomenon is not surprising, because the two datasets contain data from the same source, and most of the forum posts in the two datasets are identical.

What is common to all the datasets in terms of the best result, is that the best combination of preprocessing methods include the **C** and **L** preprocessing methods. That is to say, the combination of spelling correction (C) and lowercase conversion (L) preprocessing methods enable better classification for all examined datasets. For all the datasets, some of the preprocessing methods (and combinations of them) not only did not improve the baseline results, but even worsened them. That is to say, not every preprocessing method contributes to better classification. Some of them even negatively affect the quality of the classification. Possible explanations of the difference between the significant improvement in the 2015 dataset and the minimal and insignificant improvements in the 2016-7 datasets might be: the larger size of the 2015 dataset that enabled better learning, and probably a much higher incidence of spelling mistakes the 2015 dataset that enabled very significant classification improvement due to the C preprocessing method.

7 Conclusions and Future Work

In this study, we investigated the influence of all possible combinations of six basic preprocessing types (correction of commonly misspelled words, conversion of uppercase letters into lowercase letters, HTML object removal, punctuation mark removal, stopword removal, and reduction of replicated characters). We validated the proposed model on three mental medical datasets using training and test sets to determine what preprocessing combination(s) is (are) the best suited to classification tasks, if any.

We tested the combinations over three mental medical datasets. In the larger dataset, the best result showed a significant improvement over the baseline result using all the six preprocessing methods. In the two other datasets, several combinations of preprocessing methods showed a few minimal improvements over the baseline results. Possible explanations for these phenomena are (1) the two other datasets are too small to enable significant learning and (2) the CLPsych 2015 dataset consists only of tweets, the limited length of each tweet forces the poster to be very concise. This might make the identification of mental disorders easier. By contrast, the CLPsych 2016 & 2017 datasets contain forum posts that are typically much longer than tweets. As a result, the actual information might be more spread out over a larger forum post, making it harder to classify.

The general conclusions for the datasets verified are as follows. (1) There is no uniform answer to the question of whether TC of mental disorders can be improved using a certain combination of preprocessing types. The answer depends on a variety of criteria such as the selected domain, dataset, ML method, and size of the BOW representation, and the tested combination of preprocessing methods. (2) It is recommended to try at least each preprocessing method alone, and then combinations of successful preprocessing methods, in order to find an improvement (hopefully a significant one). (3) It should be known that there are preprocessing combinations that can impair the quality of the classification and should not be used. (4) The best combination of preprocessing methods for all three datasets include the **C** and **L** preprocessing methods and include **S** for two datasets. The **L** preprocessing method was also applied by systems which won the shared tasks, as well as other methods such as the **S** and **H**.

Future research proposals include (1) implementing TC experiments using various combinations of the number of selected word n-grams and various combinations of preprocessing methods; (2) implementing TC experiments using additional feature types, e.g., word/character n-grams, skip word/character n-grams while working with TF-IDF values; (3) implementing TC experiments for combinations that include more complex types of preprocessing such as lemmatization of words and expansion of common abbreviations (e.g. [20]); (4) applying other ML methods such as deep learning methods; and (5) conducting experiments on additional mental medical datasets written in English, as well as datasets written in other languages.

Acknowledgments. This work was partially funded by an internal research grant from Jerusalem College of Technology, Lev Academic Center. The authors thank two anonymous reviewers for their reviews and fruitful comments. Thanks also to Shalom Mashbaum for his English editing.

References

1. Altszyler, E., Berenstein, A. J., Milne, D., Calvo, R. A., Slezak, D. F.: Using contextual information for automatic triage of posts in a peer-support forum. In Proceedings of the Fifth Workshop on Computational Linguistics and Clinical Psychology: From Keyboard to Clinic, pp. 57-68 (2018).
2. Ayedh, A., Tan, G., Alwesabi, K., Rajeh, H.: The effect of preprocessing on Arabic document categorization. Algorithms, 9 (2), 27 (2016).
3. Breiman, L.: Bagging predictors. Univ. California Technical Report No. 421 (1994).
4. Breiman, L.: Random forests. Machine Learning. 45, 5–32 (2001).
5. Bloom, D. E., Cafiero, E. T., Jané-Llopis, E., Abrahams-Gessel, S., Bloom, L. R., Fathima, S., Feigl, A. B., Gaziano, T., Mowafi, M., Pandya, A., Prettner, K., Rosenberg, L., Seligman, B., Stein, A., Weinstein, C.: The global economic burden of noncommunicable diseases (No. 8712). Program on the Global Demography of Aging (2012).
6. Bolton, D. What is mental disorder?: an essay in philosophy, science, and values. Oxford University Press (2008).

7. Brew, C.: Classifying ReachOut posts with a radial basis function SVM. In Proc. of the third workshop on computational linguistics and clinical psychology, pp. 138-142 (2016).
8. Coppersmith, G. A., Harman, C. T., Dredze, M. H.: Measuring post traumatic stress disorder in Twitter. In ICWSM (2014).
9. Coppersmith, G., Dredze, M., Harman, C., Hollingshead, K., Mitchell, M.: CLPsych 2015 shared task: Depression and PTSD on Twitter. In Proceedings of the 2nd Workshop on Computational Linguistics and Clinical Psychology: From Linguistic Signal to Clinical Reality, pp. 31–39, Denver, Colorado, June 5. ACL (2015A).
10. Coppersmith, G., Drede, M., Harman, C., Hollingshead, K.: From ADHD to SAD: Analyzing the language of mental health on Twitter through self-reported diagnoses. In Proceedings of the 2nd Workshop on Computational Linguistics and Clinical Psychology: From Linguistic Signal to Clinical Reality, pp. 1-10 (2015B).
11. Cortes, C., Vapnik, V.: Support-vector networks. Machine Learning, 20 (3), 273–297 (1995).
12. De Choudhury, M., Gamon, M., Counts, S., Horvitz, E.: Predicting depression via social media. ICWSM, 13, 1-10 (2013).
13. Forman, G.: An extensive empirical study of feature selection metrics for text classification. Journal of Machine Learning Research, 3, 1289–1305 (2003).
14. Fox, C.: A Stop List for General Text. ACM SIGIR Forum, 24, 1–2, 19–35 (1989).
15. Gonçalves, C. A., Gonçalves, C. T., Camacho, R., Oliveira, E. C.: The impact of preprocessing on the classification of MEDLINE documents. In Proceedings of the 10th International Workshop on Pattern Recognition in Information Systems, 53–61 (2010).
16. Hall, M., Frank, E., Holmes, G., Pfahringer, B., Reutemann, P., Witten, I. H.: The WEKA data mining software: an update. ACM SIGKDD Explorations Newsletter, 11, 1, 10–18 (2009).
17. Heckerman, D.: Bayesian networks for data mining. Data mining and knowledge discovery, 1(1), 79-119 (1997).
18. HaCohen-Kerner, Y., Beck, H., Yehudai, E., Rosenstein, M., Mughaz, D.: Cuisine: Classification using stylistic feature sets &/or name-based feature sets. Journal of the American Society for Information Science and Technology 61 (8), 1644–57 (2010A).
19. HaCohen-Kerner Y., Beck, H. Yehudai, E., Mughaz, D.: Stylistic feature sets as classifiers of documents according to their historical period and ethnic origin. Applied Artificial Intelligence, 24(9), 847-862 (2010B).
20. HaCohen-Kerner, Y., Kass, A., Peretz, A.: HAADS: A Hebrew Aramaic abbreviation disambiguation system. Journal of the American Society for Information Science and Technology, 61(9), 1923-1932 (2010C).
21. HaCohen-Kerner, Y., Rosenfeld, A., Tzidkani, M., Cohen, D. N.: Classifying papers from different computer science conferences. In Proc. of the International Conference on Advanced Data Mining and Applications (pp. 529-541). Springer, Berlin, Heidelberg, (2013).
22. HaCohen-Kerner Y., Mughaz, D., Beck, H., Yehudai, E.: Words as classifiers of documents according to their historical period and the ethnic origin of their authors. Cybernetics and Systems: An International Journal, 39(3), 213-228 (2008).
23. HaCohen-Kerner, Y., Dilmon, R., Friedlich, S., Cohen, D. N.: Classifying True and False Hebrew Stories Using Word N-Grams. Cybernetics and Systems, 47(8), 629-649 (2016).
24. Jashinsky, J., Burton, S. H., Hanson, C. L., West, J., Giraud-Carrier, C., Barnes, M. D., Argyle, T.: Tracking suicide risk factors through Twitter in the US. Crisis (2014).
25. Jaynes, E. T.: Notes on Present Status and Future Prospects. In Maximum Entropy and Bayesian Methods, edited by W. T. Grandy and L. H. Schick. Kluwer, 1-13 (1990).

26.Joachims, T.: Text categorization with support vector machines: Learning with many relevant features. In Proceedings of the European Conference on Machine Learning (ECML). 137–142 (1998).
27.Keerthi, S. S., Shevade, S. K., Bhattacharyya, C., Murthy, K. R. K.: Improvements to Platt's SMO Algorithm for SVM Classifier Design. Neural Computation, 13 (3), 637–649. http://doi.org/10.1162/089976601300014493 (2001).
28.Kessler, B., Nunberg, G., Schutze, H.: Automatic detection of text genre. In Cohen P. R., Wahlster W. (eds.). In Proc. of the 35th Annual Meeting of the ACL and Eighth Conference of the European Section of the Association for Computational Linguistics. 32–38 (1997).
29.Kim, S. M., Wang, Y., Wan, S., Paris, C.: Data61-csiro systems at the clpsych 2016 shared task. In Proceedings of the Third Workshop on Computational Linguistics and Clinical Psychology, 128-132 (2016).
30.Knight, K.: Mining online text. Commun. ACM. 42, 11, 58–61 (1999).
31.Landwehr, N., HECK, M., Frank, E.: Logistic model trees. Machine Learning, 59(1-2), 161–205 (2005).
32.Liaw, A., Wiener, M.: Classification and regression by randomForest. R news, 2(3), 18-22 (2002).
33.Liparas, D., HaCohen-Kerner, Y., Moumtzidou, A., Vrochidis, S., Kompatsiaris, I.: News articles classification using random forests and weighted multimodal features. In Information Retrieval Facility Conference (pp. 63-75). Springer, Cham (2014).
34.McCallum, J.: Python 3 Spelling Corrector. From https://pypi.python.org/pypi/autocorrect/0.1.0 (2014).
35.Milne, D. N., Pink, G., Hachey, B., Calvo, R. A.: CLPsych 2016 Shared Task: Triaging content in online peer-support forums. In Proceedings of the 3rd Workshop on Computational Linguistics and Clinical Psychology: From Linguistic Signal to Clinical Reality, pp. 118–127, San Diego, California, June 16. Association for Computational Linguistics (2016).
36.Quinlan R.: C4.5: Programs for Machine Learning. San Mateo, CA: Morgan Kaufmann Publishers (1993).
37.Quinlan, J. R.: C4. 5: programs for machine learning. Elsevier (2014).
38.Pourret, O., Naïm, P., Marcot, B. (eds.): Bayesian networks: a practical guide to applications (Vol. 73). John Wiley & Sons. (2008).
39.Platt, J. C.: Sequential minimal optimization: A fast algorithm for training support vector machines. Advances in Kernel Methods: Support Vector Learning, 208, 1–21 (1998).
40.Salton, G.: Developments in automatic text retrieval. Science, 974-980 (1991).
41.Sebastiani, F.: Machine learning in automated text categorization. ACM Computing Surveys, 34 (1), 1–47 (2002).
42.Song, F. X., Liu, S. H., Yang, J. Y.: A comparative study on text representation schemes in text categorization. Pattern Analysis and Applications, 8, 199–209 (2005).
43.Srividhya, V., Anitha, R.: Evaluating preprocessing techniques in text categorization. International Journal of Computer Science and Application, 47 (11), 49–51 (2010).
44.Sumner, M., Frank, E., Hall, M.: Speeding up logistic model tree induction. In Proc. of Knowledge Discovery in Databases: PKDD 2005 (Vol. 3721, pp. 675–683). Springer (2005).
45.Toman, M., Tesar, R., Jezek, K.: Influence of word normalization on text classification. In Proceedings of the 1st International Conference on Multidisciplinary Information Sciences & Technologies (2), 354–358. Merida, Spain (2006).
46.Witten, I. H., Frank, E.: Data Mining: Practical machine learning tools and techniques. Morgan Kaufmann (2005).

Suggestion of Density-based Geometric One-Class Classifier using Genetic Algorithm

Do Gyun Kim[1[0000-0002-5149-9417]] and Jin Young Choi[1[0000-0001-6397-3107]]

[1] Department of Industrial Engineering, Ajou University, Suwon, Korea
{rlaehrbs90,choijy}@ajou.ac.kr

Abstract. In recent years, the importance of One-Class Classification (OCC) is growing up in machine learning research. Contrary to classical Multi-Class Classification (MCC) approach, OCC assumes that there exists only one class in dataset, which enables to deal with problematic dataset such as imbalanced dataset. One-Class Hyper-Rectangle Descriptor ($1 - HRD$) is a state-of-the-art OCC classifier that remedies trade-off between classification accuracy and interpretability of classification results. However, $1 - HRD$ generation methods proposed as far lack of consideration for density and distribution of dataset. In addition, they require additional procedure for tuning essential parameters which drastically influence on performance of classifier. Based on these motivations, we suggest a novel method for generation of $1 - HRD$ that can reflect density and distribution of training data, called $1 - HRD_d$. Furthermore, we design a genetic algorithm for systematical generation of $1 - HRD_d$ by allowing to tune parameters such as the number of distributions assumed for dataset. Our work is validated by a numerical experiment using UCI machine learning dataset and well-known baseline methods such as Support Vector Data Description (SVDD) are considered as control group. As a result, we can prove superiority of $1 - HRD_d$ resulted from the proposed genetic algorithm to other OCC algorithms.

Keywords: One-Class Classification, One-Class Hyper-Rectangle Descriptor, Genetic Algorithm.

1 Introduction

Classification is to distinguish data in one class from those in other classes, and it is a representative data analysis method in machine learning. Traditional classification problem assumes that dataset consists of multiple classes, called Multi-Class Classification (MCC). In contrast, One-Class Classification (OCC) is a special case such that there exists only one class, called target class. In other words, OCC divides data into target class and outlier that is not belonging to target class. OCC can be considered as outlier detection or anomaly detection due to this property. Since the numbers of classes in dataset of MCC and OCC are different, they have different ways to generate classifiers used for discriminating target class and outlier. Specifically, in case of OCC, classifiers are obtained by learning patterns of target class thoroughly, whereas classifiers of MCC are obtained by identifying the difference among classes. Based on this difference, OCC shows better performance than MCC in dealing with dataset with some problematic structure such as imbalanced data. MCC approach for such dataset causes inefficiency or degradation of classification accuracy, resulted from the difficulty of assessing difference among classes.

As a novel approach for developing OCC algorithm, One-Class Hyper-Rectangle Descriptors ($1-HRD$) have been suggested [6,7]. They can provide both prominent classification accuracy and interpretability to user, which have been considered as a trade-off in other OCC algorithms. For example, Support Vector Data Description that can guarantee high classification accuracy generates a classifier containing high degree or too complex function that cannot be interpreted by user. In contrast, $1-HRD$ generates Hyper-Rectangle (H-RTGL) consisting of geometric rules called intervals, and they are simple if-and-then shape, which can be easily interpreted by user.

These $1-HRD$ algorithms can be characterized by interval generation method. However, existing interval generation methods for generating $1-HRD$ have limitations that they do not consider density or distribution, which might be important for learning patterns of target class. In addition, they require exhaustive and inefficient search procedure such as a grid search for determining the number of intervals. Based on these motivations, we propose an efficient method for generating $1-HRD$ (i) considering density and distribution of data and (ii) resolving inefficient parameter tuning issue. Specifically, we design $1-HRD$ based on density, called $1-HRD_d$, using genetic algorithm (GA) to resolve the limitations of existing methods.

The rest of this paper is organized as follows. Section 2 describe a literature survey on OCC algorithms and Section 3 suggests $1-HRD_d$ using GA. In section 4, a numerical experiment is carried out to validate the performance of the proposed OCC classifier. In the end, we conclude this paper and address possible extensions by adding some ideas to our work in Section 5.

2 Literature Review

There have been many previous works for developing OCC algorithms, which can be approximately categorized as (i) density estimation-based OCC algorithms, (ii) decision tree-based OCC algorithms, (iii) decision boundary-based OCC algorithms. In this section, we describe their basic concepts, algorithms pertaining to each category, and limitations.

2.1 Density estimation-based OCC algorithms

Density estimation-based OCC classifies data by measuring a probability that an instance belongs to target class, where the probability is calculated by using probability density function (PDF) estimated using training dataset. Specifically, if the probability is larger than a predefined threshold, the instance is classified as target class. Otherwise, the instance is classified as outlier. Barnett and Lewis [2] assumed that PDF of dataset follows a certain normal distribution and estimated its parameters by maximum likelihood estimation. Other than normal distribution such as Gamma distribution was also used for density estimation-based OCC [1]. In addition to such parametric approaches that estimate underlying distribution, nonparametric approaches were also considered. Tarassenko et al. [11] adopted Parzen windows exploiting kernel function and approximating density for classifying patient data. Even though these methodologies showed reasonable classification accuracy and easy to implement, there was no explicit standard for how to determine the threshold used for discriminating target class and outlier.

2.2 Decision tree-based OCC algorithms

Decision tree-based OCC algorithms perform classification by formulating decision tree, which consists of rules to define target class data and to provide interpretability to user. These rules should be extracted from training dataset by considering measures calculated under MCC assumption. For instance, impurity should be computed by using degree of instances from heterogeneous classes. However, this is not possible for OCC. Therefore, DeComite et al. [3] and Denis et al. [4] performed OCC by using representative C4.5 decision tree reinforced with artificial data that can be counterpart of target class data. Random forest consisting of many decision trees was also considered in order to avoid overfitting to training dataset [5]. Even though decision tree-based OCC methods could provide clear rules with interpretability, they required artificial data or unlabelled data that might be classified as outlier. Furthermore, there existed no standard for how many artificial and unlabelled data are required.

2.3 Decision boundary-based OCC algorithms

Decision boundary-based OCC methods extract a boundary that includes data of target class and can be used to distinguish target class and outlier by learning pattern of target class. An instance is classified as target class or outlier according to whether it is in the extracted boundary or not. Most of OCC methods using decision boundary are motivated by Support Vector Machine (SVM). Tax and Duin [12,13] proposed SVDD that generates hyper-sphere including target class by considering support vectors located in the boundary of target class. In other words, an instance is classified as target class if it is within hyper-sphere. Le et al. [8] extended SVDD by considering multiple hyper-sphere simultaneously. Schölkopf et al. [9] suggested One-Class SVM (1-SVM) that finds hyper-plane dividing the origin and target class. Similar to SVM, 1-SVM maximizes the margin representing distance between the origin and hyperplane. OCC methods belonging to this category have prominent classification accuracy and can maintain the performance even if the size of dataset is small. However, their performance is easily affected by hyper-parameter, which has no explicit standard for optimization. Furthermore, resulting classifier has extremely high complexity which can hardly be understood by users.

2.4 One-Class Hyper-Rectangle Descriptor

In order to overcome these limitations, Jeong and Choi [6] proposed geometric OCC classifiers using a decision boundary with a shape of H-RTGL, which is called One-Class Hyper-Rectangle Descriptor ($1-HRD$). Because this method uses a decision boundary consisting of intervals for separating target class and outlier, the classification results can be easily interpreted by users, which is different from SVDD or 1-SVM. Specifically, Jeong and Choi [6] suggested two OCC classifiers using H-RTGLs as follows: One is to generate H-RTGLs by merging overlapped intervals, namely $1-HRD_m$, and the other is to make H-RTGLs by clustering instances, namely $1-HRD_c$. Furthermore, Jeong et al. [7] suggested a method to produce H-RTGLs by partitioning one large interval into small disjoint intervals, namely $1-HRD_p$. However, they did not consider density or distribution of dataset when generating H-RTGLs, which could be utilized to improve the classification accuracy.

3 Suggestion of $1-HRD_d$ using Genetic Algorithm

3.1 Basic Idea of $1-HRD_d$

We describe the basic idea for developing $1-HRD_d$ using genetic algorithm as follows. There exists a dataset $X=\{x_1,x_2,\cdots,x_n\}$, consisting of n instances. Each instance x_i is assumed to contain q features as $x_i=(y_{i1},y_{i2},\dots,y_{iq})$, where y_{ir} is r-th feature of instance x_i. Then, the suggested OCC classifier $1-HRD_d$ can be formulated by generating H-RTGLs, which can be obtained by conjunction of q intervals taken from each feature. Specifically, an interval from feature r is generated as follows: We divide n points $y_{ir}'s(i=1,2,\dots,n)$ into several groups based on certain criteria. Then, for each group we estimate a Gaussian distribution by computing sample mean $\bar{y}$ and standard deviation s of points in it. Based on those parameters, we can construct an interval such as $(\bar{y}-\delta\cdot s,\ \bar{y}+\delta\cdot s)$, where δ is a control parameter for determining the length of interval in order to include points in the considered group. The number of intervals generated is equal to the number of groups, which is employed as a key factor for designing GA in the following.

3.2 Flow Chart of the Proposed Genetic Algorithm

The outline of the suggested algorithm for generating GA-based $1-HRD_d$ is as depicted in Fig. 1. At first, initial population is generated and $1-HRD_d$ is formulated by using the information recorded in each chromosome. Fitness of chromosomes is assessed considering classification performance of resulted classifier. If predefined condition for termination of algorithm is satisfied, the fittest chromosome found so far is selected as a final solution. Otherwise, offspring are produced by applying crossover and mutation operation. Then, new generation is generated by selecting P chromosomes from the current population and offspring produced.

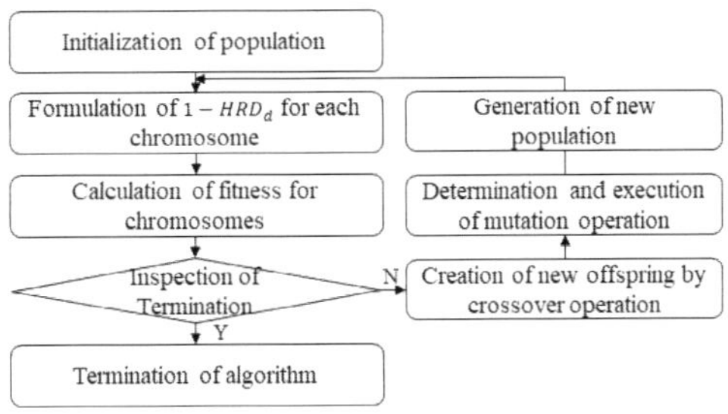

Fig. 1. Flow chart of the proposed GA.

3.3 Design of Genetic Algorithm for $1 - HRD_d$

Chromosome structure and population size. For designing GA, one thing should be considered above all is to define the representation structure of chromosome. In this paper, we devise a chromosome as a vector with size q and each element represents the number of Gaussian distributions assumed for each feature, using real-valued encoding scheme. In other words, r-th gene of chromosome represents the number of Gaussian distributions NG_r assumed for feature r, which can be depicted as Fig. 2. The population size is defined as P, and initial population is generated by randomly.

Ng_r :	3	2	3	1	4

Fig. 2. Chromosome structure.

Generation of $1 - HRD_d$. Based on the information recorded in chromosomes, $1 - HRD_d$ corresponding to each chromosome is generated as follows. At first, we generate intervals corresponding to edges of H-RTGLs composing $1 - HRD_d$ for each feature r by projecting all instances into feature r. This can be done by defining projection function $proj_r(x_i)$ of instance x_i into feature r as

$$proj_r(x_i) = y_{ir}. \forall i, r \tag{1}$$

Then, we apply k_r −means clustering algorithm to the projection points in feature r and separate them into k_r clusters, where k_r is the value of r-th gene in the considered chromosome. Then, projection points in each cluster are mapped into Gaussian distribution. In other words, instances belonging to a cluster of projection points are assumed to follow a certain Gaussian distribution, and we try to generate intervals using it. For instance, suppose that Gaussian distribution $G_r^{q_r}$ corresponding to $q_r(q_r = 1, 2, \cdots, k_r)$-th cluster of projection points in feature r is defined as

$$G_r^{q_r} \sim N(\mu_r^{q_r}, \sigma_r^{q_r}), \tag{2}$$

where $\mu_r^{q_r}$ and $\sigma_r^{q_r}$ are mean and standard deviation of the corresponding Gaussian distribution. Then, the intervals of $1 - HRD_d$ can be calculated based on such statistics of each Gaussian distribution. Specifically, we define the interval generated from Gaussian distribution $G_r^{q_r}$ as

$$ITVL_r^{g_r^{q_r}} = \left[\mu_r^{q_r} - N_\sigma \cdot \sigma_r^{q_r},\ \ \mu_r^{q_r} + N_\sigma \cdot \sigma_r^{q_r}\right], \tag{3}$$

where N_σ is a parameter to determine the length of interval by controlling the degree of reflection of $\sigma_r^{q_r}$. This procedure for generating intervals is performed for each cluster so that the number of intervals generated in feature r is the same as that of Gaussian distribution necessary for generating intervals.

Fig. 3 and Fig. 4 describe interval generation procedure mentioned above. If k_r in feature r is 3 and resulted clusters of projection points are as depicted in Fig. 3, then three intervals are generated from statistics of the corresponding Gaussian distribution as depicted in Fig. 4.

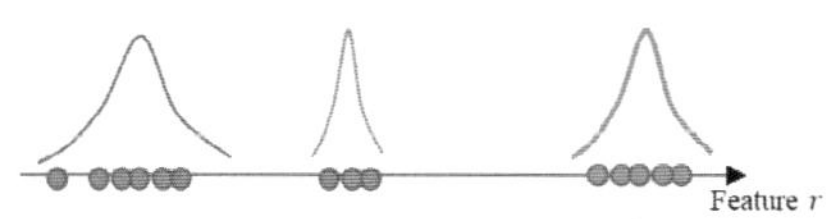

Fig. 3. Clustering projection points and mapping to Gaussian distribution.

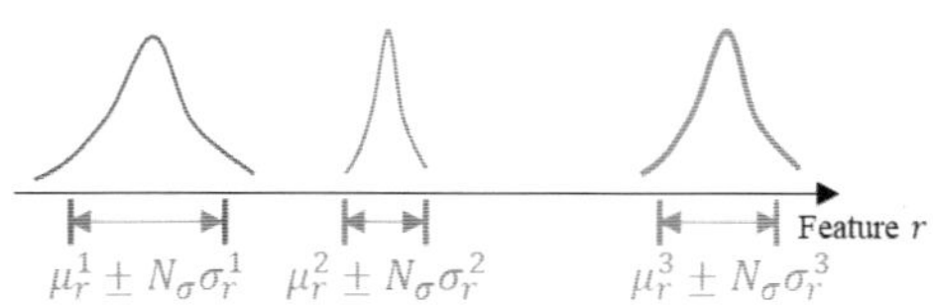

Fig. 4. Interval generation based on the statistics of Gaussian distribution.

Since projection points for each feature are clustered in k_r clusters, and there are q features in the whole dataset, the total number of resulted intervals is calculated as

$$\sum_{r=1}^{q} k_r. \tag{4}$$

Then, H-RTGLs are formulated by applying the conjunction of these intervals feature by feature. Specifically, conjunction of intervals is performed by q-fold Cartesian product operation. Since there are k_r intervals for each feature, maximally $\prod_{r=1}^{q} k_r$ interval conjunctions can be possible. However, considering all interval conjunctions is not efficient and it may generate meaningless intervals including no instance. Therefore, we only obtain interval conjunctions containing any instance as

$$\pi(q_1, q_2, \cdots, q_q) = \prod_{r=1}^{q} ITVL_r^{G_r^{q_r}} = ITVL_1^{G_1^{q_1}} \times ITVL_2^{G_2^{q_2}} \times \cdots \times ITVL_q^{G_q^{q_q}}, \tag{5}$$

where q_r is the cluster index (i.e., interval index) in feature r, and $ITVL_r^{G_r^{q_r}}$ is an interval generated by using $G_r^{q_r}$ in feature r.

Fig. 5 is an example of interval conjunction considering two features containing two intervals, respectively. Even though 4 interval conjunctions can be possible, we only use $\pi(1,1)$ and $\pi(2,2)$ since $\pi(1,2)$ and $\pi(2,1)$ contain no instance.

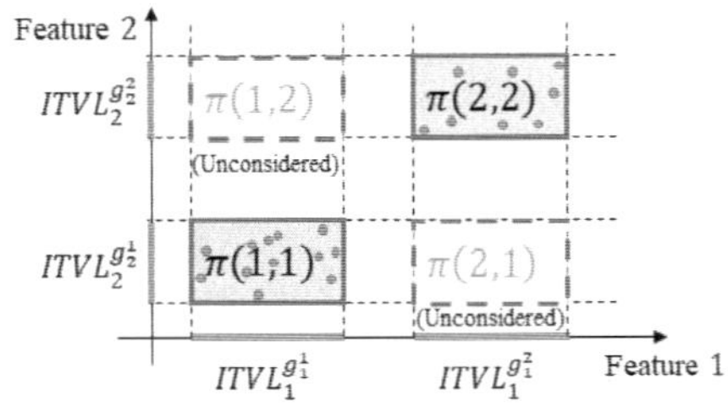

Fig. 5. An example of interval conjunction.

Such interval conjunctions reflect each of features and can be seen as H-RTGLs. However, there still exists a risk of overfitting since intervals are generated feature by feature. Thus, we apply additional fitting procedure to interval conjunctions containing instances. Specifically, intervals are tuned by fitting function based on instances in them and fitted value $Fit_r\left(\pi(q_1, q_2, \cdots, q_q)\right)$ of interval conjunction $\pi(q_1, q_2, \cdots, q_q)$ in feature r is defined as

$$Fit_r\left(\pi(q_1, q_2, \cdots, q_q)\right) = \left[\min_{x_j \in ITVL_r^{G_r^{q_r}}} proj_r(x_j) - v_r, \max_{x_j \in ITVL_r^{G_r^{q_r}}} proj_r(x_j) + v_r\right], \forall r, \tag{6}$$

where v_r is a fitting parameter. Then, H-RTGLs are formulated by logical product of fitted intervals, and they are used to classify instances as target class and outlier. If an instance is in H-RTGL, it is considered as target class or outlier otherwise. Fig. 6 depicts an example of H-RTGL as classifier.

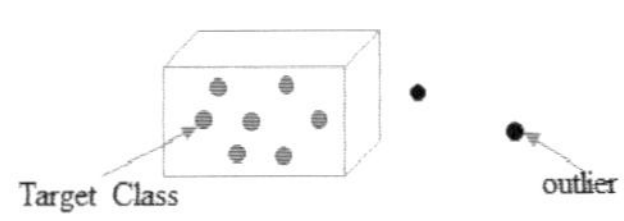

Fig. 6. Resulted H-RTGL as classifier.

Fitness function. Meanwhile, GA includes an iterative process to improve solution by handing over promising solutions to next generations. Fitness function is defined to achieve this process. It evaluates chromosomes in population in order to distinguish good and bad solutions. Since we tackle OCC problem, fitness of each chromosome should be assessed by considering classification performance of classifier. Therefore, we define fitness function as in Equation 7, where AUC is Area Under ROC Curve (AUC) that is a sort of measure to evaluate classification performance and will be described in section 4.

$$fitness\_function = AUC \tag{7}$$

Crossover Operator. After evaluating fitness function, two chromosomes should be selected as parent used for generating new offspring. We carry out roulette wheel selection that assigns each chromosome probability to be selected as parents, proportional to its fitness value. Then, new offspring chromosomes are generated by crossover operation to update population. One of the most common crossover operations is point crossover, which combines parental chromosomes according to crossover point. However, this simple crossover operation just mixing the numbers of Gaussian distribution in parents might cause inefficiency because it cannot reflect the characteristics about distribution of points in feature r. Thus, we adopt arithmetical crossover operator that generates offspring chromosomes by arithmetic operation among parental chromosomes. Specifically, we define two gene values y_r^1 and y_r^2 of offspring by using x_r^1 and x_r^2 from parental chromosomes in feature r, which is depicted as Equation 8, where α is a random number between 0 and 1 used for crossover operation. Also, Fig. 7 describes an example of our arithmetic crossover operation, which generates two offspring chromosomes $C1, C2$ by using two parents $P1, P2$. All floating points are rounded off.

$$\begin{aligned} y_r^1 &= \alpha x_r^1 + (1-\alpha)x_r^2 \\ y_r^2 &= (1-\alpha)x_r^1 + \alpha x_r^2 \end{aligned} \tag{8}$$

$P1$	3	2	3	1	4
$P2$	2	4	1	2	3
$C1$	3*0.6 +2*0.4 = 2.6 ≈ **3**	2*0.6 +4*0.4 = 2.8 ≈ **3**	3*0.6 +1*0.4 = 2.2 ≈ **2**	1*0.6 +2*0.4 = 1.4 ≈ **1**	4*0.6 +3*0.4 = 3.6 ≈ **4**
$C2$	3*0.4 +2*0.6 = 2.4 ≈ **2**	2*0.4 +4*0.6 = 3.2 ≈ **3**	3*0.4 +1*0.6 = 1.8 ≈ **2**	1*0.4 +2*0.6 = 1.6 ≈ **2**	4*0.4 +3*0.6 = 3.4 ≈ **3**

Fig. 7. An example of arithmetic crossover operation.

Mutation Operator. In genetic process in nature, sometimes chromosome in offspring is affected by mutation. It means that some offspring have different features from any of parents. Diversity of species can be preserved due to this unexpected change. GA that mimics this reproduction process in nature also has an artificial mutation operation. We use a simple integer vector mutation that can be suitable for integer-valued encoding. Specifically, we increase or decrease the value of gene by 1 if it is selected for mutation. This occurs with probability p_m.

Population Update and termination condition. After producing new generation with size P by crossover and mutation operations, we select only P chromosomes with high fitness value among $2P$ chromosomes to preserve the size of population. Moreover, as criteria for termination of algorithm, we suggest stopping the algorithm if there is no improvement of solution through the number of generations (exactly 5). Since this policy uses computation resources more efficiently than other conditions [10].

4 A Numerical Experiment

4.1 Experimental Design

To evaluate classification performance of suggested $1 - \mathrm{HRD}_d$ using GA, we designed a numerical experiment with datasets provided by UCI machine learning repository. We used four datasets namely Iris, Breast, Biomed, Liver. Since there exist multiple classes in those datasets, we chose one class as target class and other classes as outlier. Table 1 summarizes the number of features, selected target class, the number of instances in target class, and the number of instances in outlier.

Table 1. Information of datasets.

	Iris	**Breast**	**Biomed**	**Liver**
Number of features	4	9	5	6
Target class	Virginica	Malignant	Normal	Healthy
Size of target class	50	241	127	145
Size of outliers	100	458	67	200

Moreover, we used 50% of instances belonging to target class as training dataset to learn $1 - HRD_d$, whereas the rest of instances in target class and outliers were used as test dataset to verify the classifier. In Iris dataset, for instance, training dataset consists of 25 instances randomly selected from target class and test dataset consists of the remaining 25 instances in target class and 100 outliers. By performing pre-experiment, we set $P = 20$, and probability of mutation $p_m = 0.01$.

For performance measure, we considered AUC that can assess $1 - HRD_d$ in terms of the ability of excluding outliers as well as including instances of target class. AUC can be calculated by drawing ROC curve, which consists of true positive rate (TPR) representing the ratio of instances classified as positive among actual positive instances and false positive rate (FPR) representing the ratio of instances classified as positive among actual negative instances. In general, a classifier with high TPR may not be desirable if FPR of the classifier is also high since the classifier might not be capable of separating positive and negative classes. AUC can properly evaluate such undesirable classifier as low AUC value. Therefore, for each $1 - HRD_d$, we drew ROC curve by increasing v_r in fitting function, determining the length of intervals, until all instances of target class in test dataset are covered. Fig. 8 depicts one ROC curve and

AUC value obtained by using one $1 - HRD_d$, which was constructed by using one chromosome for Biomed dataset.

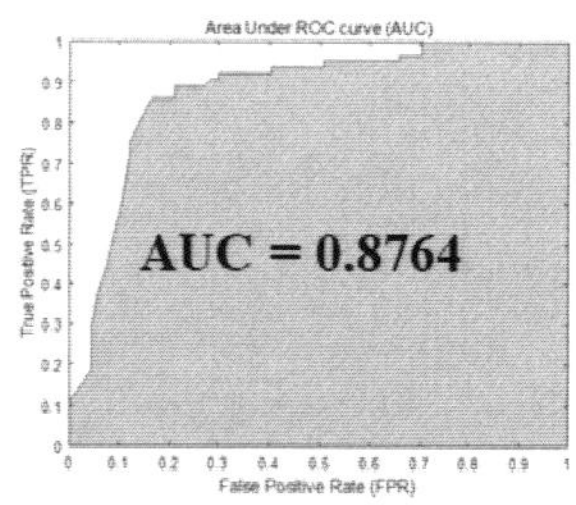

Fig. 8. Example of ROC curve and AUC calculated.

4.2 An Experimental Result

Table 2 displays an experimental result of 20 replications used to measure classification performance of proposed classifier generated by GA compared to other OCC algorithms. Results of existing $1 - HRD$s and representative OCC algorithms were taken from references [7,14].

Table 2. Comparison of AUC obtained from $1 - \mathrm{HRD}_d$ and other OCC algorithms

	Iris	Breast	Biomed	Liver
	AUC * 100 (standard deviation)			
$1 - \mathrm{HRD}_d$	98.2 (1.0)	96.2 (0.8)	90.3 (1.1)	61.1 (1.4)
$1 - \mathrm{HRD}_m$	96.1 (1.1)	95.1 (1.2)	89.6 (1.2)	61.6 (1.6)
$1 - \mathrm{HRD}_p$	97.6 (0.9)	96.2 (0.7)	85.2 (1.2)	59.4 (2.3)
Naïve Parzen	95.4 (1.1)	96.5 (0.4)	93.1 (0.2)	61.4 (0.7)
Gauss	97.8 (0.6)	82.3 (0.2)	90.0 (0.4)	58.6 (0.5)
PCA	90.9 (4.7)	30.3 (1.0)	89.7 (0.5)	54.9 (0.5)
SVDD	98.1 (0.8)	70.0 (0.6)	2.2 (0.3)	4.7 (1.4)

We could observe that the classification accuracy of $1 - HRD_d$ was better than or similar to that of existing $1 - HRD$s in most of datasets, except for Liver dataset. These results support that there exists obvious improvement in $1 - HRD_d$, although more datasets should be considered to confirm the superiority of it. In addition, due to application of GA , these results are desirable since $1 - HRD_d$ does not require exhaustive and inefficient grid search for tuning parameter carried out in $1 - HRD_m$ and $1 - HRD_p$. Meanwhile, $1 - HRD_d$ showed competitive performance compared to other OCC algorithms as well. Especially, classification performance of $1 - HRD_d$ was the highest in Iris dataset among all OCC algorithms. Although performance of $1 - HRD_d$ was slightly lower than Naïve Parzen classifier, it can provide interpretability of classification results important for post analysis of dataset.

4.3 Interpretability Example

This subsection contains how resulted H-RTGLs of $\mathbf{1-HRD_d}$ can be interpreted by user. We considered Iris dataset and Setosa class not used in the numerical experiment as target class. Table 3 describes information of H-RTGL obtained by $\mathbf{1-HRD_d}$.

Table 3. Information of H-RTGL describing Setosa species.

Feature	Interval of each feature
Sepal Length	4.1 – 6.0
Sepal Width	2.4 – 4.8
Petal Length	1.1 – 1.9
Petal Width	0.0 – 0.8

If an unidentified instance has (i) Sepal Length between 4.1-6.0, (ii) Sepal Width between 2.4 – 4.8, (iii) Petal Length between 1.1 – 1.9 and (iv) Petal Width under 0.8, it is classified as target class. Fig. 9 visualizes H-RTGL into feature space, with scatter plot of Iris dataset. Since this H-RTGL covers all instances in Setosa class marked as * and includes no outliers as depicted in Fig. 9, resulted H-RTGL can be considered as representative pattern of Setosa class.

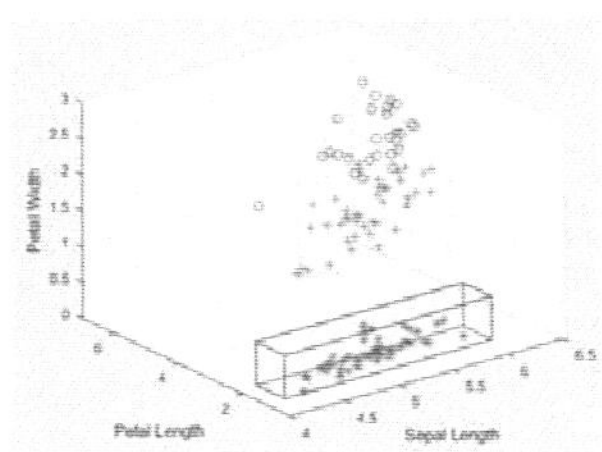

Fig. 9. H-RTGL visualized in feature space with scatter plot of Iris dataset.

In addition, we can observe Petal Width of Setosa class is far from that of other classes. Therefore, Petal Width of Iris is concluded as essential feature to distinguish instances of Setosa Class from those belonging to other classes. In this way, H-RTGL can be used to get useful insights such as key features for feature selection.

5 Conclusion

In this paper, we proposed an efficient OCC classifier $1-HRD_d$ by using GA. Application of GA allowed systematic generation of $1-HRD_d$ and was expected to be a remedy for parameter tuning problem of it. Especially, we devised encoding scheme that could represent the number of Gaussian distributions assumed in each feature r and other operators such as crossover and mutation. As a result, we could achieve desirable classification performance compared to other OCC algorithms as well as existing $1 - HRD$s.

Moreover, some further ideas and possible extensions as future works to elaborate our research are as follows. At first, we intend to consider large and complex dataset since dataset used in this paper may not be sufficient to assess robustness and scalability of the suggested algorithm. Also, we may substitute the GA as other population-based metaheuristics such as Particle Swarm Optimization (PSO). In terms of interval generation method, we plan to refine clustering procedure of projection points. Since k-means clustering is vulnerable to convergence to local optima, strategies for global searching is required. Various distribution other than Gaussian distribution can be also considered in order to handle dataset not following Gaussian distribution.

Acknowledgements

This work was supported by the National Research Foundation of Korea (NRF) grant funded by the Korea government (MSIT) (No. NRF-2017R1A2B4009841).

References

1. Agusta, Y., Dowe, D. L.: Unsupervised learning of gamma mixture models using minimum message length. In: Proceedings of the 3rd IASTED Conference on Artificial Intelligence and Applications, pp. 457-462. ACTA Press, Benalmádena (2003)
2. Barnett, V., Lewis, T.: Outliers in statistical data. Wiley, New York (1994)
3. De Comite, F., Denis, F., Gilleron, R., Letouzey, F.: Positive and unlabeled examples help learning. In: International Conference on Algorithmic Learning Theory, pp. 219-230. Springer, Heidelberg. (1999)
4. Denis, F., Gilleron, R., Letouzey, F.: Learning from positive and unlabeled examples. Theoretical Computer Science, 348(1), 70-83 (2005)
5. Desir, C., Bernard, S., Petitjean, C., Heutte, L.: A random forest based approach for one class classification in medical imaging. In: International Workshop on Machine Learning in Medical Imaging, pp. 250-257. Springer, Heidelberg (2012)
6. Jeong, I. K., Choi, J. Y.: Design of One-Class Classifier Using Hyper-Rectangles. Journal of Korean Institute of Industrial Engineers, 41(5), 439-446 (2015)
7. Jeong, I., Kim, D. G., Choi, J. Y., Ko, J.: Geometric one-class classifiers using hyper-rectangles for knowledge extraction. Expert Systems with Applications, 117, 112-124 (2019)
8. Le, T., Tran, D., Ma, W., Sharma, D.: Multiple distribution data description learning algorithm for novelty detection. In: Pacific-Asia Conference on Knowledge Discovery and Data Mining, pp. 246-257. Springer, Heidelberg (2011)
9. Scholkopf, B., Williamson, R. C., Smola, A. J., Shawe-Taylor, J., Platt, J. C.: Support vector method for novelty detection. In: Advances in neural information processing systems, pp. 582-588. MIT Press, Denver (2000)
10. Sivanandam, S.N., Deepa, S.N.: Introduction to genetic algorithms, Springer, Heidelberg (2008)
11. Tarassenko, L., Hann, A., Young, D.: Integrated monitoring and analysis for early warning of patient deterioration. BJA: British Journal of Anaesthesia, 97(1), 64-68 (2006)

12. Tax, D. M., Duin, R. P.: Support vector domain description. Pattern recognition letters, 20(11-13), 1191-1199 (1999)
13. Tax, D. M., Duin, R. P.: Support vector data description. Machine learning, 54(1), 45-66 (2004)
14. Tax, D.M.J., One-class classifier results, http://homepage.tudelft.nl/n9d04/occ/

Comprehensibility for Decision Intelligence Engineering

Inna Kolyshkina[1] and Simeon Simoff[2[0000-0001-9895-4109]]

[1] Analytikk Consulting Pty LTD 20, 9-19 Nickson St, Sydney NSW 2010, Australia
[2] Western Sydney University, Penrith, NSW 2751, Australia
inna@analytikk.com

Abstract. The broad application of machine learning methods and algorithms in diverse range of organisational settings led to the adoption of legislations, like European Union's General Data Protection Regulation, which require firm capabilities to explain algorithmic decisions. Currently in the machine learning literature there does not seem to be a consensus on the definition of interpretability or comprehensibility of a machine learning solution as well as of the necessary level of comprehensibility (or interpretability) of such solution and on how this level can be determined, measured and achieved. In this article, we provide such definitions based on our extensive experience of building machine learning solutions for various organisations across industries. We present a detailed step-by-step methodology for establishing and achieving the right level of comprehensibility for an end-to-end machine learning solution. The methodology provides guidance on creating the necessary level of comprehensibility at each stage of the machine learning solution building process and is consistent with best practices of project management in the machine learning setting. We illustrate the suggested methodology with a recent case study in the insurance industry and discuss how its versatility and intuitive approach that is consistent with best project management practices allows it to become effortlessly applicable across variety of industries and types of machine learning projects.

Keywords: data analysis, machine learning, comprehensibility, comprehensibility matrix, case study, insurance.

1 Introduction

The advent and rapidly increasing application of artificial intelligence (AI) methods, algorithms and systems in diverse range of human endeavours and organisational settings are having a profound impact on human society. This has led to an increased consideration of our capability to assess and ensure the explainability of the performance of AI systems and the interpretability of the results they produce. A special interest for those who deal with data analysis is the level of interpretability of machine learning (ML) output and respective solution models. This has been driven by the fact that the leadership of the organisations who use ML applications or ML consultants, require provided solutions to be easily understandable in order to foresee the impacts and mitigate risks in implementing them, under diverse legislation protections. For instance, the European Union's General Data Protection Regulation (GDPR), which entered into force in May 2018 (GDPR, 2016), has several articles related to the right to explanation. For instance, articles 13–15 of the GDPR include sub-articles related to cases involving automated decision-making. These sub-articles translate into obligations to companies and/or individuals to be able to provide either detailed explanations of individual algorithmic decisions or general information about how the algorithms make decisions (Wallace and Castro, 2018). These and similar developments increase the pressure on the development of methodologies, which can enable and ensure the explainability of the results. Such explainability is closely related with two concepts: *interpretability* and *comprehensibility*.

In this paper we will focus on comprehensibility of ML solutions rather than interpretability of individual models. The objective of this paper is to introduce a definition of comprehensibility of an end-to-end industry ML solution, provide a methodology for establishing the necessary level of comprehensibility of such solution and ensuring that this level is achieved as we go through the stages of the ML solution building process. The methodology, presented in the paper, is consistent with best practices of project management in the ML setting and is applicable both in industrial and applied research settings. We illustrate it in details with a recent case study in the insurance industry.

1.1 Interpretability and Comprehensibility of ML Solutions

While the concept of interpretability of a model is intuitively easy to understand, there is no consensus on the definition of interpretability, on whether the term "interpretability" or "comprehensibility" should be used instead and in what settings. Additionally, there is insufficient clarity in terms of the scope that the concept covers: while some authors narrow the focus of interpretability to the model only, others prefer to look at the interpretability of the overall ML solution. Doshi-Velez and Kim (2017) provide compact and refined overview of the state-of-the art around interpretability.

Sometimes the term "interpretability" is used interchangeably with "comprehensibility". Their definitions vary from one article to another, but often are very similar. For example, in earlier works comprehensibility is described as ability of the "learning algorithm to encode its model in such a way that it may be inspected and understood by humans." (Craven, 1996) while interpretability is described as "the ability to explain or to present in understandable terms to a human" (Doshi-Velez and Kim, 2017).

Often such definitions tend to narrow the focus to the model itself, which is only one phase of the larger modelling process (Gleicher, 2016).

While succinct and intuitive, the definitions similar to those mentioned above are very broad; they leave out the overall organizational context and related practical aspects of the operationalisation of comprehensibility. For example, they do not take into account the fact that different groups of "humans" might be interested in different aspects of the information produced by the ML solution and to a different extent: say, for the model delivery team it might be more important to understand the data specifics and choose a suitable ML algorithm for the underlying ML model, while for the company executives it may be necessary to understand how the model output can be used to inform and improve their business decisions.

1.2 The "Comfortable" Level of Comprehensibility of a Business ML Solution

In this paper we will discuss interpretability/comprehensibility of an *end-to-end ML solution* i.e. an end-to-end business solution that directly informs business decisions and processes based on the use of ML tools and techniques.

Gleicher (2016) uses the term "comprehensibility" and defines it as the "ability of stakeholders to understand relevant aspects of the modeling process" (Gleicher 2016, p.1). Further expanding on this, we suggest comprehensibility of a ML solution to be defined as "*ability of the key stakeholders of a ML project to understand the required relevant aspects of the ML solution*". This definition reflects the fact that a necessary part of the business process is to establish the key stakeholders and their required level of understanding based on the project objectives.

What should be the "right" or necessary level of comprehensibility of a business ML solution? In current literature there is no definite answer to this question. We define it as *the level of comprehensibility that is required to achieve the project goals*. If this comprehensibility level is not achieved, the solution will be inadequate for the purpose. This level needs to be established and documented at the initiation stage of the project as part of requirement collection.

Obviously, this level will differ from one project to another depending on the business goals.

For example, while sometimes the ability of the solution to explain individual predictions can be important - for example, in medical diagnosis or terrorism detection, in many cases the need to understand and trust the internal logic of the model is of more value (Ribeiro et al, 2016). In our practice we found that if the solution is needed to inform business decisions about policy, strategy or interventions aimed to improve the business outcome of interest (e.g. increase sales volume, marketing campaign conversion rate or reduce insurance claim cost), then transparency and end-to-end auditability of the ML solution is directly stated by the organisation as a necessary requirement (later we discuss such a situation when describing the case study). Sometimes, on the other hand, it is the accuracy of the solution that is of the most importance, for example, in an image-classifying project, where it is important to identify as many as possible images of a certain type and where misclassifying an individual image is not of great concern.

2 Proposed Methodology of Establishing and Building the Comfortable Level of ML Solution Comprehensibility

The methodology of building comprehensibility of a solution is based on our solution development methodology (SDM), which seven stages are described in **Table 1** and

Fig. 1. Whilst SDM has some overlapping elements with earlier methodologies, like SAS Institute SEMMA and CRISP-DM, it structure accommodates conveniently the necessary elements to take care about comprehensibility through the whole process.

Table 1. Solution development methodology (SDM)

Stage	Description
1	Project initiation stage (determining business objectives, key stakeholders, collecting business requirements, agreeing what data to use, etc.)
2	Data audit and data checks
3	Data predictive potential evaluation
4	Data enrichment (if needed)
5	Model Development (determining the algorithms to use, data pre-processing, feature selection. feature engineering, model building and evaluation)
6	Deriving the needed business insights
7	Documentation development (if required). Deployment, monitoring and updating (if required)

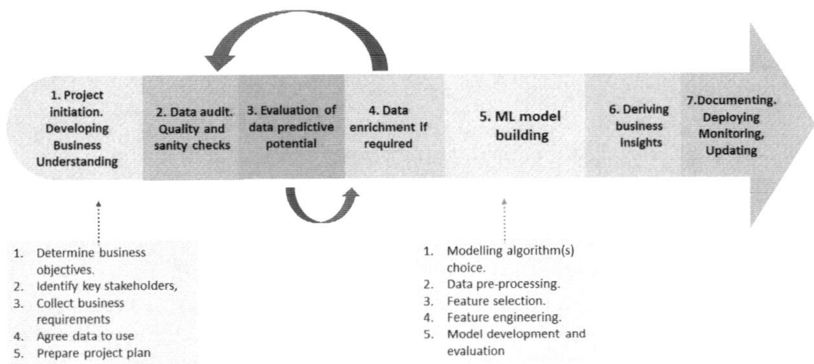

Fig. 1. Macro process diagram of SDM.

We will now discuss how to ensure that the comfortable level of solution comprehensibility is met by going through each project stage.

2.1 The Project Initiation Stage and Comprehensibility Matrix

The project initiation stage is crucial from the solution comprehensibility building perspective. It begins by establishing the project objectives and key stakeholders.

For example, typical business objectives may include building an ML solution that will:

- explain what factors and to what extent drive the business outcome of interest;

- allow the organisation to derive business insights that will help make data-driven accurate decisions regarding what changes can be done to improve the outcome of interest by a specified percentage;
- be accurate and robust, and use real-world organisational data;
- have easy to understand outputs that will make sense to the users and that the users can trust;
- be implementable to the organisational data without disrupting the work of the IT team and other professional teams.

In terms of key stakeholders some typical stakeholder groups in our experience are: executive team, data providers team (e.g. IT team); subject matter expert (SME) team; modelling team. Sometimes external groups such as industry regulators, are also included.

Once the goals and the stakeholders are established, the process of business requirement collection begins. As part of this process we work with the stakeholders to determine what is the necessary level of solution comprehensibility (as defined above). For example, the established comfortable level of comprehensibility may require that the relevant organisational stakeholders need to have understanding of:

- What are the **data inputs -** are they relevant, of suitable quality and representative of the real-world data
- The **high-level modelling approach**, its validity and whether it is proven and is likely to work in this industry
- **Solution outputs:** are they consistent with the project goals in terms of accuracy, format, ease of understanding for the end users, level of potential business insight etc, and are they valid from ML and business points of view
- How the solution will be **implemented, monitored and updated.**

When the right level of the solution comprehensibility is agreed, the next step is to establish what needs to be done by which stakeholder at each project stage in order to ensure that the solution we are building will have the right degree of comprehensibility. To achieve this, we fill out the **comprehensibility matrix** in **Table 2**.

Table 2. Comprehensibility matrix structure

	Key Stakeholder 1	Key Stakeholder 2	…	Key Stakeholder *n*
Project Stage 1				
Project Stage 2				
…				
Project Stage 7				

In each cell of the matrix we need to document what has to be done by this stakeholder at this project stage to ensure that the required solution comprehensibility will be achieved. This matrix, once completed, becomes part of the business requirements document (BRD). The activities it outlines are integrated into the project plan. They then are performed, updated and monitored along with the project plan as needed.

We will now discuss some typical entries to the comprehensibility matrix at each stage of the ML solution building process, and in a later chapter we will illustrate this in detail with a case study.

2.2 Stages 2-4. Data Understanding (Comprehension)

From the perspective of interpretability/comprehensibility stages 2, 3 and 4 form the data understanding (comprehension) mega-stage.

Stage 2. Data Audit (and Gaining Data Understanding), Data Cleansing. If achieving user trust in the solution is part of the required level of comprehensibility, usually the users will want to be certain that the data used by the solution is of adequate quality and representative of the real-world data that the model will be deployed on. If this is the case, at this stage we need to ensure that the data satisfies these requirements.

In terms of comprehensibility matrix, at this stage the following stakeholder groups are typically involved in the ways described below.

Modellers usually need to learn from SMEs the subject matter aspects that would allow them to gain data understanding and perform data audit and cleansing more effectively (for example, they might want to understand data definitions, acceptable data values and ranges etc), they might need to provide a data extraction template to the data providers; SMEs usually need to conduct any required data "sanity checks". Data provider team extracts the data in the required format and might need to share with SMEs and modellers the necessary information about data availability/accessibility, known issues etc.

Stage 3. Predictive Potential Evaluation of the Data. At this stage we assess whether the available data is sufficient for achieving the business goals. The cleansed and otherwise prepared data is used for evaluation of its predictive potential using powerful ML methods like gradient boosting, random forests or complex method ensembles.

In terms of comprehensibility matrix, at this stage the following groups are involved in the following ways: modellers may need to establish the predictive potential of the data from the statistical point of view (for example by establishing what percentage of target variability can be explained by the data). They then share this knowledge with other relevant stakeholders (SMEs, data providers, etc) to determine if it is sufficient to achieve the right level of comprehensibility. Additionally, any sanity checks required may need to be done at this stage by SMEs and modellers.

Stage 4. Data Enrichment. At this stage if it has been previously determined that the initially provided data is not sufficient for the project purposes, data enrichment is conducted. Additional internal and external data sources are identified, the new data is extracted, audited and cleansed and added to the previously used data. Then predictive potential of the enriched data is again assessed. This stage is repeated until the necessary level of predictive potential is achieved.

From the comprehensibility matrix perspective, the key stakeholder groups that are usually involved in this stage are SMEs, data providers and modellers.

SMEs might need to help identify additional data to enrich the model, data providers extract it in the specified format, modellers add the data to the model and assess the predictive potential from the statistical perspective. SMEs need to design and perform "sanity checks" and, when satisfied with the check results, determine whether the predictive potential of the enriched data is sufficient to achieve the right level of comprehensibility.

Stage 5. Modelling. At this stage the ML technique to be used for modelling needs to be selected, the data needs to be pre-processed, the model needs to be applied to the data and its results need to be evaluated.

It is crucial to choose a technique that will allow us to achieve the right comprehensibility level. When making this choice, it is important to keep in mind that, as Freitas (2013) mentions, there is a trade-off between model accuracy and flexibility on one hand, and ease of its ability to be interpreted on the other hand.

Some modelling methods produce output that is relatively easy to explain to an ML layman – these are, for example, decision trees, association rules and other classification rules-related techniques, as well as model agnostic techniques which provide local explainability via additive feature attribution, like SNAP (Lundberg and Lee, 2017), additive models (Lou et al., 2012), attention-based networks or sparse linear models. In our experience, such methods are useful when the business goals require the solution to be transparent and easily audited (for example, when it needs to be assessed by the industry regulator), or when the solution needs to be used to guide strategy, policy or business interventions.

Other algorithms, for example, deep neural networks, complex ensemble models or random forests with large numbers of trees (Ribeiro et al, 2016) are functionally "black boxes" i.e. their internal logic is difficult to explain to a non-expert however their accuracy level is usually very high.

If the project goals require accuracy more than the ease of explaining of the logic of the output derivation, for example, when analysing audio and images data, then the choice of "black box" ML techniques that accurately model such data such as deep neural networks will be more suitable.

Finally, if both accuracy and comprehensibility are required (for example, in medical diagnostics or terrorist detection) then a "black box" model can be chosen and model-agnostic interpretability methods may be used (Ribeiro et al, 2016).

From the comprehensibility matrix perspective, the key stakeholder groups that are usually involved in this stage are modellers and SMEs. The modellers need to ensure that the chosen algorithm(s), the methods of feature selection and feature engineering, the model evaluation methods and the results they produce are in line with building the right level of comprehensibility.

Once the model is built, "sanity checks" might need to be performed by SMEs and modellers.

Stage 6. Deriving Business Insights. At this stage business insights necessary to achieve the project goals are derived. From the comprehensibility matrix perspective typically at this stage the following stakeholders are involved as follows. End users (e.g. executive team) need to gain understanding of the business insights derived from the solution, check that the insights are valid and valuable and build trust in these insights. To achieve this, the modelling team in consultation with SMEs may prepare a presentation, demonstration and/or a report that serves this purpose. Such a presentation might cover the insights gained, a high-level description of the solution, the data used, the scenarios is can cater for, its performance evaluation and how its outputs can be interpreted to help inform the needed business decisions.

Stage 7. Documentation. Deployment and Monitoring. To ensure that the achieved comprehensibility level is maintained during the future use of the solution, usually a technical report will need to be created. The necessary comprehensibility aspects that should be covered by the report need to be documented in the comprehensibility matrix. For example, the matrix might state that the report needs to include a solution manual and a glossary; that the modellers need to produce this report and that the SMEs and end users need to review and sign off on the report.

If the solution needs to be deployed, in terms of comprehensibility matrix, the teams that will be involved would typically be the deployer team and the modelling team. The former will need to understand the project goals, the data used and any information necessary for the solution deployment and maintenance, for example the relevant data extraction, cleansing and pre-processing that needs to performed; the model formula; any built-in model performance evaluation criteria etc. They typically will need to document the way the model was deployed and distribute the documentation to the other stakeholders. The latter team may deliver a presentation for the deployers or provide consultations on the model specifics if required.

3 Demonstration of Proposed Methodology - A Case Study in Workers Compensation Insurance

3.1 Project Background and Objectives

A large Australian Workers Compensation insurer wanted to build a ML solution that would enable the organisation to gain data-driven insights into risk factors of workers compensation claims lasting longer than a year. Claim duration is the major cost driver in workers compensation insurance, and the ability to identify high risk claims is of major importance for targeting case management effort.

Business objectives of building an ML solution project were as follows. The solution had to

- Identify the most important factors and their combinations that at early stage of claim lodgement drive the risk of claim duration being a year or longer; rank these factors in order of importance and quantify their influence

- Enable a case manager to identify at early stages of a claim development the claims at risk to last longer than a year and inform what can be done to help reduce the risk. Develop human-interpretable business rules for the case manager to use for this purpose
- Be easy for the organisational IT team to deploy, and for the BI team to be able to develop in-depth understanding of it as well as monitor and update it as required

The data agreed included: claimant information (gender, occupation, income estimate, age at the time of injury, etc); employer and industry data; injury information (injury date, nature of injury, body part, etc); previous claims history of the same claimant etc.

3.2 Comprehensibility Process Building at Each Stage

We present the comprehensibility process building at each stage. We will label each stage in order to refer to it in the appropriate area of the comprehensibility matrix in **Fig. 2**.

Project Initiation Stage. Comprehensibility Matrix (3.2.1). First, the **key stakeholders** were identified as follows: the executive team including representatives of case management team; SME team, business intelligence (BI) team who would do data extraction and develop skills and knowledge that would enable them to monitor and update the solution), IT team who would deploy the solution and ML modellers.

Then, the **necessary comprehensibility level of the solution** was established in workshops and discussions with the stakeholders as follows.

- The business rules produced by the solution needed to make sense to SMEs and be easy to understand for end users (executives and case managers).
- End users (executives and case managers) should be able to develop understanding of the results and trust in them. Specifically:
  - It should be clear to the executives what scenarios the solution can work with and what business questions it would be able to help address.
  - The solution should be transparent, easily auditable and its results should be visualised
- The BI team should be able to:
  - Gain in-depth knowledge of how the solution works and be able to update and monitor it. Fully understand the workings of the underlying ML model.
  - Understand what data and in what format needs to be used and how it has to be pre-processed before being included into model development. Check that the data inputs to the solution were audited and preprocessed in the way that ensured their integrity as well as effective treatment of noise and errors
  - Understand the model outputs and the way they can be used to produce business insights
- The IT team needed to have a high-level understanding of how the solution works and establish the best way to deploy it for the organisational use

- The SMEs needed to check the model inputs for integrity and relevance; suggest additional data for model enrichment if the enrichment is required, gain a high-level understanding of how the solution will work and what data will be used. They also needed to use this understanding to help executive and case managers build trust in the model.
- The solution needed to be fully transparent and well documented to ensure ease of familiarising of new team members in executive, BI, IT and case management teams.

Comprehensibility Matrix. Comprehensibility matrix, presented in **Fig. 2**, was then developed via workshops and discussions with the stakeholders. The level of the involvement of each stakeholder team to ensure the right level comprehensibility for the project was established as follows:

Modelling team needed to

- gain understanding of the subject matter relevant to the project goals achievement
- gain understanding of the available data,
- establish whether the data is sufficient for the project purposes: whether data enrichment will be needed; if enrichment is needed, understand what data would be suitable to add for the enrichment purposes
- Express the model output as human-interpretable rules
- Create a technical report, documented solution code, a solution manual for BI team and a user manual for case managers.

All stakeholders other than the ML modelling team in order to build trust in the solution needed to gain a high-level understanding of the ML solution building process (see diagram 1) and of what happens at each step of the process.

As the detailed comprehensibility matrix spelling out each task that each team had to do at each project stage is too large to show on a page, we will provide below a high-level diagram. Each cell of the diagram indicates the established level of involvement of each stakeholder at each stage and specifies the section of the article where the relevant details of who needed to do what are given.

The labels "High", "Med" and "Low" describe the established level of involvement of each stakeholder in developing of shared understanding of the project team. Such a high-level diagram has its own use as it allows the project team to grasp quickly the overall level of comprehensibility across the project as well as immediately identify any weak areas or bottlenecks, and establish how they should be addressed.

Additionally, at the project initiation stage the modelling team held a brief presentation for other teams to explain the ML project methodology we use based on **Fig. 1**.

Project Stage 2. Data Audit and Cleansing (3.2.2). The stakeholders involved in this stage were **BI team** who extracted and prepared the data, **modelling team** who did data audit and **SME team** who explained various data meaning aspects and performed "sanity checks". Specifically, it was recorded in the matrix that:

- **Modelling team** needed to develop data understanding (via getting familiar with metadata etc) to enable effective data audit and cleansing.
- **SMEs** needed to
  - gain high-level understanding of the modelling approach (e.g. the ways in which machine learning approaches differ from generalised linear models that were previously used by the organisation and that SMEs grew familiar with).
  - participate at data sanity checks and in solving of any issues related to data understanding
- **BI team** needed to understand data requirements and explain to the modelling and SME teams any data issues or limitations that can affect the project objective and suggest the ways of solving the issues.

		Key Stakeholders				
	Project stages	Executive team	SME team	BI team	IT team	ML modelling team
1	Project initiation	High (agreeing business goals and establishing requirements)	High (agreeing business goals and establishing requirements)	High (agreeing business goals and establishing requirements)	High (agreeing business goals and establishing requirements)	High (agreeing business goals and establishing requirements)
2	Data Extraction and Audit	Low	Med (tasks are listed in section 3.2.2)	High (tasks are listed in section 3.2.2)	Low	High (tasks are listed in section 3.2.2)
3	Predictive potential evaluation	Low	Med (tasks are listed in section 3.2.3)	Med (tasks are listed in section 3.2.3)	Low	High (tasks are listed in section 3.2.3)
4	Data enrichment	Low	Med (tasks are listed in section 3.2.4)	High (tasks are listed in section 3.2.4)	Low	High (tasks are listed in section 3.2.4)
5	Model development	Low	Med (tasks are listed in section 3.2.5)	Med (tasks are listed in section 3.2.5)	Low	High (tasks are listed in section 3.2.5)
6	Deriving business insight	High (tasks are listed in section 3.2.6)	Med (tasks are listed in section 3.2.6)	Med (tasks are listed in section 3.2.6)	Low	High (tasks are listed in section 3.2.6)
7	Documentation.	Low	Med (tasks are listed in section 3.2.7)	Med (tasks are listed in section 3.2.7)	Low	High (tasks are listed in section 3.2.7)
	Deployment and monitoring.	Low	Low	Med (tasks are listed in section 3.2.7)	High (tasks are listed in section 3.2.7)	Low

Fig. 2. Comprehensibility matrix of the project

Project Stage 3. Predictive Potential Evaluation of the Data (3.2.3). At this stage it was assessed whether the data was sufficient for achieving the business goals. The key stakeholders involved in this step were the **SME, BI** and **modelling teams**.

Specifically, it was recorded in the matrix that:

- **SMEs** needed to gain high-level of understanding of what "variability explained by a model" is and what data enrichment is.

- The **modellers** needed to find the percentage of variability explained by the preliminary model, and together with **SMEs** establish whether the data enrichment is necessary.
- **BI team** needed to develop understanding on what was done by the modelling team, how and why in order to be able to perform similar tasks when updating the solution in the future; to achieve this, **modelling team** needed to conduct knowledge transfer to the **BI team**.

Project Stage 4. Data Enrichment (3.2.4). The key stakeholders involved in this step were the **SME, BI** and **modelling teams**. The comprehensibility matrix recorded that at this stage:

- **SME team** needed to provide information to modellers on what additional factors could drive the outcome
- **modellers** needed to add it to the model and establish the updated model predictive potential.
- After the data was added to analysis, the enriched data predictive potential needed to be assessed by **SMEs** who had to decide whether it is sufficient for the project goals achievement.
- **BI team** needed to develop understanding on what was done by the modelling team, how and why in order to be able to perform similar tasks when updating the solution in the future; to achieve this, **modelling team** needed to conduct knowledge transfer to the **BI team**.

The additional information to add to the solution was identified by **SMEs** as data on use of opioids by the claimants; lag between injury and claim lodge; service provider data (identity and specialty (doctors, physiotherapists etc.); number of visits by claimant; provider location, and others.

It was established at the end of this stage that the percentage of variability explained by the enriched model was much higher than before and was sufficient for the project purposes.

Project Stage 5. Model Development (3.2.5). The key stakeholders involved in this step were the **SME, BI** and **modelling teams**. The comprehensibility matrix recorded that at this stage

- **modellers** needed to establish and apply the techniques that would produce the model that meets comprehensibility requirements.
- **SME team** needed to check that the model outputs meet the requirements and are valid from the business point of view.
- **BI team** needed to develop understanding on what was done by the modelling team, how and why in order to be able to perform similar tasks when updating the solution in the future; to achieve this, **modelling team** needed to conduct knowledge transfer to the **BI team**.

The modelling approach was developed as a hybrid of gradient boosting, association rules and decision trees. The model accuracy and performance was found suitable.

Project Stage 6. Deriving Business Insights (3.2.6). The key stakeholders involved in this step were the **executive team, SME, BI** and **modelling teams**.

The comprehensibility matrix recorded that at this stage

- **modellers and SME team** needed to derive the required business insights and develop a presentation for the **executive team**;
- **executive team** needed to develop understanding of the business insights and high-level understanding of the modelling process and ask any additional questions;
- **BI team** needed to develop understanding on what was done by the modelling team, how and why; to achieve this, **modelling team** needed to conduct knowledge transfer to the **BI team**.

The key business insights reflected in the presentation included the following information:

- The important predictors of claim duration were found to be injury nature and location; claimant age, occupation, industry; lag between injury and its report; claimant's previous history with the insurer and service provider identity and specialty. The ranking of these factors was provided as well. Enriching the data with provider information significantly improved predictive outcome;
- Derived business rules that would identify claims that have high risk of long duration were intuitive and easy to use.

Project Stage 7. Documentation and Deployment (3.2.7). The key stakeholders involved in this step were the **IT team, BI team** and **modelling teams**.

The comprehensibility matrix recorded that at this stage

- **modellers** needed to document the relevant aspects of the solution and produce the technical report including the model code and a manual for the end users;
- **IT team** needed to develop understanding of the business rules and deploy them in the organisational data;
- **BI team** needed to familiarise themselves with the technical report, identify and and bridge any knowledge gaps with the help of the modelling team.

The relevant documentation was created and the IT team successfully deployed the solution.

4 Conclusion

This article contributes to addressing the problem for providing companies with capabilities to explain algorithmic decision making. It has introduced a definition of comprehensibility of an end-to-end business solution that directly informs business deci-sions and processes based on the use of machine learning tools and techniques as the ability of the key stakeholders of an ML project to understand the required relevant aspects of the ML solution. We suggested a definition of the necessary level of com-prehensibility of a business ML solution as the level of comprehensibility that is re-quired to achieve the project goals. This level needs to be established and documented at the initiation stage of the project as part of requirement collection. Finally, we pre-sented the methodology of achieving the necessary level of comprehensibility of a ML solution. The methodology is based on our extensive experience in delivery of business ML solutions across industries. It adds value to the organisation by establishing shared understanding across all key stakeholders of what the solution needs to do and who needs do what to ensure the required level of performance; allows to build trust of the stakeholders in the solution outputs; helps getting buy-in from all relevant parts of or-ganisation and allows the end users to easily interpret the solution results, confidently make successful evidence-based business decisions and if needed, explain these deci-sions to any external party, for example industry regulator.

We have successfully applied it in commercial projects across a variety of industries including banking, insurance, utilities, retail, FMCG, government, high education, public health, transport, to name some areas, for ML solutions used for marketing cam-paign improvement, sales volume increase, credit risk, fraud detection, student attrition minimisation, image classification, road safety improvement, facility management, as-set management, designing interventions to improve early childhood development lev-els, social media analysis, workers compensation claim management and others.

It effortlessly accommodates the diversity of industry specifics as well as variety of organisational goals, machine learning techniques and data types. Of course, the nec-essary comprehensibility level of a solution as well as entries into the comprehensibility matrix will differ depending on the project goal, the industry and the data nature.

For example, in a recent project we needed to classify outdoor asset images to iden-tify those with specific external damage. The business goals required accuracy of clas-sification of the asset as damaged or not to ensure that the maintenance team concen-trates the repair effort on the assets that appeared to be damaged, while the logic behind an individual asset image being classified as damaged or not was of little importance to the organisation. The comprehensibility matrix reflected this in the following way: the predictive potential evaluation stage included SMEs labelling a sample of asset images as "damaged" or "not damaged"; and data enrichment stage consisted of ensuring that the size of the labelled sample was sufficient to achieve the required level of accuracy. At the project stage 5 the model we chose was a "black box" classifier (a deep neural net), and the derived business insight was presented as the list of assets that were at risk of being damaged and needed immediate attention of maintenance team.

Our approach worked even in a case that was quite unusual from the comprehensi-bility building point of view. A grocery manufacturer needed to recalibrate their mar-keting mix model to help improve the allocation of marketing spend and increase sales volume. A generalised linear model (GLM) was implemented three years earlier by a modeller who since left the company, and the model documentation was lost. The model performance declined with time. The organisation wanted to build a new GLM-based solution that performed similarly to the old one and was easy to understand, maintain, deploy and recalibrate.

Obviously, for this fairly unusual project the comprehensibility matrix was different from a typical one. Specifically, at the project initiation stage it was established what data source the old solution used, but it was not known what variables and in what form were included in the model. So, it was determined that stage 2 only needed to involve developing of data understanding by the modelling team (since the data inputs to the old model were of excellent quality, well pre-processed and filtered); the stages 3 and 4 were skipped as only one data source was used by the old model, and at the stage 5 the choice of model was directly dictated by the requirement of the modelling technique to be of the GLM type that the stakeholders were familiar with.

As shown, this methodology is intuitive, easy to use and is applicable to any industry or research ML project. Its versatility, flexibility and common-sense approach that is also consistent with best practices of project management allows it to be seamlessly applied in any organisational environment. It provides organisations with a reliable, pressure-tested across industries tool to successfully establish the necessary level of a solution comprehensibility and then to achieve it in a step-by-step coordinated way.

References

1. Gleicher, M.: A framework for considering comprehensibility in modeling. Big data 4(2), 75–88 (2016).
2. Doshi-Velez, F., Kim,B.: Towards a rigorous science of interpretable machine learning. arXiv preprint arXiv:17-2.08608v2 (2017).
3. Craven M.: Extracting comprehensible models from trained neural networks. Ph.D. Dissertation, University of Wisconsin–Madison (1996).
4. Ribeiro, M. T., Singh, S., Guestrin, C.: "Why should I trust you?": Explaining the predictions of any classifier. In: Editor, Proceedings of the 22nd ACM SIGKDD International Conference on Knowledge Discovery and Data Mining (KDD'16), pp. 1135–1144, ACM, New York, NY, USA (2016).
5. Freitas, A.: Comprehensible classification models: A position paper. ACM SIGKDD Explorations Newsletter 15(1), 1-10, (June 2013)
6. Lou, Y., Caruana, R., Gehrke, J.: Intelligible models for classification and regression. In: Proceedings of the 18th ACM SIGKDD International Conference on Knowledge Discovery and Data Mining (KDD'12), 150–158, ACM, New York, NY, USA (2012).
7. General Data Protection Regulation (Regulation (EU) 2016/679 of the European Parliament Parliament and of the Council of 27 April 2016), https://eur-lex.europa.eu/legal-content/EN/TXT/PDF/?uri=CELEX:02016R0679-20160504&from=EN, last accessed 2019/03/15.
8. Wallace, N., Castro, D.: The Impact of the EU's New Data Protection Regulation on AI. Center for Data Innovation (March 27, 2018), http://www2.datainnovation.org/2018-impact-gdpr-ai.pdf, last accessed 2019/03/15.
9. Lundberg, S. M., Lee, S.-I.: A unified approach to interpreting model predictions. In Guyon, I., Luxburg, U. V., Bengio, S., Wallach, H., Fergus, R., Vishwanathan, S., Garnett, R. (eds) NIPS 2017, Advances in Neural Information Processing Systems 30, pp. 4765–4774, Curran Associates, Inc. (2017).

Recognition of the Experimental Design of Laboratory Scale Wine Fermentations Using ANN

Gonzalo Hernandez[1], Alejandra Urtubia[2,3,4], Roberto Leon[5]

[1] Universidad de Santiago de Chile, Departamento de Ingeniería Industrial, Santiago, Chile
[2] Universidad Técnica Federico Santa María. Departamento de Ingeniería Química y Ambiental, Valparaíso, Chile
[3] Centro Regional de Estudios en Alimentación Saludable, Valparaíso, Chile
[4] Centro Científico Tecnológico de Valparaíso, CCTVaL, Valparaíso, Chile
[5] Universidad Andres Bello, Facultad de Ingeniería, Viña del Mar, Chile
gonzalo.hernandez.o@usach.cl

Abstract. In wine production, the applications of Artificial Neural Networks have been concentrated in different problems, such as: classification of different classes of wines, selection of variables that identify of denominations of origin of samples of different rose wines, classification of varieties of wines produced in different years by different producers. In this work we studied the performance of Artificial Neural Networks to detect the experimental design that was used to develop 38 laboratory scale Cabernet Sauvignon wine fermentations, 8 of which were normal and the rest problematic. Our main result establishes that for different training/testing/validation configurations and several sizes of the hidden layer with an average overall prediction rate error almost zero, considering a wide range of the parameters.

Keywords: Laboratory Scale Wine Fermentations, Experimental Design, Neural Networks.

1 Introduction

Chile is one of the top ten wine-producing countries and among the top five major wine-exporting countries, [1]. This success is mostly explained because of the excellent quality of the Chilean wine in relation with its price. Usually, in winemaking processes, alcoholic fermentations are monitored with standard and easy to obtain measurements (density, reduced sugars, total and volatile acidity, pH, temperature, etc.) made daily. However, when its normal behavior is affected for some stress condition, and the fermentation could be stuck or sluggish, the action of the enologist is try to correct the problem in the moment, with the previous information. Many times, it can be solved with the employment of traditional practices such as inoculations and nutrient additions. In addition, in the last 10 years several authors have develop and applied Computational Intelligence Methods in order to identify and classify wine fermentation processes solving problems such as classify chemometrically different classes wines, classify wines according to the denominations of origin, identify the wine's variety of grapes, harvest year and originating winery, etc., see for instance [2-8].

The authors of this work have applied different methods coming from Multivariate Statistics and Computational Intelligence to early detect normal and problematic fermentations, see refs. [9-13]. In [9,10] the following statistical methods were applied: Principal Component Analysis, Clustering k-means, Linear Discriminant Analysis, Multiway Principal Component Analysis, Multiway Partial Least Squares. In this case was built by means of laboratory scale wine fermentations a database that contains approximately 22000 data which come from 22 normal, sluggish and stuck fermentations of Cabernet Sauvignon wine. The main result of [9,10] establishes that considering the measurements of sugars, alcohols and density, the statistical methods can predict, with low error, normal and problematic fermentations but using data of the first 96 hours. This result was improved in [11,12] by applying a multilayer perceptron ANN to timely detect the behavior of wine fermentations. It was used the same database of [9,10] and the ANN was defined with one input layer with neurons corresponding to predictor variables, one or two hidden layer and one output layer with two neurons represented the dependent variables: 1: normal fermentations; 0: problematic fermentations. The training algorithm was back-propagation with gradient descent and the transition function was the sigmoid function. It was computed the ANN prediction rates using data of the first 72, 96 and 256 hrs. By several computational experiments it was demonstrated, that ANNs can be applied to detect problematic wine fermentations at 72 hrs. with good accuracy. A similar methodology of [11,12] but with a different prediction method was applied in [13]. In this work the SVM method was used considering three different kernels: linear, third degree polynomial and radial basis function. For the training and testing phase, it was used the same database of [9-12]. The main result of [13] establishes that the SVM method with third degree polynomial and radial basis kernels predict correctly 88% and 85% respectively. These results were achieved for an 80–20% training/testing percentage configuration and a time cutoff of 48 hrs. Therefore, this work improves the previous results obtained in [9-13].

In this paper we applied the ANN method to detect the conditions under which the wine fermentations were developed, i.e., we determine the condition of the wine fermentations applying a simple feedforward neural network. The determination of these conditions is our first attempt to explain why normal and problematic wine fermentations occur from the point of view of ANN.

2 Neural Networks for the Detection of the Initial Conditions of Laboratory Scale Wine Fermentations

An Artificial Neural Network (ANN) is a well-known Computational Intelligence model of a biological neural network, see for instance refs. [14-19]. By the application of a supervised or unsupervised learning building method, the ANN have shown in numerous cases coming from different applications the capacity to detect complex deterministic relationships between inputs and outputs in problems that belongs to the following areas: Pattern Recognition, Clustering, Regression, Fitting, etc. In figure 1 is shown the main stages of a supervised learning schema.

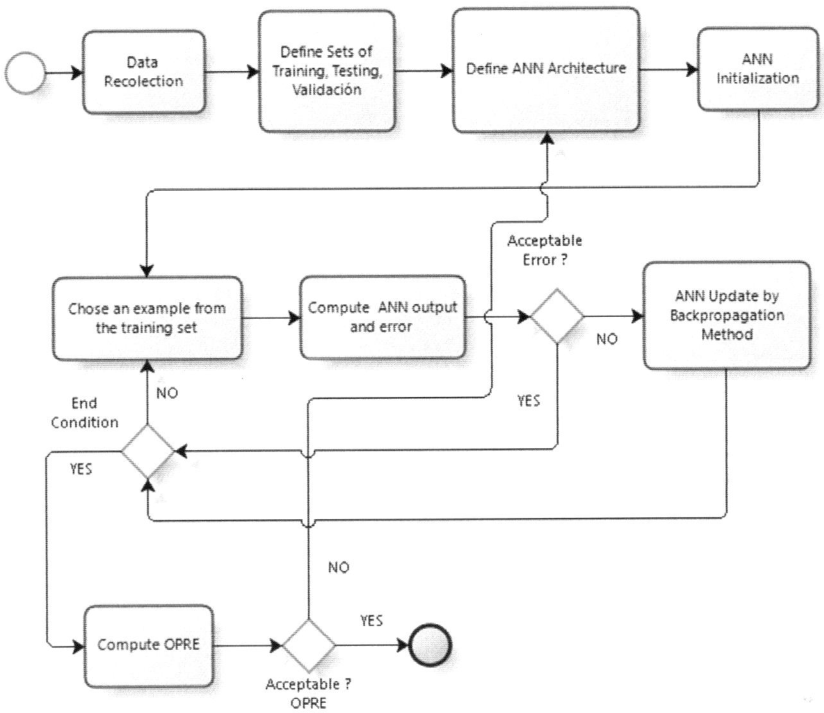

Fig. 1. Main steps of a supervised learning schema of an ANN.

For the application of the ANN in order to detect the initial conditions of laboratory scale fermentations of cabernet sauvignon, it was used the data of the main chemical variables of 8 normal fermentations and 30 problematic fermentations (stuck and sluggish), with a total amount of 1476 measurements distributed in the following way:

- Density and Brix: 342 data for each chemical variable corresponding to 38 fermentations and 9 measurements every 12 hours, for each fermentation, corresponding to the first 4 days of the process.
- Fructose, Glucose, Ethanol and Glycerol: 198 data for each chemical variable corresponding to 22 fermentations and 9 measurements every 12 hours, for each fermentation, corresponding to the first 4 days of the process.

The initial conditions of the wine fermentations are temperature, YAN adjustment, initial sugar concentration (brix), and aeration. In our case, these conditions were coded as +1 for High Level, 0 for Central Level, -1 for Low Level. The exact values of these initial conditions are shown in table 1.

Table 1. Initial condition values of the fermentation processes.

Fermentation Parameter (IC)	High Level +1	Central Level 0	Low Level -1
Temperature (C°)	32	28	24
YAN adjustment (mg N/l)	Time 0: 350 Exponential phase: 350	Time 0: 200 Exponential phase: 350	Without adjustment
Sugar concentration (brix)	28	25	22
Aeration (min)	Time 0: 15 Exponential phase: 15	Time 0: 15 Exponential phase: 0	Without aeration

A program was developed in Matab© using the Neural Network Pattern Recognition Toolbox for the computation of the overall prediction rate error (OPRE), considering only the measurements of one variable at one time:

$$OPRE = 1 - \left(\frac{Number\ of\ Correct\ Classifications}{Number\ of\ Total\ Cases} \right) \tag{1}$$

The program determines this error considering a simple network architecture with only one hidden layer, the mean squared normalized error as performance function, and the update of the weights and biases by the Levenberg - Marquardt training function optimization. The best OPRE was determined for 5 training/testing/validation configurations (40%,30%,30%; 50%,25%,25%: 60%,20%,20%; 70%,15%,15%; 80%,10%,10%) with each set of examples chosen at random in a balanced way among all the fermentations; and for each training/testing/validation configuration for several hidden layer sizes: from 4 to 20 neurons. A schema of the Matlab program is the following:

```
%Matlab Program
load data;
Initializations of matrices that recollect the results of the ANN constructed
Definitions of the parameters of the ANN: ttv (training/testing/validation), hls (hidden layer size)
Loop for different ttv configurations
        Loop for different hls
                Computing of the ANN for each ttv and hls
                Computing of the outputs of the ANN
                Computing of the OPRE of the ANN
                Computing of the confusion matrix
        end
end
Computing of the best ANN with respect to the OPRE
Plot of the performance function and confusion matrix of the best ANN
Printing all the results obtained: best ANN, best OPRE, best performance, etc.
```

Using only the first two days of data of the evolution of the main chemical variables (density, brix, fructose, glucose, ethanol and glycerol) considering only the measurements of each chemical variables at the time, the data of the initial conditions (temperature, YAN adjustment, brix, aeration) and the characteristic of each fermentation as normal +1, or problematic 0 (to compute the prediction error), we obtain the following results with respect to the OPRE, see table 2:

Table 2. OPRE results obtained for predicting the normal and problematic fermentations.

Initial Condition	Chemical Variable	OPRE
Temperature (C°)	Density	0.0000
YAN adjustment (mg N/l)		0.0313
Sugar concentration (brix)		0.0313
Aeration (min)		0.1563
Temperature (C°)	Brix	0.0313
YAN adjustment (mg N/l)		0.0313
Sugar concentration (brix)		0.0938
Aeration (min)		0.1250
Temperature (C°)	Fructose	0.0455
YAN adjustment (mg N/l)		0.0455
Sugar concentration (brix)		0.0455
Aeration (min)		0.0000
Temperature (C°)	Glucose	0.0000
YAN adjustment (mg N/l)		0.0909
Sugar concentration (brix)		0.0455
Aeration (min)		0.0000
Temperature (C°)	Ethanol	0.0000
YAN adjustment (mg N/l)		0.0000
Sugar concentration (brix)		0.0000
Aeration (min)		0.0000
Temperature (C°)	Glycerol	0.0455
YAN adjustment (mg N/l)		0.0455
Sugar concentration (brix)		0.0909
Aeration (min)		0.0455

From these results, considering the results of the best ANN obtained considering several values of the parameters of its architecture, we can affirm that:

- The best initial conditions to predict the main causes of normal and problematic fermentations are temperature, aeration and YAN, considering the measurement of the evolution of all the chemical variables.
- The best chemical variables that can be used to predict normal and problematic fermentations are: density, glucose, ethanol and glycerol.
- For obtain excellent results, with respect to the OPRE, they are only needed the data of the first two days of data of the evolution of the main chemical variables.

In figure 2 is shown an example of a feedforward ANN obtained in this work.

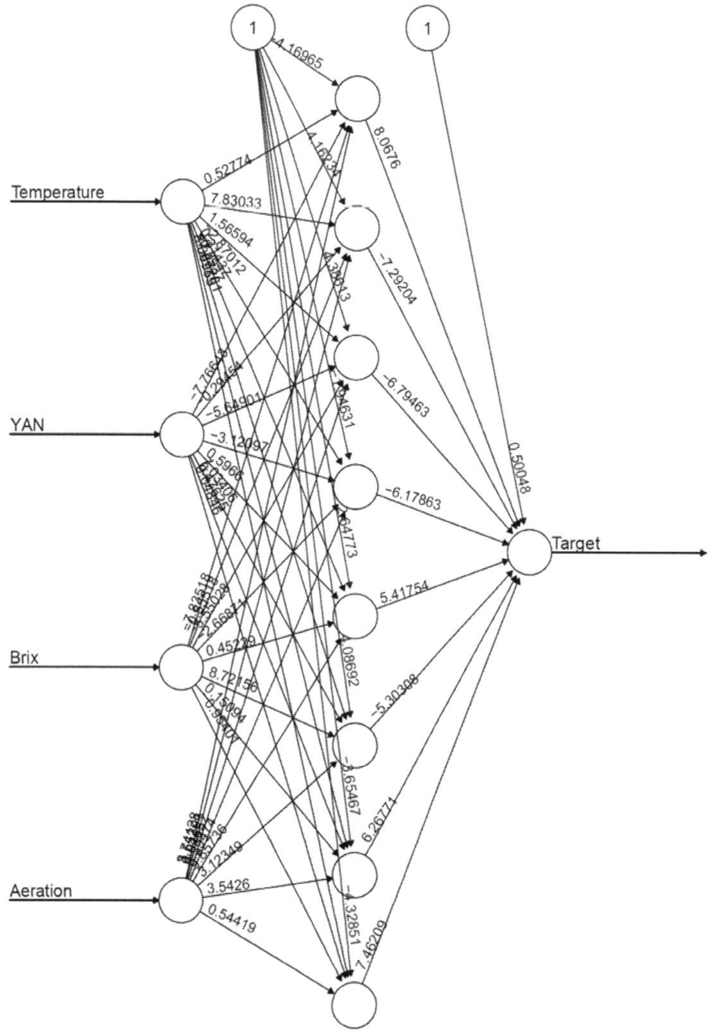

Fig. 2. Example of a feedforward ANN with 8 neurons in the hidden layer obtained in this paper.

3 Conclusions

The performance of feedforward Artificial Neural Networks was applied to detect the experimental design of laboratory scale normal and problematic wine fermentations, using the data of the typical chemical variables (density, brix, fructose, glucose, ethanol and glycerol). This experimental design can be interpreted as the main causes that explain the success or failure of a wine fermentation process. A simple Matlab© program that use the Neural Network Pattern Recognition Toolbox was developed to compute the overall prediction for several values of the main parameters of the ANN: training/testing/validation configurations and hidden layer sizes. Our main results establish that, first, the best initial conditions to predict the main causes of normal and problematic wine fermentations are temperature, aeration and YAN, second, the best chemical variables that can be used to predict the evolution of wine fermentations are density, glucose, ethanol and glycerol, and third, it is only needed the first two days of measurements to obtain excellent results with respect to the overall prediction rate error. Finally, the results achieved allow us to affirm that simple feedforward ANNs can be used to obtain a second order information about a chemical process, i.e., not only if a wine fermentation will evolve as a normal or problematic process, but also the causes that produces this behavior.

Acknowledgments. Research supported by grants: FONDECYT 1120679 and Conicyt PIA/Basal FB0821.

References

1. Executive Report Chilean Wine Production, Servicio Agrícola y Ganadero de Chile, (2017).
2. Beltran, N., et al, Feature extraction and classification of Chilean wines, J. Food Eng. 75, 1-10 (2006).
3. Marini, F., R. Bucci, A. Magri, Artificial neural networks in chemometrics: History, examples and perspectives, Microchemical Journal 88, 178-185, (2008).
4. Penza, M., G. Cassano, Chemometric characterization of Italian wines by thin-film multisensors array and artificial neural networks, Food Chemistry 86, 283-296, (2004).
5. Perez-Magariño, S., at al, Comparative study of artificial neural network and multivariate methods to classify Spanish DO rose wines, Talanta 62, 983-990, (2004).
6. Kruzlicova, D., et al, Classification of Slovak white wines using artificial neural networks and discriminant techniques, Food Chemistry 112, 1046-1052, (2009).
7. Hosu, A., V.M. MirceaCristea, C. Cimpoiu, Analysis of total phenolic, flavonoids, anthocyanins and tannins content in Romanian red wines: Prediction of antioxidant activities and classification of wines using artificial neural networks, Food Chemistry 150, 113-118, (2014).
8. Fernandes, A.M., et al, Brix, pH and anthocyanin content determination in whole Port wine grape berries by hyperspectral imaging and neural networks, Computers and Electronics in Agriculture 115, 88-96, (2015).

9. Urtubia, A., M. Emparan, C. Roman, G. Hernández, J.M. Roger, Multivariate Statistic and Pattern Recognition to detect abnormal fermentations in wine process, Journal of Biotechnology 150 (1), 328 (2010).
10. Urtubia, A., J.M. Roger, Predictive power of LDA to discriminate abnormal wine fermentations, Journal of Chemometrics, 25 (7), 382-388, (2011).
11. Urtubia, A., G. Hernández, C. Román, Prediction of problematic wine fermentations using artificial neural networks, Bioprocess and Biosystems Engineering 34, 1057-1065, (2011).
12. Urtubia, A., G. Hernández, J.M. Roger, Detection of abnormal fermentations in wine process by multivariate statistics and pattern recognition techniques, Journal of Biotechnology 159, 336-341, (2012).
13. Hernández, G., R. Leon, A. Urtubia, Detection of Abnormal Wine Fermentation Processes by Support Vector Machines, Cluster Computing 19, 1219 – 1225, (2016).
14. Engelbrecht A.P., Computational Intelligence: An Introduction, 2nd Edition, John Wiley & Sons, (2007).
15. Kruse, R., et al, Computational Intelligence: A Methodological Introduction, Springer, (2013).
16. Bishop, C.M., Neural Networks for Pattern Recognition, Oxford University Press, (1996).
17. Bishop, C.M., Pattern Recognition and Machine Learning, Springer, (2006).
18. Theodoridis, S., K. Koutroumbas, Pattern Recognition, Fourth Edition, Academic Press, (2008).
19. Ripley, B.D., Pattern Recognition and Neural Networks, Cambridge University Press, (2008).

Data Mining for the Internet of Things

Tausifa Jan Saleem[1], Mohammad Ahsan Chishti[1]

[1] National Institute of Technology Srinagar, India

Abstract. Internet of Things is an idea that will eventually lead to the creation of a smart world. It is a concept that allows things/objects to talk to each other, work in co-ordination with other things to create novel applications, and attain common targets. The massive volume of data generated by IoT devices is considered of immense value. Hence, extracting hidden correlations and insights from this data is highly crucial. Data mining will certainly play a role in generating valuable inferences from this humongous volume of data and hence, will assist in creating smarter IoT. This paper begins with a brief discussion on the knowledge discovery process in IoT. Then, a concise review of data mining for IoT is provided. Finally, a number of challenges faced by data mining in IoT are discussed.

Keywords: Internet of Things (IoT), Data Mining, Classification, Clustering, Association Rule Mining.

1 Introduction

The major characteristics of IoT are interconnectivity, things related services, heterogeneity, dynamism in the environment, and enormous scale. These concepts more or less allow the progress of the internet of things to "internet of everything", because almost everything can be connected to the internet at anyplace, and from anywhere. As IoT penetrates more and more into the various aspects of human life, the number of devices that require communication and management increase substantially. As such, the ratio of human-generated communication to device generated communication will shift more towards the device initiated communication. The amount of data generated will be enormous. IoT is striving to make our environment an intelligent one that has smart homes, smart transportation, smart industries, smart healthcare, smart agriculture, smart grid, etc. by deploying a plethora of sensors everywhere. Fig. 1 depicts the various applications of IoT.

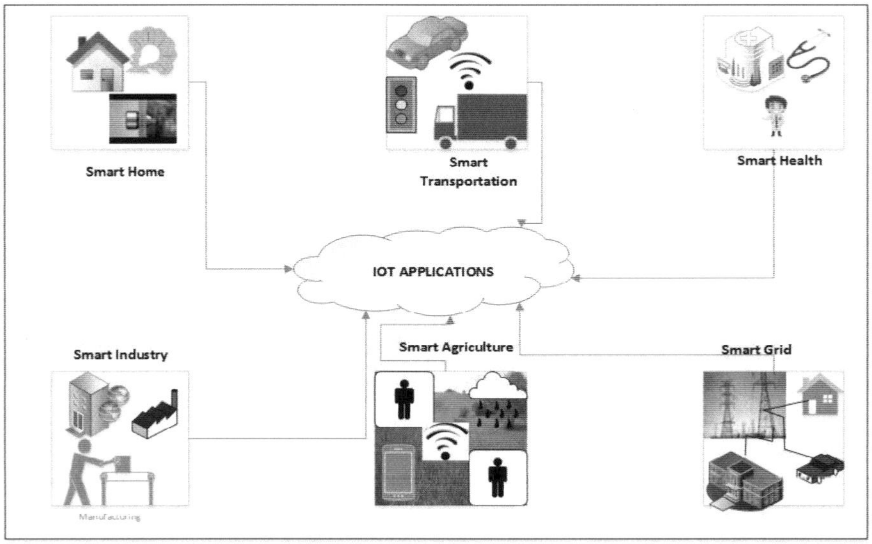

Fig.1. IoT Applications

The data generated by IoT devices exhibit the following characteristics:

- Large-scale data: IoT data are characterized by huge volume, as a myriad of sensors deployed in IoT environments continuously emanate large magnitude of data, which need to be processed and analyzed within a certain lapse of time [1, 2, 3].
- Time and space correlation: unlike conventional data, data from IoT has a position and time stamp for all data points in order to depict the change of location of an object with time [1, 2, 3].
- Redundancy: The data produced from IoT environments contain highly redundant information. Hence, to improve the data quality, effective data pre-processing techniques need to be employed [4, 3].
- Highly noisy: IoT data are subjected to noise during data acquisition and data transmission as IoT data are generated by highly constrained devices. Experiments demonstrate that RFID devices only generate 60% to 70% accurate data [5, 6].
- Weak semantics: Data produced by IoT devices are of weak semantics. Hence, intricate semantics ought to be extracted from the collection of weak semantic data so as to assist diverse IoT applications including smart transportation, smart healthcare, smart factory, etc. [5, 6].
- Massive real-time data: A multitude of sensors deployed in highly dynamic IoT environments continuously generate huge real-time streaming data [5, 6]. For example, an airplane with an average 12-hour flight-time generates up to 844TB of real-time streaming data [7].

- Heterogeneity: Data generated from heterogeneous and distributed sensing systems in IoT are highly diverse, and may be of structured, unstructured or semi-structured nature [1, 2, 3, 5, 6].

2 Knowledge Discovery Process in IoT

Knowledge discovery is a crucial process for revealing effective, novel, valuable, and comprehensible patterns in data. The prime objective is to extract valuable knowledge from weak semantic data. The raw data produced by IoT devices may be of structured, unstructured or semi-structured nature. Hence, recognizing and extracting knowledge from IoT data is an arduous job [8]. Fig. 2 shows an overview of knowledge discovery in IoT environments. Knowledge discovery in IoT includes following steps:

- Data Acquisition: It is a process of capturing signals that measure physical parameters like temperature, pressure, humidity etc.
- Data Integration: In this process, data from diverse sources with different formats are combined.
- Data pre-processing: Data generated by IoT devices may contain noisy data, ambiguities, and missing values. Hence it is crucial to deal with such issues before processing the data. In data pre-processing, noisy data are smoothened, ambiguities in the data are removed, and missing values are filled, thus making it suitable for further processing. Moreover, data pre-processing is indispensable for removing redundancy in the captured sensor data in order to efficiently utilize the transmission link and reduce energy wastage.
- Data Mining: It is a vital step in the process of knowledge discovery. It is used to extract trends, hidden correlations, inferences, and actionable insights by applying different data analysis algorithms.
- Data Visualization: It is a process of displaying data in a lucid and comprehensible manner by presenting outcomes in the form of statistical representations like charts, graphs, etc.

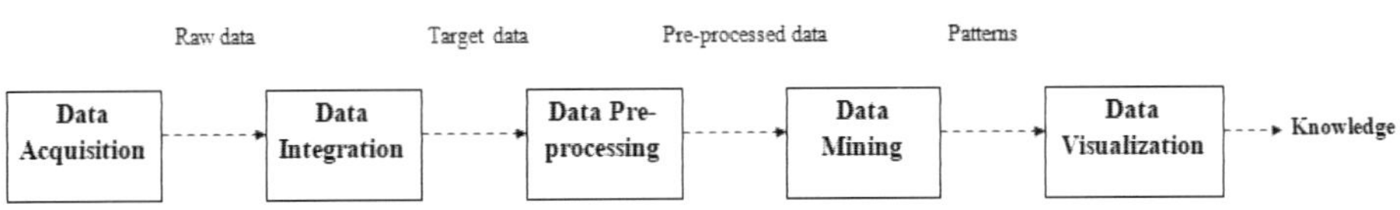

Fig.2. Knowledge discovery in IoT environments.

3 Data Mining for IoT

As mentioned in the previous section, data mining is a crucial step for extracting the valuable information from the data generated by IoT devices. Data mining techniques are grouped into the following types:

3.1 Classification: Classification is one of the most popular and highly employed data mining techniques for analyzing IoT data. The data items are classified into groups based on supervised learning. Examples of IoT use cases that utilized classification as a data mining method include real-time ECG monitoring [9], ebola virus outbreak control [10], automatic people counter in stores [11], defect detection in machines [12], video surveillance [13], real-time condition monitoring of machines [14], etc.

3.2 Clustering: Clustering is a data mining technique that forms groups of data items on the basis of different characteristics. The data items that display same features are put in one cluster. Clustering employs an unsupervised learning method for creating the clusters. Examples of IoT use cases that harnessed clustering include heart disease survival prediction [15], behavior visualization of Sybil attacker in IoT [16], wormhole attack detection in IoT [17], weather data analysis and sensor fault detection [18], safe driving [19], gesture recognition [20], etc.

3.3 Association Rule Mining: Used in the applications of decision-making and market analysis, it includes recognizing the relationships among various events, entities or objects to help improve decision making capabilities of business and offer a better analysis of the market. Examples of IoT use cases that utilized association rule mining include human activity recognition [21], extraction of usage patterns of IoT devices [22], etc.

Table 1 provides a summary of the use cases mentioned in this section.

Table 1. Data Mining in IoT use cases

IoT Use Case	Data Mining Method	Purpose of data mining	References
Real-time ECG monitoring	Classification	To classify ECG data into different cardiovascular conditions.	[9]
Ebola virus outbreak control	Classification	To assess the intensity of infection in a user based on the symptoms.	[10]
Automatic people counter in stores	Classification	To categorize people into adults and children based on their height.	[11]
Defect detection in machines	Classification	To categorize products into defected and non-defected classes.	[12]
Video surveillance	Classification	To categorize traffic into five classes: non-critical traffic, little	[13]

		critical traffic, rather critical traffic, critical traffic, very critical traffic.	
Real-time condition monitoring of electric machines	Classification	To formulate condition monitoring decisions for electric machines based on the vibration patterns of the shaft.	[14]
Heart disease survival prediction	Clustering	To categorize data items into two clusters based on the attribute value similarity.	[15]
Behavior visualization of Sybil attacker in IoT	Clustering	To group compromised identities and deploy the sybil node for corresponding identities without violating the set of adjacent nodes.	[16]
Wormhole attack detection in IoT	Clustering	To divide the nodes into various clusters based on their location from the root node.	[17]
Weather data analysis and sensor fault detection	Clustering	To categorize the regions with different weather data characteristics.	[18]
Safe driving	Clustering	To identify accident-prone areas.	[19]
Gesture recognition	Clustering	To detect the presence of an event.	[20]
Human activity recognition	Association Rule Mining	To mine frequent patterns.	[21]
Extraction of usage patterns of IoT devices	Association Rule Mining	To extract device co usage patterns.	[22]

4 Challenges

In case of IoT, data quality means how appropriate the captured data are for dispensing smart services to the IoT users [23]. Therefore, high-quality data is mandatory for making efficient control decisions in smart IoT environments [24]. Nevertheless, several issues like the huge scale of IoT data, intermittent loss of connection and resource-constrained nature of sensor devices imperil the quality of generated IoT data [25]. Poor data quality affects decision making in IoT environments that lead to poor IoT services. Following provides a description of the factors that are vital for effective data mining. However, ensuring these factors is challenging in IoT environments.

- Accuracy: The data collected from across the network of sensor devices in IoT should correctly reflect what was captured at each device.
- Completeness: Because of the constrained nature of IoT sensors and intermittent loss of connectivity, IoT data may contain missing and incomplete values which lead to poor data quality [22]. Hence, ensuring completeness in IoT data is vital for efficient data mining.
- Timeliness: Timeliness is an important data quality requirement as most of the IoT applications are time stringent demanding fast analytics [26]. Hence, the data generated from such applications should be analyzed at the right time with minimal delay.
- Uniqueness: The closely deployed sensor nodes in IoT tend to capture similar information which leads to redundancy in IoT data. Redundant data not only leads to energy wastage but also dissipates the storage space. Moreover, it also affects the feature extraction process [3]. Hence, removing redundancy in IoT data and ensuring its uniqueness is crucial for its data quality.

5 Conclusion

Data mining is crucial for extracting the valuable information from the data generated by IoT devices. This paper briefly discusses three important data mining methods namely, classification, clustering, and association rule mining and reviews a number of research studies that have applied these data mining methods for extracting valuable insights from the IoT data. Moreover, various factors that are vital for effective data mining were discussed. These factors include accuracy, completeness, timeliness, and uniqueness. However, ensuring accuracy, completeness, timeliness, and uniqueness of data is challenging in case of IoT environments. Hence, it is concluded that data mining is indispensable for creating smarter IoT, however, because of the intricate nature of IoT data, a number of challenges are yet to be resolved.

References

1. M. Chen, S. Mao, Y. Liu. Big Data: A Survey. Mobile Networks and applications, Springer, Vol. 19 (2014) 171-209.
2. Tingli Li, Yang Liu, Ye Tian, Shuo Shen, Wei Mao. A Storage Solution for Massive IoT Data Based on NoSQL. International Conference on Green Computing and Communications, Conference on Internet of Things, and Conference on Cyber, Physical and Social Computing, IEEE, Besancon, France (2012) 50-57.
3. Sai Xie, Zhe Chen. Anomaly Detection and Redundancy Elimination of Big Sensor Data in Internet of Things [online]. Available: https://arxiv.org/abs/1703.03225 (2017)
4. Mervat Abu-Elkheir, Mohammad Hayajneh, Najah Abu Ali. Data Management for the Internet of Things: Design Primitives and Solution. Sensors, Vol. 13 (2013) 15582-15612.
5. Meng Ma, Ping Wang, Chao-Hsien Chu. Data Management for Internet of Things: Challenges, Approaches and Opportunities. International Conference on Green Computing

and Communications and IEEE Internet of Things and IEEE Cyber, Physical and Social Computing, IEEE (2013) 1144-1151.
6. Hongming Cai, Boyi Xu, Lihong Jiang, Athanasios V. Vasilakos. IoT-based Big Data Storage Systems in Cloud Computing: Perspectives and Challenges. IEEE Internet of Things Journal, Vol. 4, No. 1 (2016) 75-87.
7. Bhoopathi Rapolu. Internet of Aircraft Things: An Industry Set To Be Transformed [online]. Available: http://aviationweek.com/connected-aerospace/internet-aircraft-things-industry-set-be-transformed (2016).
8. Constante Nicolalde F., Silva F., Herrera B., Pereira A. Big Data Analytics in IOT: Challenges, Open Research Issues and Tools. Trends and Advances in Information Systems and Technologies. WorldCIST'18 2018, Advances in Intelligent Systems and Computing, Springer, Cham, Vol. 746 (2018).
9. R. Varatharajan, Gunasekaran Manogaran, and M. K. Priyan . A big data classification approach using LDA with an enhanced SVM method for ECG signals in cloud computing,. Multimed Tools Appl, Springer.
10. Sina Dami, and Mahtab Yahaghizadeh. Efficient Event Prediction in an IOT Environment Based On LDA Model and Support Vector Machine. 6th Iranian Joint Congress on Fuzzy and Intelligent Systems (CFIS), IEEE, Kerman, Iran (2018).
11. Kabilan N, and Dr. M. Senthamil Selvi. Surveillance and Steering of Irrigation System in Cloud using Wireless Sensor Network and Wi-Fi Module. Fifth International Conference on Recent Trends in Information Technology, IEEE, Chennai, India (2016).
12. Z. Huang, K.-J. Lin, B.-L. Tsai, S. Yan, and C.-S. Shih. Building edge intelligence for online activity recognition in service-oriented IoT systems. Future Generation Computer Systems, Elsevier (2018).
13. Eduardo Viegas, Altair Santin, Luiz Oliveira, Andr´e Franca, Ricardo Jasinski, and Volnei Pedroni. A Reliable and Energy-Efficient Classifier Combination Scheme for Intrusion Detection in Embedded Systems. Computers & Security, Elsevier, Vol. 78, (2018) 16-32.
14. Henry Friday Nweke, Ying Wah Teh, Mohammed Ali Al-garadi, and Uzoma Rita Alo. Deep Learning Algorithms for Human Activity Recognition using Mobile and Wearable Sensor Networks: State of the Art and Research Challenges. Expert Systems With Applications, Elsevier, Vol. 105 (2018) 233-261.
15. Mohammad Malekzadeh, Richard G. Clegg, and Hamed Haddadi. Replacement AutoEncoder: A Privacy-Preserving Algorithm for Sensory Data Analysis. Third International Conference on Internet-of-Things Design and Implementation, IEEE, IEEE/ACM, Orlando, FL, USA (2018).
16. Mohammad Kachuee, Anahita Hosseini, Babak Moatamed, Sajad Darabi, Majid Sarrafzadeh. Context-Aware Feature Query To Improve The Prediction Performance. Global Conference on Signal and Information Processing (GlobalSIP), IEEE, Montreal, QC, Canada (2017).
17. Homayoun S., Ahmadzadeh M., Hashemi S., Dehghantanha A., and Khayami R. BoTShark: A Deep Learning Approach for Botnet Traffic Detection. Cyber Threat Intelligence, Advances in Information Security, Vol 70. Springer, Cham.
18. Guifang Liu, Huaiqian Bao, and Baokun Han . A Stacked Autoencoder-Based Deep Neural Network for Achieving Gearbox Fault Diagnosis. Mathematical Problems in Engineering, Hindawi.
19. Lianbing Deng, Daming Li, Xiang Yao, David Cox, and Haoxiang Wang . Mobile network intrusion detection for IoT system based on transfer learning algorithm. Cluster Computing, Springer, (2018).
20. G.Nagarajan, R.I.Minu, B Muthukumar, V.Vedanarayanan, and S.D.Sundarsingh. Hybrid Genetic Algorithm for Medical Image Feature Extraction and selection. International Conference on Computational Modeling and Security (CMS), Procedia Computer Science, Elsevier, Vol. 85 (2016) 455-462.

21. Sourabh S. Patil, and Dr. Mrs. A. S. Bhalchandra. Pattern Recognition Using Genetic Algorithm. International conference on I-SMAC (IoT in Social, Mobile, Analytics and Cloud), IEEE, Palladam, India.
22. Jonathan Reynolds, Yacine Rezgui, Alan Kwan, Solène Piriou, and A ZoneLevel. Building Energy Optimisation Combining an Artificial Neural Network, a Genetic Algorithm, and Model Predictive Control. Energy, Elsevier, Vol. 151 (2018) 729-739.
23. Aimad Karkouch, Hajar Mousannif, Hassan Al Moatassime, Thomas Noel . Data quality in internet of things: A state-of the-art survey. Journal of Network and Computer Applications, Elsevier, Vol. 73 (2016) 57-81.
24. Li Cai1, Yangyong Zhu. The Challenges of Data Quality and Data Quality Assessment in the Big Data Era. Data Science Journal, Vol. 14, No. 2 (2015) 1-10.
25. Aimad Karkouch, Hajar Mousannif, Hassan Al Moatassime, Thomas Noel. Data Quality Enhancement in Internet Of Things Environment. 12th International conference of computer systems and applications, IEEE, Morocco (2015).
26. Mehdi Mohammadi, Ala Al-Fuqaha, Sameh Sorour, Mohsen Guizani. Deep Learning for IoT Big Data and Streaming Analytics: A Survey. IEEE Communications Surveys & Tutorials (2018).

Large-Scale Vertex-Centric Network Embedding via Apache Spark

Sara Riazi and Boyana Norris

Department of Computer and Information Science
University of Oregon,
Eugene, OR 97403
{riazi,bnorris2}@uoregon.edu

Abstract. Network embedding is an important step in many different computations based on graph data. However, existing approaches are limited to small or middle size graphs with less than a million edges. In practice, web or social network graphs are orders of magnitude larger, thus making most current methods impractical for very large graphs. To address this problem, we introduce a new distributed-memory parallel network embedding method based on Apache Spark and GraphX. We demonstrate the scalability of our method as well as its ability to generate meaningful embeddings for vertex classification and link prediction on both real-world and synthetic graphs. To the best of our knowledge, we are the first to train network embeddings for graphs with billions of edges.

1 Introduction

Network embedding is an important step in solving many graph problems including link prediction, vertex classification, and clustering. Network embedding aims to learn a low dimensional vector representation for vertices of a graph. However, existing approaches do not scale to very large graphs with billions of vertices and edges. One solution is to use distributed memory systems and out-of-core computation. Among distributed memory systems, frameworks such as the Apache Spark-based GraphX [1] are of particular interest to us because they offer a map-reduce-based approach to expressing distributed-memory parallel algorithms for graph computations.

However, to take advantage of such distributed graph processing frameworks, we need to design new map-reduce [2] network embedding algorithms. In general, following the previous work for learning general network embedding [3–5], we use the structural properties of a network to train an embedding. A common assumption underlying existing methods and our new algorithm is that we expect that the embedding of a vertex is more similar to the embeddings of its neighbors rather than to the embedding of a random vertex outside of its neighborhood. We enforce this objective with approximate maximum likelihood training of the embedding in which the partition function is approximated using negative samples. This training requires lookup access to the embedding of

Our **key contributions** include the following.

- A discussion of the limitations of GraphX for implementing existing network embedding algorithms.
- A new map-reduce-friendly message propagation model for learning vertex-centric network embeddings, which propagates the gradients instead of the embedding.
- The use of random graphs to construct negative sampling, which is necessary for approximate maximum likelihood training.
- A new Graph-X based vertex-centric network embedding (VCNE) algorithm based on gradient propagation and random graphs that performs well on a range of real-world problems and synthetic graphs and can be applied to large-scproblems that cannot be handled by current embedding approaches.

2 Parallel Graph Frameworks

Running traditional graph algorithms over extremely large graphs requires distributed processing as well as out-of-core computation. Therefore, several parallel graph frameworks such as GraphX [1] or Giraph [6] have been developed on top of data-parallel systems Apache Spark or Hadoop, respectively. As a result, they provide graph processing APIs using distributed data processing models such as map-reduce [2]. In map-reduce, data is converted to key-value pairs and then partitioned onto nodes. A map-reduce system consists of a set of workers that are coordinated by a master process. The master process assigns partitions to workers, and then workers apply a user-defined map function to the key-value pairs, resulting in intermediate key-value pairs stored on the local disks of workers. Apache Spark defines the map-reduce model in term of operation over distributed collection objects called resilient distributed datasets (RDDs). RDDs [7] are immutable collection of objects that are partitioned across different Spark nodes in the network.

An RDD is transformed to another RDD using transformation instructions such as *map* and *filter*. Transformations in Spark are lazy, which means that Spark does not apply transformations immediately. It, instead, constructs a directed acyclic graph (DAG) of data parts and transformations followed by final steps as actions. Then it executes the formed DAG by sending it as several tasks to Spark nodes. The actions in Spark reduce RDDs to values. For example, *count* computes the number of records in RDDs, so it needs all the transformation to be applied first, and then it returns the result.

Because Spark is a data-parallel computation system, GraphX implements graph operations based on the data-parallel operations available in Spark, such as join, map, and reduce. GraphX represents graphs using two RDDs, one for vertices and another for edges.

However, handling graphs in a data-parallel computation system is more complex than map-reduce operations since the vertices should be processed in the context of their neighbors. To address that, GraphX introduces edge triplets, which joins the structure of vertices and edge RDDs. Each triplet carries an edge attribute and the attributes of vertices that incident with that edge. Therefore, by grouping the triplets on the id of the source or destination vertex, one can access the value of all the neighbors of each vertex. Moreover, since the triplets are distributed, if the neighbors of a vertex are located on different machines, then Spark workers have to communicate to each other to construct the result. Therefore, different strategies for distributing graphs over partitions result in significant differences in communication and storage overheads. GraphX supports both edge-cut and vertex-cut graph partitioning strategies.

GraphX also provides a vertex-centric programming model for developing distributed graph algorithms. Vertex-centric programming models such as Pregel [8] are widely used for reimplementing sequential algorithms in graph-parallel frameworks such as Apache Giraph or GraphX. In a vertex-centric programming model, we develop an algorithm from a vertex point of view, which in general includes three different steps: gathering messages from its neighboring vertices, updating its state, and generating messages for its neighbors. The graph-parallel framework iteratively executes these steps in one super-steps until no vertex produces any message. GraphX implements all this functionality using map-reduce operations over edge triplets.

3 Vertex-Centric Network Embedding

The goal of vertex-centric network embedding is to learn a low-dimensional vector for each vertex in the graph such that the vector representation carries the structural properties of the graph. Formally, for graph $G(\mathcal{V}, \mathcal{E})$ of vertex set $\mathcal{V}$ and edge set $\mathcal{E}$, we want to learn a d-dimensional vector representation $\mathbf{u}_i$ for each $i \in \mathcal{V}$ such that $d \ll |\mathcal{V}|$.

Many approaches have been introduced to learn a vector representation [3–5, 9, 10] aiming to encode a vertex's neighborhood (its structural properties) into a low-dimensional space. Other properties of vertices, such as attributes, labels, and relations can also incorporated into the vector representation of the vertex [11–14].

In general, a graph embedding approach is vertex-centric friendly if the embedding of each vertex is a function of only the embeddings of its neighbors. For example, LINE-1st [4] computes the embedding using first-order proximity by optimizing the following objective function:

$$\max_{\mathbf{u}} \sum_{(i,j)\in E} w_{ij}\sigma(\mathbf{u}_i^T \mathbf{u}_j), \tag{1}$$

$$\max_{\mathbf{u}} \sum_{i} \sum_{j \in N(i)} w_{ij} \sigma(\mathbf{u}_i^T \mathbf{u}_j), \tag{2}$$

where $N(i)$ is the set of neighbors of vertex i.

More powerful representation learning methods, such as LINE second-order proximity, consider the embeddings of neighbors *and* the embeddings of random vertices selected among non-neighbor nodes (negative samples), contrasting them to learn the embedding of each vertex:

$$\max_{u} \sum_{j \in N(i)} w_{ij} \sigma(\mathbf{u}_i^T \mathbf{u}_j) + \frac{-1}{k} \sum_{j \notin N(i)}^{k} w_{ij} \sigma(\mathbf{u}_i^T \mathbf{u}_j) \tag{3}$$

Negative samples make sure that the objective function does not find a trivial solution (e.g., the embedding of all vertices become the same). Negative sampling simply forces the embeddings of non-neighbor nodes to become different.

In a vertex-centric paradigm, we are required to decompose the algorithm such that each vertex is responsible for its part of the objective function evaluation, providing all the necessary information, e.g., the current state of its neighbors. In other words, we look at the computation from a vertex point of view. We can simply view network embedding of Eq. 3 in a vertex-centric paradigm: "As a vertex, I want my embedding to be similar to my neighbors' embeddings, while it differs from the embeddings of other non-neighbor vertices". A vertex-centric network embedding requires the objective function to decompose as partial objectives computable at individual vertices, but unfortunately the objective of Eq. 3 does not decompose over vertices.

In a vertex-centric setting for optimizing based on Eq. 3, each vertex needs to access the embeddings of vertices that are not directly connected to it (negative sampling). Parallel graph frameworks do not provide efficient lookup of random vertices that are distributed among different machines. Moreover, each computing node does not have a lookup dictionary that can be used to locate and ship the attributes of required vertices, but there are routing tables for vertices based on the edges that are connecting them, so accessing the neighboring vertices is efficient (compared to random lookup access).

To benefit from this efficiency, we define a random graph, in which each vertex is connected to k randomly selected vertices in the graph with a negative weight, which can be uniformly set to one. We construct a new graph as the union of the current graph and the random graph. In the new augmented graph, each vertex has access to the embedding of k randomly chosen vertices. Therefore, we can rewrite Eq.3 with our augmented graph:

$$O_i = \max_{u} \sum_{j \in A(i)} w_{ij} \sigma(e_w \mathbf{u}_i^T \mathbf{u}_j), \tag{4}$$

where e_w is negative one for negative samples and positive one for the actual neighbors, and $A(i)$ is the set of neighbors of vertex i in the augmented graph. We can derive Eq. 4 from Eq. 3 by using the symmetry in the sigmoid function: $\sigma(-x) = -\sigma(x)$ and absorbing k in the weights.

The objective function of Eq. 4 decomposes over vertices in the augmented graph, so it can be computed in a vertex-centric approach unlike the negative sampling-based approach in the original graph, whose objective function is not decomposable.

3.1 Vertex-Centric algorithm

A data-parallel vertex-centric graph algorithm typically involves three steps: sending messages among neighbors (sendMessage), reducing all the messages to a single vertex to one message (mergeMessage), and executing a vertex related function given the final reduced message and the current state of the vertex (vertexProgram).

In order to compute the partial objective O_i on each compute node, a naive implementation sends the embedding of each neighbor to vertex i as sendMessage, keeps the union of embeddings as the reduceMessage, and optimizes O_i in the vertexProgram. However, in a map-reduce framework, combining the embedding vectors can result in prohibitively large collections since there is no bound on the degree of the vertices.

We use a simple trick to avoid the construction of these large collections by propagating the gradient instead of the embeddings. However, we first have to make sure that the total gradient of Eq. 4 can be computed by the vertex programs.

The gradient of O_i can be written as

$$\nabla O_i = \sum_{j \in A(i)} \nabla O_{i \leftarrow j}, \tag{5}$$

where

$$\nabla O_{i \leftarrow j} = e_w * \mathbf{u}_j * \sigma(e_w * \mathbf{u}_i^T \mathbf{u}_j)(1 - \sigma(e_w * \mathbf{u}_i^T \mathbf{u}_j). \tag{6}$$

Finally we can update the embedding using gradient ascent:

$$\mathbf{u}_i = \mathbf{u}_i + \eta \nabla O_i \tag{7}$$

Using edge triplets, each vertex in the augmented neighborhood $A(i)$ has access to data structures needed for computing $\nabla O_{i \leftarrow j}$. Therefore, defining $\nabla O_{i \leftarrow j}$ as a sendMessage function and sum as the mergeMessage operation, the final reduced message for vertex i is Eq. 5. Finally, vertexProgram executes the gradient update. In this vertex-centric design, the size of the data structures remains bounded and no large collection would be constructed in the intermediate steps. Therefore, we can optimize Eq. 4 for very large graphs with large vertex degrees. Algorithm 1 shows the definition of these functions.

Algorithm 1 Vertex-Centric Network Embedding

//e_{ji} : edge from j to i.
//d: embedding dimension
//msg: (m: $|\mathbb{R}|^d$)
//vertex attributes: (u: $|\mathbb{R}|^d$)
//$m_{i\to j}$: means the message from i for j
procedure SENDMESSASGE(e_{ij}, u_i, u_j)
    $m_{j\to i}$: $\nabla O_{i\leftarrow j}$ //Eq. 6
procedure MERGEMESSAGES($m_{i\to j}$, $m_{k\to j}$)
    $m_{i\to j} + m_{k\to j}$ //Eq. 5
procedure VERTEXPROGRAM(u, m)
    $u \leftarrow u + \eta m$ // Eq.7

4 Experiments

We compare our network embedding algorithm, VCNE, with LINE [4] and Node2vec [5] on mid-size datasets to show the capability of VCNE to learn meaningful representation. Then, we apply VCNE to very large graphs for the task of link prediction. Table 1 reports the characteristics of the graphs used in our experiments.

Table 1. The number of vertices and edges of the real-world graphs in our test suite.

Name	Num. of Vertices	Num. of Edges
Friendster	68,349,466	2,586,147,869
Twitter-MPI	52,579,682	1,963,263,821
Twitter	41,637,597	1,453,833,084
LiveJournal	5,193,874	48,682,718
Reddit	232,965	11,606,919
PPI	56,944	793,632

4.1 Vertex Classification

The vertex classification goal is to classify each vertex into different groups, which includes both multi-class and multi-label classification.

We use two datasets of protein-protein interaction (PPI) and Reddit posts. In PPI, the goal is to assign a set of activated protein functions to each vertex, which are represented using positional gene sets, motif gene sets, and immunological signatures [9]. The total possible protein functions are 121 and the vertex feature set size is 50.

Reddit is an online discussion forum in which people publish posts and comment on others' posts. In the Reddit graph, the vertices are the posts and two vertices are adjacent if a user comments on the posts corresponding to the vertices [9]. The node features include the average word embedding of the title, all comments of the post and the score of the post as well as the number of comments on the posts. The total number of features is 602, and the goal is to assign each vertex to one of 41 communities. For both PPI and Reddit, we used the same set of train/val/test as provided by [9]. Table 1 shows the characteristics of these two graphs.

We first generate vertex embedding using LINE, Node2Vec, and VCEmb, and then concatenate the vertex embedding to the vertex features, and use it as input to a logistic regression classifier to predict labels. As a baseline, we also train logistic regression using only the vertex features. Although more complex classifiers such as multi-layer perceptron would be possible and may result in higher accuracy, we use simple logistic regression to better isolate the impact of vertex embedding.

We used an embedding dimension of 100 for all algorithms.

Table 2. F_1 score of vertex classification tasks using different embedding algorithms.

	PPI	Reddit
Vertex features	43.3	51.2
LINE	**53.08**	63.9
Node2vec	49.8	65.4
VCNE	51.4	**66.2**

Table 2 shows the performance VCNE, LINE, Node2Vec, and raw vertex features in terms of F_1 score. For all embedding algorithm, using embedding in addition to vertex features helps, so we can conclude that the embedding is meaningful and encodes structural properties of the graph. For Reddit, VCNE is more accurate than LINE and Node2Vec, but for PPI, it only better than Node2vec. We also show the learned embedding by VCNE using t-SNE [15] in Figure 1. VCNE can capture clear clusters in the graph.

4.2 Link Prediction

Link prediction is an import graph analytic problem, in which we wish to predict the potential edges in the network. This problem is of particular interest for social network friend suggestion or predicting the evolution of graphs in the future.

We constructed a synthetic link prediction dataset, for which we dropped one percent of the current edges of the graph and kept the dropped edges as the test set combined with another set of vertex pairs as the true negative. The size of our negative set is equal to the size of the dropped set making sure that we have balanced test set. The remaining edges of the graph constitute the core graph, which the network embedding algorithms have been trained on. We emphasize that the training algorithms have not seen the dropped edges.

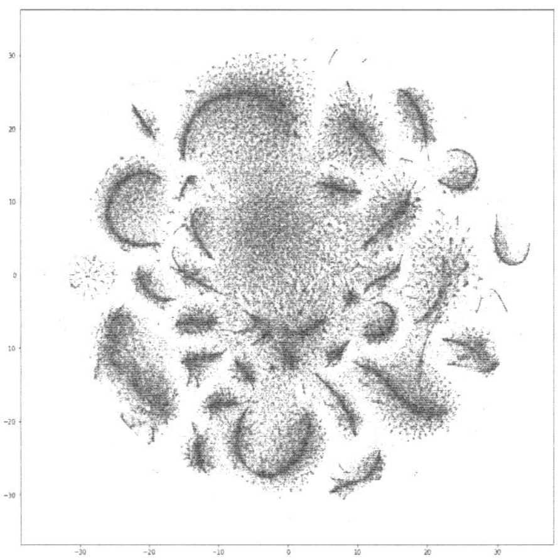

Fig. 1. The embedding of the Reddit graph generated by VCNE.

We report the performance of link prediction using the embedding generated by VCNE in Table 3.

Table 3. The performance of link prediction using VCNE.

	Precision	Recall	F_1
Friendster	69.3	98.0	81.2
Twitter MPI	67.8	94.7	79.0
Twitter	72.4	93.9	81.7
LiverJournal	67.3	81.7	73.8

Because the existing embedding algorithms cannot scale to our very large graphs, we try to use Jacard index to predict an edge: $J(u, v) = \frac{N(u) \cap N(v)}{N(u) \cup N(v)}$, where $N(u)$ is the set of neighbors of vertex u. Computing the Jacard index requires constructing triplets whose vertex attributes are sets of neighbor IDs, and for very large social networks, this results in prohibitively large messages given the power-law degree distribution of social networks. Nevertheless, we could compute the Jacard index for LiveJournal graphs, but not for the other larger graphs. For LiveJournal, using the Jacard index results in 99.2% precision, 71.1% recall, and F_1 score of 83.1%. We should also mention that for link prediction using VCNE, we just use pure embedding and the sigmoid function to classify the edges. However, one can train a classifier given the embedding of the vertices on both sides of an edge, which would result in a much more accurate prediction.

4.3 Scalability

To measure the scalability of VCNE over Apache Spark, we run VCE for Friendster, Twitter MPI, Twitter, and LiveJournal with different numbers of Spark workers: 10, 20, 30, and 40. Each worker has access to 20 cores and 75GB of memory (for a total number of cores ranging between 200 and 800 and memory ranging from 750GB to 3TB). The University of Oregon Talapas cluster where we peformed the experiments consists of dual Intel Xeon E5-2690v4 nodes connected with an EDR InfiniBand network.

Figure 2 reports the average runtime for one learning iteration, which includes generating the random graph, combining the random graph with the original graph, and updating the embedding using Algorithm 1. We observe that the overhead of using data-parallel systems such as Apache Spark for processing mid-size graphs such LiveJournal is considerable, but increasing the number of workers significantly helps the processing of larger graphs such as Twitter-MPI and Friendster.

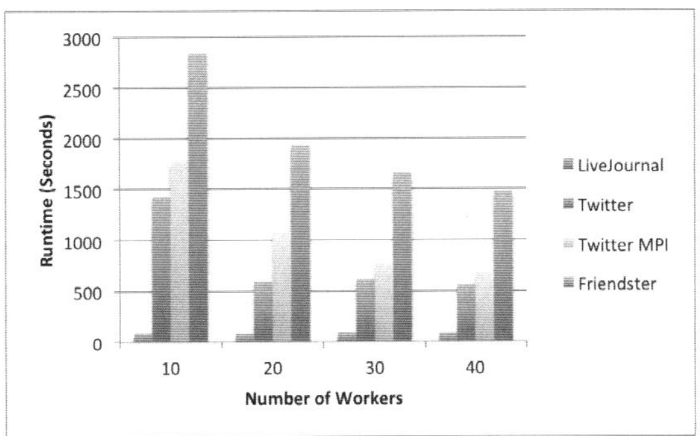

Fig. 2. Average runtime for one training step of VCE with 10 to 40 Spark workers.

4.4 Implementation Details

Working with iterative algorithm over very large graphs may result in replicating large collections such as EdgeRDDs in the memory. It is very important to unpersist the collection from memory in order to avoid exceeding the available memory capacity. For example, in the pipeline operations such graph construction followed by groupEdge, Apache Spark materializes the first graph and we lose the pointer to it as it is followed by map operation. It is necessary to observe the storage memory profile provided by Apache Spark as a part of its Web UI to make sure that no large collections are left behind in an iteration.

Moreover, operations such as aggregateMessage, which is used for message passing over graphs requires significant amount of data shuffling for shipping vertex attributes (embeddings) among workers. This results in a large amount

7 Acknowledgments

This research was supported by NSF CCF Award #1725585.

References

1. Gonzalez, J.E., Xin, R.S., Dave, A., Crankshaw, D., Franklin, M.J., Stoica, I.: GraphX: Graph processing in a distributed dataflow framework. In: Proceedings of the 11th USENIX Conference on Operating Systems Design and Implementation. OSDI 14, Broomfield, CO, USA (2014) 599–613
2. Dean, J., Ghemawat, S.: MapReduce: Simplified data processing on large clusters. Communications of the ACM **51**(1) (2008) 107–113
3. Perozzi, B., Al-Rfou, R., Skiena, S.: Deepwalk: Online learning of social representations. CoRR **abs/1403.6652** (2014)
4. Tang, J., Qu, M., Wang, M., Zhang, M., Yan, J., Mei, Q.: Line: Large-scale information network embedding. In: Proceedings of the 24th International Conference on World Wide Web, ACM (2015) 1067–1077
5. Grover, A., Leskovec, J.: node2vec: Scalable feature learning for networks. In: ACM SIGKDD International Conference on Knowledge Discovery and Data Mining (KDD). (2016)
6. Tian, Y., Balmin, A., Corsten, S.A., Tatikonda, S., McPherson, J.: From think like a vertex to think like a graph. Proceedings of the VLDB Endowment **7**(3) (2013) 193–204
7. Zaharia, M., Chowdhury, M., Das, T., Dave, A., Ma, J., McCauley, M., Franklin, M.J., Shenker, S., Stoica, I.: Resilient distributed datasets: A fault-tolerant abstraction for in-memory cluster computing. In: Proceedings of the 9th USENIX conference on Networked Systems Design and Implementation, USENIX Association (2012)
8. Malewicz, G., Austern, M.H., Bik, A.J., Dehnert, J.C., Horn, I., Leiser, N., Czajkowski, G.: Pregel: A system for large-scale graph processing. In: Proceedings of the 2010 ACM SIGMOD International Conference on Management of data. (2010) 135–146
9. Hamilton, W., Ying, Z., Leskovec, J.: Inductive representation learning on large graphs. In: Advances in Neural Information Processing Systems. (2017) 1024–1034
10. Veličković, P., Cucurull, G., Casanova, A., Romero, A., Lio, P., Bengio, Y.: Graph attention networks. (2018)
11. Duran, A.G., Niepert, M.: Learning graph representations with embedding propagation. In: Advances in neural information processing systems. (2017) 5119–5130
12. Lin, Y., Liu, Z., Sun, M., Liu, Y., Zhu, X.: Learning entity and relation embeddings for knowledge graph completion. In: Twenty-ninth AAAI conference on artificial intelligence. (2015)
13. Yang, C., Liu, Z., Zhao, D., Sun, M., Chang, E.Y.: Network representation learning with rich text information. In: IJCAI. (2015) 2111–2117
14. Pan, S., Wu, J., Zhu, X., Zhang, C., Wang, Y.: Tri-party deep network representation. In: IJCAI. (2016)
15. Maaten, L.v.d., Hinton, G.: Visualizing data using t-sne. Journal of Machine Learning Research **9**(Nov) (2008) 2579–2605
16. Wang, D., Cui, P., Zhu, W.: Structural deep network embedding. In: Proceedings of the 22Nd ACM SIGKDD International Conference on Knowledge Discovery and Data Mining. KDD '16, New York, NY, USA, ACM (2016) 1225–1234

17. Zhu, X., Lafferty, J., Rosenfeld, R.: Semi-supervised learning with graphs. Carnegie Mellon University, language technologies institute, school of computer science (2005)
18. Sen, P., Namata, G., Bilgic, M., Getoor, L., Galligher, B., Eliassi-Rad, T.: Collective classification in network data. AI magazine **29**(3) (2008) 93
19. Zhu, X., Ghahramani, Z.: Learning from labeled and unlabeled data with label propagation. (2002)
20. Kipf, T.N., Welling, M.: Semi-supervised classification with graph convolutional networks. arXiv preprint arXiv:1609.02907 (2016)

Leveraging Multiple Online Sources for Accurate Income Verification

Chirag Mahapatra[1] and Kedar Bellare[1]

[1] Airbnb, San Francisco CA 94103, USA

Abstract. Income verification is the problem of validating a person's stated income given basic identity information such as name, location, job title and employer. It is widely used in the context of mortgage lending, rental applications and other financial risk models. However, the current processes surrounding verification involve significant human effort and document gathering which can be both time-consuming and expensive. In this paper, we propose a novel model for verifying an individual's income given very limited identity information typically available in loan applications. Our model is a combination of a deep neural network and hand-engineered features. The hand-engineered features are based upon matching the input information against income records extracted automatically from various publicly available online sources (e.g. payscale.com, H-1B filings, government employee salaries). We conduct experiments on two data sets, one simulated from H-1B records and the other from a real-world data set of peer-to-peer (P2P) loan applications obtained from one of the world's largest P2P lending platform. Our results show a significant reduction in error of 3-6% relative to several strong baselines. We also perform ablation studies to demonstrate that a combined model is indeed necessary to achieve state-of-the-art performance on this task.

Keywords: Knowledge Acquisition, Web Data Mining, Financial Applications.

1. Introduction

In this paper, we address the problem of income verification: given a person's basic identity attributes (e.g. name, date of birth), current employment information (e.g. job title, company, location), and stated income we attempt to accurately validate the income of the given individual within a certain threshold. We define income as sum of earnings such as base salary and bonus in a year. We do not include rent, stocks, interest payments, dividend payments and other forms of income in our modeling. We would like to note that we use identity attributes such as name only to look up relevant income records via database queries or web searches. We do not use names for modeling to avoid .

One of the foremost use-cases of income verification is to identify creditworthy and fraudulent users during loan applications. Several recent pay-day loan and peerto-peer loan companies provide instant/pre-approved loans, powered by models behind the scenes that can accurately assess the risk involved with an application. An individual's validated income is an important feature in these risk models. Banks and lending institutions need to make these checks in a cost-effective and time-efficient manner. Currently applicants need to provide documents which have to be manually verified which can be both time-consuming and expensive. We present an approach that can algorithmically validate the input information quickly and accurately.

The main component of an income verification system is income prediction from a given input identity. We leverage the power of publicly available data sources on the web to solve the prediction problem. Obviously, using the public web comes with the following challenges:

- **Search, Extract, and Match:** We need to build queries from input to get a candidate set of web documents and database records that contain income information. We then have to extract data from structured and unstructured sources and filter the sources to keep only those which have the closest match to the input identity.

- **Partial and ambiguous information in the input and the Web:** An example of this is acronyms and alternate names of companies. For example, "United States Postal Service" can be represented as "USPS", "U.S.P.S", "US Postal Service" etc. We need to be able to identify that these are all the same entity.

- **Erroneous data on the Web:** Not all sources on the web are accurate. Some web sources misrepresent salary information or are out dated.

We have built a robust system that addresses all the aforementioned issues. First, our algorithm leverages search engines to surface salary content on tail entities; the surfaced content includes domains such as payscale.com, salary.com, H1-B data, etc. We have also crawled a large number of public government databases and indexed the available information in a structured format so that they can be searched directly. Each of these domains pose a different extraction challenge. For example, in some cases we need to extract content from unstructured text, whereas in other cases we can directly use wrappers based on XPath expressions tailored to specific websites.

Second, to address the issue of partial information (either in the input or on the Web), we often "expand" the scope of our identity: for example, we infer the industry from the company, the experience/level from job title and date of birth if present, and then generalize our search to the given position and industry.

Finally, to address the issue of possibly incorrect information on the Web, we build a model that aggregates salary ranges across several domains, and then computes one unified range by factoring in (a) frequencies of occurrence, (b) trustworthiness of sources, and (c) strength of identity match between the input and a source. For example, if multiple sources indicate that the median salary of a software engineer in San Francisco is around $100,000, but one source indicates the median salary is $50,000, the algorithm would center the range around $100,000.

Table 1. Example Input

Attribute	Example
Name	Barack H Obama
Address	Washington DC
Date of Birth	August 4, 1961
Employer	United States Government
Position	President
Stated Income	$400,000

We have made the following assumptions in our work:

- Employment information is available and correct.

- Identity information is available and correct.
- Verified income provided by the client does not include rent, interest payment, dividends, debts etc.

We introduce the model and delve into each component in detail in Section 2. We discuss the experiments used to validate our model in Section 3. We cover the previous literature in income modeling in Section 4 and conclude the paper in Section 5.

2. Method

In this section, we first describe the input provided for income verification (Section 2.1) and outline our overall approach to tackling it (Section 2.2). Then in Section 2.4 we delve into the system design and describe the individual system components at a high-level. Sections 2.3 and 2.5 lay out the crux of this paper by describing the systems utilizing online sources and input data respectively in detail.

2.1. Input Description

Table 1 gives an example input to our system. Each row in the input has personally identifiable information (e.g. name, address, dob), employment information (e.g. employer, job title) and the individual's stated income. Our goal in this paper is to verify that the stated income is accurate. There are two things to note about the input information here.

- Firstly, some of the information may be missing or incomplete. For example, the second row in the table has an incomplete address. However, we are always provided with the employment and income information although in some cases this information may be noisy or incomplete. In this paper, we focus on the problem of verifying the income assuming that the employment information is correct. In practice, we have observed that a very small percentage (i.e. roughly 1%) of people provide incorrect employment details but nearly 25% state a significantly higher income than their actual verifiable income.
- Secondly, we do not use sensitive information such as social security number, email, phone and the experience level for verifying income. This makes our approach broadly applicable since it can be applied in scenarios where the users are averse to giving out such private information. Of course, this information could help improve our models and in the future we would like to explore the possibility of using private information and even previous employment information to improve our models.

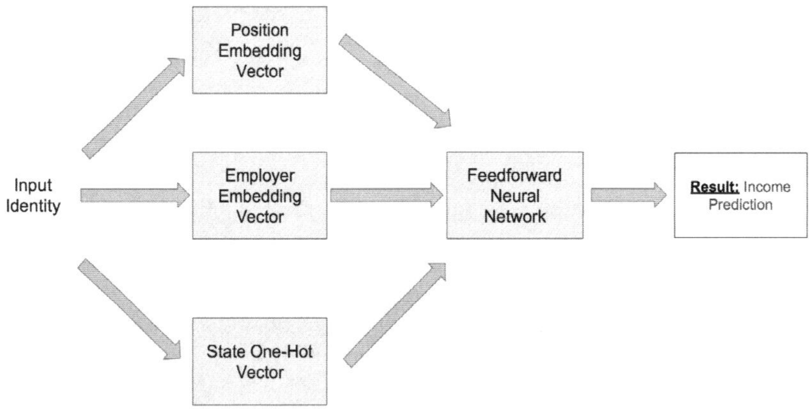

Fig. 1. Flowchart for internal model

2.2. Overall Approach

As described in the previous section, we want to determine whether the stated income is accurate for a user with the given identity and employment details. We cast the problem as a regression problem and use both the input data (e.g. employer, position, location) and online sources (e.g. payscale.com, Government databases) to predict the true income. Our model processes input and external data separately and combines the result. Initially, we built an internal model using only the input data. Figure 1 shows the model architecture for the processing of input data. Then we experimented with online sources and saw that it significantly improved model performance. Figure 2 shows the system architecture to utilize external data. It consists of several parts including, the input canonicalizer, a query generator for web and database records, data extractor, employment matcher, and feature extractor. The combined model is presented in Figure 3. We describe the individual components in the following sections.

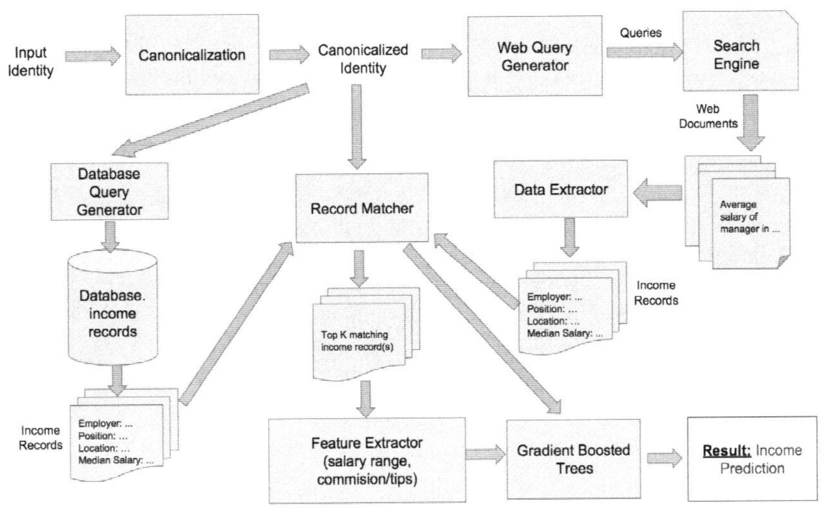

Fig. 2. Flowchart for external model

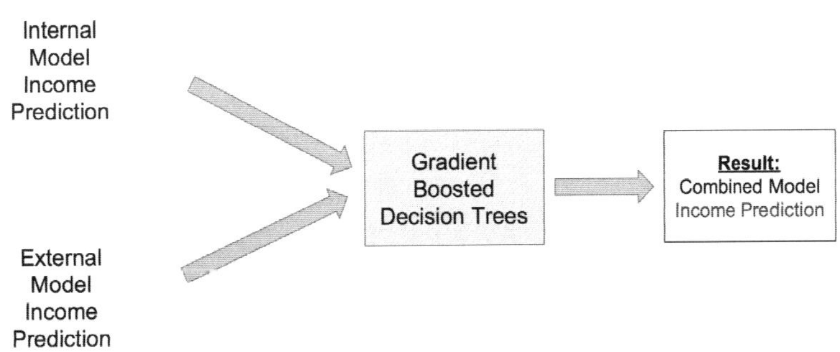

Fig. 3. Flowchart for combined model

2.3. Internal Model

For the internal model we create the word embeddings trained on the job title and employer using word2vec model (Mikolov et al. 2013). The job title and the employer embeddings were further trained separately using publicly available position and user stated income data and publicly available employer and user stated income data. The original word embeddings were used as the embedding layer of a neural network which consisted of a LSTM layer, a dropout layer and a dense layer. LSTM recurrent neural networks are useful for sequential modeling tasks. LSTM units were developed by (Hochreiter and Schmidhuber 1997) to overcome gradient vanishing problem. They introduced the adaptive gating mechanism which decides the degree to which

LSTM units keep the previous state and memorize the extracted features of the current data input.

We currently assume that user's location plays a role in determining the outcome. Currently we only incorporate information at the state-level by modeling user's state as a categorical variable. We use a one-hot encoding of the state as an indicator of user's location. In the future, we want to encode much finer-grained location information based on metropolitan statistical areas (MSAs) since they are widely used by Bureau of Labor Statistics.

The embedding dimensions were 300 each for employer and job title while the state encoding had a dimension of 50. This 650 dimension vector formed the input to a feed forward neural network. The network consisted of one hidden layer of size 200. We model the problem as a regression problem and our target is the income given by the input vector. We use Mean Absolute Error as the loss and otpimize the network parameters using gradient descent. We were able to get reasonable estimates of the income using the internal model. However, this did not use the wide range of sources available in the web.

2.4. External Sources Overview

Recently, there has been a growing number of online sources collecting and disseminating income information (e.g. payscale.com, salary.com). The main reason for this push has been the need for pay transparency and accountability from both private and public institutions. In some cases such as government sources point estimates of the salary and bonus are available (see Table 2). Other sources collect compensation details from individuals willing to report such information and expose only anonymized ranges for individual income components (see Table 3).

In this paper, we describe a system to exploit such resources in order to improve income verification.

2.5. External Model

The main components of the External Model are:

- *Canonicalizer*: In a large number of cases we find different representations of the same employer, job title. There were also spelling errors in the user input. Hence, the first step was to normalize the input. Some examples of noisy input and their normalized form is in Table 4. The transformation was performed using a lookup table. The table was manually created and consisted of the most common examples found in the dataset. In the future, we plan to explore better string and similarity models.
- *Web Query Generator:* Our main source of income records is from the web. We use targeted web queries as show in Table 5 to get the records of interest. E.g. if we want salaries for software engineers in XYZ company, the query would be 'XYZ Company Software Engineer Salary'. While there would be records available for large companies, for the long tail of companies we would rely on generic queries such as 'Software Engineer Salary'.
- *Record Matcher*: In this step, we extract the identities from the candidate records generated from database income records and search engines. We then choose the five best matches. The extraction system depends on the type of record. For records from structured sources such as Feds Data Center and Payscale, the identities were extracted using xml paths. For unstructured sources such as web snippets and text, we used pattern-based information extraction to extract the identity.

From the source identity and input identity we create features such as name match, address match, employment match, and industry match. To compute the name match score we use the normalized edit distance between the names of the input and the source. We also add a penalty for middle name dissimilarities (E.g. James Ryan Smith is not equal to James S Smith). We compute the address match by considering string similarity metrics for city, street match, and county, and exact matches for zipcode and country. We bucketed the matches into different confidence levels based on different points on the precision-recall curve. To compute the employment match we consider the cosine distance between the employer strings and the position strings.

We used a decision tree to match record pairs. In order to train our record matcher we annotated thousand input and source identity pairs. We then used different thresholds to bucket the model scores and assigned a confidence value to each bucket. E.g. A score of above 0.8 is a high match.

- *Feature Extractor*: We rank the sources according the match score and select the top 5 sources. We extract the base salary median, base salary low, base salary high, total compensation median, total compensation low and total compensation high for each of these sources. The total compensation consists of bonus, stock awards and profit sharing. In many cases only a subset of the salary attributes existed. We aggregated the employments by industry and found the industry wide ratio of each salary value to the other values. In cases of missing values, we filled it by multiplying the known salary attribute with the industry wide ratio. If none of the attributed existed, we discarded the source. We then used ratio of the attribute and the stated income as a feature. Each source generated 6 features. We also added the match score to the feature set. For each user, we had an feature dimension of 35.
- *Model*: We used the features from above and stacked them with the income pre-

diction from the input model and passed it to the gradient boosted decision tree as the final model.

3. Experiments

3.1. Datasets

We evaluated our model on two income datasets. The statistics of the dataset are provided in Table 6.

Client Dataset This dataset was obtained from one of the largest peer-to-peer lending companies. The input information includes names, home address, date of birth, employer name and job title. The client manually verified the salary information using the following methods:

- Requiring the loan applicants to submit documents such as paystubs, W-2 forms, or other tax records that verify the income stated in their loan request.
- Electronically checking their income data through a third party provider.
- Verifying the income with employer.

H1-B Dataset This dataset was obtained from the United States Department of Labor website[10] . The input information includes employer name, job title and address. The Department of Labor has been disclosing information about the H1- B visa class from 2008. This dataset was created from disclosure data as of 2016 and is only used to show the income prediction results since it does not contain a stated income as input.

Table 2. Example of Government source with fake names

Name	Salary	Bonus	Agency	Location	Occupation	Year
James Bond	$73,482	$0	Department of Homeland Security	SELLS	Medical Technologist	2016
Harry Potter	$84,443	$10000	Department of Agriculture	AMES	General Engineering	2016

Table 3. Example of information found online for software engineers of a random company

	Mean	Min	Max
Base Salary	150,000	90,000	234,000
Total Compensation	265,000	90,000	1,000,000
Cash Bonus	38,000	10,000	500,000
Stocks	100,000	10,000	800,000

Table 4. Canonicalization examples

Input	Mean
U.S.P.S, U.S. Postal Service	United States Postal Service
GE, G.E	General Electric
Acc. Manager	Account Manager
Sr. Manager, Snr. Manager	Senior Manager

3.2. Baselines

We compare our model with several methods such as neural networks and gradient boosted trees (GBT) with both input and external sources with different types of preprocessing. The model architectures and hyperparameters are the chosen based on the minimization of cross-validation error.

Bag of Words (BOW) with Gradient Boosted Trees. The top 200 words based on frequency are each selected from job title and employer name and the word counts are used as a feature. The city and state state are treated as categorical variables. The total input dimension is 402.

The model is a gradient boosted tree with a linear regression objective, a max depth of 5, and an initial learning rate of 0.01.

Mean Word Vectors with Feed-forward network. The mean 300 dimension word2vec vectors (Mikolov et al. 2013) for job title and employer name trained on the input data are used as the feature set. The feature state is used as a one-hot encoded vector. The total input dimension is 650.

The model is a feed-forward network with two hidden layers of size 300 and 100 respectively.

Mean Word Vectors trained on external data with Feedforward network. The word2vec vectors are trained on the input data and external data from Lending Club's loan application dataset [11] . The data contains around 850,000 examples of job titles and 42,000 examples of employer names. This will generalize the word vectors on a larger dataset. The feature state is used as a one-hot encoded vector. The total input dimension is 650.

The model is a feed-forward network with two hidden layers of size 300 and 100 respectively.

Tuned Mean Word Vectors trained on external data with Feed-forward network. The word vectors are trained on the input and external data as in the previous model. The job title vectors are further trained by using it as an embedding in a deep neural network model predicting the user income in the Lending Club's loan application dataset mentioned above. The model has an embedding layer, a LSTM layer (128 dimensions), a dropout layer (rate of 0.5), and a hidden layer (200 dimensions). The model is trained on 520,000 examples and validated on 58,000 examples. The employer name vectors are trained in the same way as the previous model. The mean employer name, job title word vectors and the one-hot encoded state feature form an input dimension of 650.

The model is a feed-forward network with a hidden layer of size 200.

External data with Gradient Boosted Trees. The 5 best external sources with their salary low, median, high, and total compensation low, median, high are taken along with their match scores. The input dimension is 35.

The model is a gradient boosted tree with a linear regression objective, a max depth of 5, and an initial learning rate of 0.003.

3.3. Results

The experimental results on the datasets for the task of income prediction are presented in Table-7. The three metrics which we evaluate our model on are Cross Validation Mean Absolute Error (CV MAE), Test Set Mean Absolute Error (Test Set MAE) and the Test Set Mean Relative Error (Test Set MRE). The results show that the combined model performs the best on all metrics on both datasets with the exception of the MRE of the Client dataset. It outperforms the next best model by 2.8% on the Client dataset and 6% on the H1-B dataset.

From Table 7 we also observe that the performance of the model using only external data falls in the H1-B dataset where it is the fourth best model as compared to being the second best model in the client dataset. We hypothesize this is due to the lack of names and phone numbers in the input identity. This results in poor matches with database records. Despite this it is able to outperform the baseline model by 7.5%.

We also show the results of various models for the task of income verification in Table 8. This experiment was only performed on the Client dataset. Similar to the income prediction results, the combined model performs the best on this task as well.

Table 5. Example of search engine queries

Query Template	Example

<Employer> <Job Title> Salary	XYZ Company Software Engineer Salary
<Job Title> Salary	Software Engineer Salary
<Industry> <Job Title> Salary	Travel Software Engineer Salary

Table 6. Dataset Statistics

Dataset	Size	Mean	Stddev	Skew
Client Train	3108	77571.760	57979.323	5.694
Client Test	1037	78930.494	52488.707	3.576
H1-B Train	7500	91411.177	46969.135	1.878
H1-B Test	2500	90648.067	44355.742	1.407

3.4. Ablation studies

We perform a number of experiments to study the impact of the number of sources, and the importance of each feature in the internal and external models. Our first experiment was to observe the variation in Test Set MAE with the number of web sources used as a feature. Figure 4 presents the graph of how the Test Set MAE varies with the number of sources. The data for the graph is presented in Table 9. The mean absolute error decreases while we increase the number of sources and then stabilizes after four sources. This makes intuitive sense because we expect the improvement from adding more sources to reduce after a certain threshold.

The second experiment we performed was to identify the importance of each feature in the input identity. This was evaluated by running the BOW + GBT model by removing one feature at a time. The results are shown in Table 10. We observe that removing the job title feature leads to the maximum increase in the Test Set MAE. One surprising result here is that removing the Employer Name does not degrade the model's performance significantly.

The third experiment we performed was to identify the impact of the different features which we extract from web and database records. The different features include low, median, high salary and total compensation. We remove each feature group (i.e. one of low, median and high) and retrain the External model. The results are presented in Table 11. We notice that removing the median leads to the maximum degradation in performance while there is no significant change on removing low and high. We hypothesize this is because most people earn close to the median and the median feature has the largest coverage in our dataset.

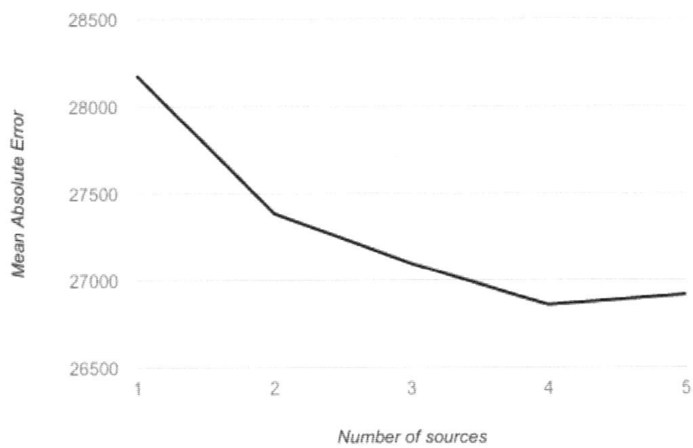

Fig. 3. Graph of the Test Set MAE vs. number of sources

4. Related Work

(Kohavi 1996) used a hybrid of Naive Bayes and Decision Tree to predict whether a person makes over $50K a year in the Census Income dataset. The census dataset consists of categorical variables like education (e.g. Bachelors, Some-college, High school graduate), relationship (e.g. Wife, Own-child, Husband, Not-in-family) and continuous values like hours-per-week, age, capital gains. This dataset was collected from the 1994 Census. (Lazar 2004) applied Support Vector Machines on the same dataset to achieve superior results. However, in many cases banks and lending companies do not have access to all these features and need to build alternate approaches to model an individual's income.

Some of the recent work in predicting salaries has been motivated by the Kaggle's Adzuna Job Salary Prediction competition. The dataset provides 240,000 UK job postings each of which consist of title, job description, location, contract details, company as features. The goal of this competition is to model income based on the details available in the posting. There are no details about the individual's identity. (Li, Liu, and Zhou 2013) compared models such as Support Vector Regression, Linear Regression, K Nearest Neighbors Regression and Random Forest Regression and concluded that Random Forest works the best. (Jackman and Reid 2013) modeled the unstructured text fields as unigram bag of words and compared methods such as Maximum Likelihood, Dropout Neural Network and Random Forest. They reached the same conclusion that Random Forests outperform the other models.

(Preotiuc-Pietro et al. 2015) conducted a study to predict the income of social media users from their online behavior. They used profile features, psycho-demographic features, inferred emotion features, and text features. They discovered that emotional content, gender, race and education level have correlation with income. They were also able to highlight topics that distinguish users by income, such as politics, technology topics and swear words.

(Kibekbaev and Duman 2016) predict incomes of bank customers. Their work benchmarks various regression algorithms on five datasets provided by Turkish banks. However, the paper does not mention the features used and hence, it is difficult to compare their results against ours.

Recently, (Chen et al. 2018) proposed an approach to infer salary insights in the LinkedIn graph when there are limited or no user-reported salaries available for a given company. Their approach learns an embedding vector for each company based on employees transitioning between different companies and then applies a Bayesian statistical model to infer salary ranges based on similar companies in the embedding space. Our approach can definitely leverage some of the techniques used in this paper. However, a key advantage of our approach is that we are able to make accurate predictions without having access to the large amount of information within the LinkedIn graph.

Table 7. Experiment results of various models for the income prediction task (BOW = Bag of Words, GBT = Gradient Boosted Trees, WV = Word vectors, NN = Feed-forward neural network)

Model	Client Dataset			H1-B dataset		
	CV MAE	Test Set MAE	Test Set MRE	CV MAE	Test Set MAE	Test Set MRE
BOW + GBT	31222.990	30126.355	0.425	23848.233	22611.401	0.251
Mean WV + NN	31536.852	30492.682	0.407	22812.092	21718.642	0.248
External Mean WV + NN	29834.140	28606.042	0.378	20055.863	18744.684	0.216
Tuned Mean WV + NN	30021.129	27917.228	**0.361**	19961.718	18591.964	0.212
External data + GBT	28402.790	26858.992	0.389	22639.001	20911.111	0.254
Combined + GBT	**27710.378**	**26100.232**	0.375	**19000.542**	**17466.239**	**0.207**

Table 8. Results of various models for the income verification task on the Client dataset

Model	Precision	Recall	F1 score
BOW + GBT	0.8196	0.6218	0.7072
Mean WV + NN	0.8328	0.5945	0.6938
External Mean WV + NN	0.8420	0.5833	0.6892
Tuned Mean WV + NN	**0.8490**	0.5945	0.6993
External data + GBT	0.8230	**0.6766**	**0.7427**

Combined + GBT	0.8230	**0.6766**	0.7427

Table 9. Results of external data model by the number of sources

# sources	CV MAE	Test Set MAE	Test Set MRE
1	28800.476	28179.456	0.422
2	28529.557	27384.617	0.393
3	28408.582	27096.461	0.394
4	28402.790	**26858.992**	**0.389**
5	**28401.768**	26916.694	0.390

Table 10. Results of BOW + GBT by removing one feature at a time

Features	CV MAE	Test Set MAE	Test Set MRE
All features	31222.990	30126.355	0.425
- Job Title	**33651.446**	**33892.304**	**0.515**
- Employer Name	31434.002	30000.765	0.453
- State	31500.645	29873.344	0.451
- City	31503.394	30121.302	0.454

Table 11. Results of External model by removing one feature group at a time

Features	CV MAE	Test Set MAE	Test Set MRE
All features	28401.768	26916.694	0.390
- Low	28566.334	26997.413	0.389
- Median	**28810.107**	**27972.642**	**0.404**
- High	28385.222	27026.328	0.394

5. Conclusions

In this paper, we introduce the problem of income verification and propose a model which used internal features such as position, employer, location along with external features such as salary information in web documents and government database records. Our experiments showed that the combined model performed better than all the other models. We found that job title is the most important input feature and salary median is the most important external feature. We also found that the model MAE depends on the number of external sources used.

References

1. Chen, X., Liu, Y., Zhang, L., Kenthapadi, K: How LinkedIn economic graph bonds information and product: Applications in LinkedIn salary. In Proceedings of the 24th ACM SIGKDD International Conference, 120–129. (2018).
2. Hochreiter, S., Schmidhuber, J: Long short-term memory. Neural Computation 1725-1780. (1997).
3. Jackman, S., Reid, G: Predicting job salaries from text descriptions. (2013).

4. Kibekbaev, A., Duman, E: Benchmarking regression algorithms for income prediction modeling. Information Systems 61:40–52. (2016).
5. Kohavi, R: Scaling up the accuracy of naive-bayes classifiers: A decision-tree hybrid. In Proceedings of the Second International Conference on KDD, 202–207 (1996).
6. Lazar, A.: Income prediction via support vector machines. In Proceedings of the International Conference on Machine Learning and Applications, 143–149. (2004).
7. Li, L., Liu, X., Zhou, Y: Prediction of Salary in UK. http://cseweb.ucsd.edu/\~jmcauley/cse190/reports/fa15/012.pdf. (2013)
8. Mikolov, T., Sutskever, I., Chen, K., Corrado, G., Dean, J: Distributed representations of words and phrases and their compositionality. In Proceedings of the 26th International Conference on NIPS, 3111–3119. (2013).
9. Preotiuc-Pietro, D., Volkova, S., Lampos, V., Bachrach, Y., Aletras, N., Braunstein, L. A: Studying user income through language, behaviour and affect in social media. In PLoS ONE. (2015).
10. US Department of Labor Website, https://www.foreignlaborcert.doleta.gov/performancedata.cfm
11. Lending Club Website, https://www.lendingclub.com/info/ download-data.action

Methods for Solving the Challenges Observed in the Multiplatform Setup for Self-Driving Cars Contribution

Mirza Mujtaba Baig

University of the Cumberlands, McLean, USA
mujtaba961989@gmail.com

Abstract. Artificial Intelligence (AI) is evolving rapidly and one of the areas which this field has influenced is automation. The automobile, healthcare, education and robotic industries deploy AI technologies constantly and the automation of tasks is beneficial to allow time for knowledge-based tasks and also introducing convenience to everyday human endeavors. The paper reviews the challenges faced with the current implementations of autonomous self-driving cars by exploring the machine learning, robotics and artificial intelligence techniques employed for the development of this innovation. The controversy surrounding the development and deployment of autonomous machines e.g., vehicles begs the need for the exploration of the configuration of the programming modules. This paper seeks to add to the body of knowledge of research assisting researchers in decreasing the inconsistencies in current programming-modules.

Keywords: Artificial Intelligence; Automation; Big Data; Self-driving Cars; Machine Learning; Neural Networking Algorithm

1 Introduction First

The Cloud Computing and Data Science platform, robotics environment and AI are developing rapidly, and it brings its advantages to everyday activities. However, many uncovered gaps are found in the industry (Yang, & Coughlin, 2014). The current challenges faced by the current implementations of the self-driving cars are related to safety, security, privacy, performance, user's experience, reliability and economic value and a one-to-many relationship between the attribute and its properties. Also, the challenges in the implementations of controllers, deficiency, malfunctions, and inconsistencies that occur during data transmission, and, the threats detected while performing the implementations for the self-driving vehicles have been discussed. This paper addresses the lack of sufficiency in data modeling activities for the self-driving cars implemented within the autopilot modes, also discussed are the lazy evaluation mechanisms included for the design of multimodal dialogue systems by combining input modules to generate next-generation autonomous machines as part of Artificial Intelligence and IoT technologies. The paper discusses about the creation of patterns related to gesture recognition, speech recognition, dialogue system, and conversational knowledge base for enhancing the existing functionality of the autonomous system. These technical advancements can be an enhancement to the field of robotics, healthcare, education system, security access control systems, advertising, driving, aviation, and personal assistance image recognition. The activities associated with machine learning, complex planning, decision-making methods, verification and guaranteed performance of autonomous driving pipeline have become ever so involved with the presence of the cars in the challenging environments. The approaches considered for implementing the module of the cars includes sequential planning, behavior-aware planning, end-to-end planning, advanced perception, motion planning, control.

Self-driving vehicles which are in the prototypical stage are being put into public traffic and soon will be available to put on display and start being sold. Public awareness and media coverage are already in the stages on unfolding the discussions about self-driving cars from the perspectives of Waymo developed by Google which are developed based on computer simulations and feeds what it learns from those into a smaller real-world fleet, autopilot self-driving vehicle developed by Tesla which are incorporating huge amounts of data (Uhlemann, 2016). The reports have been published about the situations of accidents caused by autonomous vehicles. The programming of the software embedded within the Electronic Control Units (ECUs) is playing a key role in the modern vehicles as well as the self-driving vehicles. The discussion has already been in place to describe
about the software engineering activities as well as the production and manufacturing activities encompassed within the electrical and software architecture of the car.

The challenge of the current automation construction for self-driving cars lies within handling the integration between technical areas and integrated approach required for the autonomous driving related to decision-making and real-time control of the driving situation. The components of the models can include creativity, emotional knowledge, self-awareness along with the incorporation of the neural networks, fuzzy systems, evolutionary computation, and computational models. The current model with the help of AI is able to produce intelligent decisions in variable, real-time traffic conditions. Also, the simulation-based learning situations along with neural networks and artificial intelligence systems are able to address properly to the emergency situations in real life events. Combination of robotics, automation, AI, machine learning, data science and Big Data benefits to the automobile industry and transportation safety. The advances made in the sensor capabilities of the self-driving cars system was able to improve the event-based vision, which was involved with the broad-set of visual pattern recognition.

In contrast to traditional machines, smart machinery is being employed by the system to handle the behavior, operations, circumstances, and feedback of the autonomous machines. Taking into consideration, the devices handling wireless sensors as well as universal connectivity enables the flow of data to be monitored while being sent to the autonomous machines; onboarding processors can handle the operations on the data as well as provide appropriate responses and as such it is required for new software architecture to be developed. The capacities of this model can include creativity, emotional knowledge, self-awareness incorporating the technologies from computational intelligence related to neural networks, fuzzy systems, evolutionary computation, computational models. This level of intelligence can be extended to handle tasks with the proper level of rationality to supersede humans thinking capability. Autonomous vehicles have been provided with proper sensors, cameras for enabling recognition of 3D environment as well as providing the capability to make intelligent decisions in variable, real-traffic conditions.

Artificial Intelligence platform when combined with virtualized environments have the ability to respond to the situations in real-time taking into consideration voice recognition, facial recognition, text analytics and natural language processing, virtual assistants, robotic process automation, biometric recognition, hardware optimization. By combining robotics and automation, it has been possible to merge traditional programming and learning modules with developing applications that are more robust, efficient, and provide safe automation. Mobile robotics include the platforms for localization, mapping, planning, image recognition, reinforcement learning modules, focus on prior knowledge about the structures of tasks and environments. Within the framework of autonomous computing, deep RL-methods for end-to-end computing has been enabled to provide optimal adversarial policy (i.e., mapping of states to actions) for autonomous motion planning. By employing optimal motion planning strategy it is possible to avoid collisions within the trajectory surface for the self-driving vehicles. With a help of suitable choices of optimality criteria as well as employing a reward function, it will be capable to enable the adoption of powerful state-space exploration and policy optimization techniques developed using deep Reinforcement Learning applications. Furthermore, we argue that both the training and test-time procedures of adversarial policies provide quantitative measures of reliability, which can be used for benchmarking of behaviors in worst-case scenarios.

In this proposal, the design is based on the technical combinations of machine learning techniques including: deep learning, neural networks, sensor networks, computer vision, natural language processing, and, additional forms of processing the data including databases, networking, security, memory, and infrastructure capabilities. The produced outputs are presented in the form of graphical displays, navigation systems, motions and control devices. The different test case scenarios will be conducted by setting the appropriate measures for the test performance. The proposed model shows the architecture flow of Big Data, Data Science, Robotics, AI technologies along with programming modules. In the long run, the benefit will be provided to the transportation system by decreasing the number of incidents and improving the driving conditions.

Using the technical combinations in cloud computing, data science and analytics, robotics and Artificial Intelligence platforms, the paper aims to uncover the challenges faced by the implementations of these algorithms for the model in the real-time environment. As a matter of fact, it also focuses to provide solutions to some of these challenges. The paper is organized in 4 sections. Section 2 is related to the literature review and the previous works related to the industry. The section 3 describes the methods and technologies used in developing the model, and the results and benefits from the produced module. The section 4 provides the conclusion on the innovation of the current method and advantages for the automobile industry.

2 Literature Review

According to a recent research conducted by the team of Modular and Integrated approach, an algorithm was developed using the technologies which include Sensing, perception and Decision-making where, in addition, the operating system and cloud platform deliberately are designed in accordance with HD mapping of the sensor data. Sensors like LiDAR, GPS, IMU, radars and GNSS helped in determining the reflection time based on the distance and enabling in creating High-Definition (HD) maps, real-time localization, as well as map projection and update process respectively. Action prediction and path planning mechanisms are integrated with the autonomous systems to generate an effective action plan in real time. The driving conditions are challenging in the complex traffic environments. Irrespective of an action plan based on predictions the stochastic model of the reachable position sets of the other traffic participants and associate within the reachable sets. Searching all possible paths is the best approach within the given dataset, and, a cost function can be utilized to identify the best approach. However, this requires enormous computational resources which may make it incapable of delivering real-time navigation plans. To ensure that the processing pipeline is effective, sensor data generates faster results, and, if a part of the system fails, it needs to be robust enough to recover from the failure and the system needs to perform all the computations under energy and resource constraints.

The paper describes the state-of-the-art technologies used to implement machine learning including deep reinforcement learning (RL) for optimal regulation and tracking of single and multi-agent systems (Wulfmeier, 2018). The proposal draws on the effectiveness of uncertainty-based information-theoretic approach for performing optimal searches within the data. The algorithm related to iteration-based Q-learning is guaranteed to excel in the implementations of critical-only structures which requires the neural networks to be combined with the Q-function for analytical purposes. The theory is proved using Lyapunov techniques for the algorithmic implementations. Subsequently, the RADP algorithms are proposed to transform the nonlinear optimal control problems with closed loop systems to be stable. There are three groups based on extended Kalman filters, particle filters, and graph optimization paradigms for the algorithmic implementations. The global features are able to extract information in the form of raw pixels, shape signatures, color information. Sequences of image can be matched based on deep convolutional neural networks modeling.

On the other hand, local features utilize a detector to locate points of interest (e.g., corners) in an image and a descriptor to capture local information of a patch centered at each interest point. The Bag-of-Words (BoW) model is often used as a quantization technique for local features in order to construct a feature vector in place recognition applications. The image-to-image matching, which localize the most similar individual image that best matches the current frame obtained by the robot. Combining pair wise similarity scoring, nearest neighbor search, and sparse optimization provides reliable solutions. This has been demonstrated by being able to integrate information from a sequence of frames that can significantly improve place recognition accuracy and decrease the effect of perceptual aliasing. This method uses rasterized vehicle context (including the high-definition map and other actors) as a model input to predict actor's movement in a dynamic environment. As the vehicle is approaching the intersection the multimodal model (where we set the number of modes to 2) estimates that going straight has slightly less probability than a right turn.

There are major contributions that can be seen in the form of machine learning techniques including: deep learning, reinforcement learning, Markov decision processes, robotics, psychology etc. (Kuutti, Fallah, Katsaros, Dianati, Mccullough, Mouzakitis, 2018). Starting with the machine learning techniques, the necessary factors were taken into consideration to cleanse the data that can be handled across different Big Data sources and subsequently generate intelligence results and neural network forms related to enhancing perpetual intelligence and eliminate the necessary feature engineering options. Advances were made for improving computer vision, which was involved with the broad set of visual pattern recognition.

IoT platform collects diverse real-time valuable information of objects' concerns in objective world, forms a giant network through Internet and realizes interconnection among massive sensing devices in order to make co-fusion between data world and physical world. It has been highlighted in the context of autonomous vehicles that there are emerging trends and challenges related to performing operations in the self-driving vehicles. Trust requirements at the early stage for developing autonomous cars taking into consideration the factors of safety, security, privacy, performance, user's experience, reliability and economic value and a one-to-many relationship between the attribute and its properties is established. A safety-critical control function, such as steering, brake assist, self-parking and other functions without a direct driver input. A framework for integrating mutual trust computation with a standard human - robot interaction. The system consists of both functional and non-functional requirements. Functional requirements can be related to calculation, technical details or other specific functionality that define what a system is supposed to accomplish. Non-functional requirements for autonomous car describe properties, such as the look and feel of safety, security and privacy, which are critical to the product's success based on the user's expectations and demand. Trust requirements can be related to i) Customer's satisfaction with the technology provided, ii) Willingness of learning and using the automated features in the current autonomous technology in a car, and iii) Preferable method for learning to use the automated features.

Reinforcement learning defined as having the capability to support artificial intelligence by enabling dynamic programming to train the model using the forms of pass or failure for the situations encountered while performing technical evaluations for the model and provide mechanisms for developing mobile robots. Deep Learning, a form of artificial intelligence function is capable of processing the data and creating patterns for use in decision making, and, capable of learning unsupervised forms of data from data that is unstructured in nature. Both the technologies have contributed significantly to the autonomous systems including pedestrian, car, cyclist, traffic sign detection, semantic segmentation, and other tasks. While these systems heavily rely on learning: localization, reasoning, and planning modules that often continue to be the domain of secured rules and programs, designing and developing geometric priors and intuitions. This design usually operates with expert knowledge and repeated iterations between testing – in simulation as well as on the platform for handling and refining heuristics data as well as to reduce the manual effort and focus on the automation tasks relevant to learning decision patterns. The successful application usually requires detailed domain knowledge, systems engineering, and demands significant time for data collection and curation, experimental setup and safety arrangements. One of the AI applications, namely, Advanced Driver-Assistance Systems have been developed and consequently its full potential can be realized by the implementing self-driving vehicles.

Actors motion prediction methodologies consist of computing object's future motion based on the time progressed by using Kalman filter as well as utilizing short-term predictions using the map method. The factors considered include possible paths computation, lane connectivity, vehicle's current state estimate. Machine learning models including Hidden Markov Model, Bayesian networks, or Gaussian Processes, Inverse Reinforcement Learning approach are utilized mostly in the autonomous systems design. One line of research follows the recent success of recurrent neural networks (RNN), namely Long Short-Term Memory (LSTM), for sequence prediction tasks. Authors applied LSTM to predict pedestrians' future trajectories with social interactions and long-term dependency problem. The LSTM network has the ability to remove or add information for the state in the form of gates which have the ability to let the information pass through. This layer consists of sigmoid neural net layer and point wise multiplication operation. At the same time, the gate layers are able to look at the cell state.

Security relates to an attribute that protects the digital information and data from any danger or threat from any malicious activity. Examples of the properties that relate to this attribute are data sharing, global positioning system (GPS) and visible vehicle identification number, smart key, remote keyless entry system, and remote panic features. Safety features can be related to automatic steering, intelligent pairing assist system, blind spot system, adaptive light control and camera sensor technology. Privacy is related to the location of information, cloud storage, crash data retrieval, event data retrieval and cabin monitoring system. Reliability attribute is measured based on the rating system for head protection technology, blind spot technology, advanced safety assist technology and national highway traffic safety administration. Performance attributes are related to engine smart cities, weather-sensitive tires, tires sensor, active suspension control system and electronic transmission control. User's experience are the push start button, screen touch control, keyless entry, garage door system, design dashboard and on-board maps and navigation. Economic value are trusted brand, selling price, trend, product features and car warranty.

The measures of error of distance and error of angle from camera images, and then applying fuzzy logic to fuzzify them into a combined error degree. Autonomous driving application has features composed of low speed, short connection, fixed routes, less complicated traffic. The path tracking controller can be divided into two categories: localization-based path tracking and vision-based path tracking. Localization-based path tracking can consist of high-precision GPS or LiDAR could provide absolute global position. And one of the path tracking controllers is pure pursuit for the robotic modeling using vehicle kinematic bicycle method. Control theory controllers are also based on precise localization, using the approaches of Linear Quadratic Regulator(LQR) and Model Predictive Control(MPC). Vision-based path tracking task is defined as guiding the motion of a robot with respect to a target path based on the feedback obtained through a vision system. The following measures can be used to calculate the distance error and direction error at preview distance in the image, however they require high-precision error values. Environment factors such as daylight and whether severely affect visual detecting, path tracking. Visual Path Tracking consists of the following paths related to Inverse Perspective Mapping, Track Line Detection, Fuzzification.

To find the location of the device, the past trajectory data can be employed. In another recurrent network variant called gated recurrent unit (GRU) combined with conditional variation auto-encoder (CVAE) was used to predict vehicle trajectory. Convolutional neural networks also encompassed visual glimpses. Mixture Density Networks (MDNs) are conventional neural networks which solve multimodal regression tasks by learning parameters of a Gaussian mixture model. Contrast to the neuro-fuzzy is proposed to simulate the propagation model to predict RSS and compare the performance with empirical models of channels. RSS from the aerial platform is calculated using Hata model. However, Kaiser integrated the combination of received signal strength (RSS) and variance fractal dimensions as an input to ANN for prediction of location features. ANN was used to predict channel propagation of multi-user transmission under Rayleigh fading to maximize the efficiencies (Alsamhi, Ma, Ansari, 2018). Conditional Variational Atuo-Encoder was considered to be non-parameterized prediction method to be employed for a diverse set of prediction hypotheses to capture the multimodality of the space of plausible futures (Yin, 2018). Emergent behavior includes induced lane changes and changes in velocity at intersections and highway segments. The behavioral models are learned by maximum-entropy IRL from demonstrations of different social acceptability (Schwarting, Alonso-Mora, Rus, 2018). The maximum-entropy deep IRL framework exploits the expressive capacity of deep fully convolutional neural networks to represent the cost model underlying driving behaviors (Schwarting, Alonso-Mora, Rus, 2018). In general, deep fully convolutional neural networks, as robust, flexible, high-capacity function approximates, are able to model the complex relationship between sensory input and reward structure very well (Schwarting, Alonso-Mora, Rus, 2018).

In this manner, a range of AI techniques can reduce investigators' cognitive load and support decision-making, including: planning the assessment of the scene; ongoing evaluation and updating of risks; control of autonomous vehicles for collecting images and sensor data; reviewing images/videos for items of interest; identification of anomalies; and retrieval of relevant documentation. With the utilization of robots, associated with Micro Unmanned Aerial Vehicles (MUAV) for carrying out remote sensing in the current hazardous environments. Threats can be possibly detected using responders as well as multi-robot reconnaissance. The RAVs can be able to operate as multi-agent robot swarm for dividing the work as well as relaying information from the sensors as well as cameras to a Central Hub. The Image Analysis model can be used by utilizing a Deep Neural Network algorithm for detecting as well as identifying the objects in images taken by the RAV cameras. It is also possible to perform pixel-level semantic annotation of the terrain by using the network algorithm to support subsequent route-planning for Robotic Ground-Based Vehicles (RGVs). The Probabilistic Reasoning module assesses the likelihood of occurrence of different threats, for incoming information as well as monitoring the images and sensor readings. By deploying Information Retrieval TF-IDF module is possible to simulate with respect to the incident. The communication protocol can be developed using JSON-based real-world RAVs using RESTful APIs, cameras, sensor systems. In this way, the system can be maintained loosely coupled as well as testing can be taken into consideration the real-world scenarios. The routing algorithms employed can include hyper-heuristics which can be integrated with machine learning algorithms for optimizing the routes as well as handling the components of failure and battery usage. The documentation can be based on standard operating procedures and guidance documents from the knowledge base based on the implementations done using Elastic Search implementations.

In fact, AI works on the principle of costly hardware, as well as massive datasets to process the data, machine learning phase of deep learning, reinforcement learning, inverse reinforcement learning principles plays a major part in the software development. The computations performed are very intensive in nature and cost-effective computing resources. Object recognition AI systems can

include facial recognition on the phones as well as systems. A national approach is followed for maximizing the potential capabilities which are critical factors utilizing coordination and mobilizing key agencies to make the necessary organizational changes to take advantage of AI to the next level (Sharifzadeh, Chiotellis, Triebel, Cremers, 2016). Cognitive scientists explore mental ability of human beings through observation on aspects such as language, perception, memory, attention, reasoning and emotion. Brain-like computing aims to enable the computers to understand and cognize the objective world from the perspective of human thinking. Communication field emphasizes on transmission of information, while computer realm emphasizes on utilization of information. The data can be in the form of structured and unstructured data.

3 Discussion. Technical Implementation

With the development of network-enabled sensors and artificial intelligence algorithms, various human-centered smart systems are proposed to provide services with higher quality, such as smart health care, affective interaction, and autonomous driving. Cognitive computing consists of the domains including data science, discovery, cognitive science, and big data. The technologies of networking, cloud computing, analytics can be implemented in this domain. The applications of this technology are found in human-centered cognitive computing, including robot technology, emotional communication system, and medical cognitive system. The human-centered cognitive cycle includes machine, cyberspace and human.

The techniques of perception, data planning, decision-making, interactive planning and end-to-end learning has been proved valuable in deriving the insights for the future generation of cars. Improvements in functional capabilities have been proven to be useful for the prototypes developed as well as there is a requirement still focused on the performance and safety of the vehicles being driven under different driving conditions. The concepts of autonomous vehicles, decision-making, motion planning, artificial intelligence, verification, fleet management have proved useful for the communication to be distributed across.

Also, autonomous driving can improve the quality, performance, productivity, reliability, efficiency of the driving vehicles. The level of automation derived from human-operated vehicle to self-driving autonomic vehicles is varying in nature. The advancements made in the technical implementations of the self-driving cars have supported the drivers in making decisions for taking actions related to driving and maintaining speed, to be in a lane, performing car-driver handover. The experiments performed in this area were conducted based on real-time environment simulations. Driving in dynamic environments, needs to handle the outcomes to be dealt in an unpredictable manner for situations related to human-level reliability, and reacting safely in complex urban situations. The navigation system for the autonomous vehicles can be developed by taking into consideration the factors of perception, decision-making, control. Machine learning techniques and complex planning and decision-making methods, verification and guaranteed performance of autonomous driving pipeline have become ever so involved with the activities of challenging environments.

Within the domain of robotic programming, it includes mechanisms related to kinematic modeling consisting of scenarios related to reference path, proportional-integral-derivative control, feedback linearization, model-predictive control, nonlinear model, model predictive control, feedback-feed forward control (Khan, 2018). Operating procedures at high speeds or aggressive maneuvers employ full dynamic modeling of the vehicle which includes tier forces. Simulation modelling of the cars has been developed taking into consideration the factors of steering angle and projection trajectories. Advances made for fast nonlinear optimizers is to optimize simultaneously over steering angle and velocity or throttle input for achieving minimal intervention. Firstly is the input space discretization with collision checking, secondly is randomized planning, third is the constrained optimization and receding-horizon control and can also compute collision-free trajectories for employing a navigating device in the vehicle. The main advantage of this vehicle is in the constrained optimization for the smoothness of trajectories and direct encoding of the vehicle model utilized in the trajectory planning. The rules included can be based on the motion-planner, maximizing visibility may reduce risk, questions of rules violation arises, rules related to logic functions as well as utilizing automatic control synthesis methods can be demonstrated. Also, by utilizing the cost function, traditional motion planning methods can be employed to determine the trajectory of the lowest cost. Minimum-violation routing and single-trip scenarios to effectively monitor the flow of data. Integrated perception and planning can be done to generate the control input of the vehicle based on sensory information as well as machine learning optimizations. Perception can be based on the following technique recognition, reconstruction, motion estimation, tracking, scene understanding, and end-to-end learning. Maps have been constructed as part of handling navigational features in the autonomous engines. Object detections are done by employing bounding-box detection, semantic segmentation, deep neural networks have played a significant role in this area, effective neural network have played a significant role in the dataset's in production. Bayesian deep learning incorporates the intersection between deep learning and Bayesian probability theory, providing uncertainty estimates within deep architectures. Sensory information and actuation can be achieved in the network by enabling path proposals, perception and planning module, neural network schemas, supervised and unsupervised learning modules, GPU-computing capabilities computed using efficient learning of convolutional neural networks, improved performance of end-to-end driving capability.

The interaction model simply consists of a constant braking action triggered if a time to collision falls below a threshold. Planning on abstractions rather than detailed trajectories can lower planning complexity significantly. Solving the POMDP in a conventional way or by domain knowledge and specific simplifications, is to employ nonparametric reinforcement learning, to immediately receive an approximately optimal policy without optimization. However, generalization to arbitrary environments remains a challenge. Support vector machine for lane-change decision-making with features composed of relative position and relative velocity. If a lane-change desire is triggered, a lane-change reference trajectory is executed by a model predictive controller with the objective from minimal deviation to the reference subject to a set of safety constraints.

The end-to-end motion planning has been also applied to robotics—for example, to learn a navigation policy in simulation from an expert operator, with a 2-D laser range finder and relative goal position as inputs. It is then feasible to transfer the knowledge gained from training to unseen real-world environments to perform target-oriented navigation and collision avoidance. Socially aware collision avoidance with deep reinforcement learning was introduced to explain and induce socially aware behaviors capable of learning directly from multiagent scenarios by developing a symmetrical neural network structure. Robots that use learned perceptual models in the real world must be able to safely handle cases where they are forced to make decisions in scenarios that are unlike any of their training examples. Automated driving with humanlike driving behavior requires interactive and cooperative decision-making, socially compliant motion planning. Probabilistic approaches can be defined to include lower cost for the functions involving maximum likelihood, or, maximum a-posteriori resulting in a receding-horizon planner. Increased complexity in this model is another challenge. Decision tree grows exponentially with the number of agents such as Monte Carlo tree search algorithm. Markov decision process can be applied for scenarios related to making decisions in the highway platform. Factors related to maximum acceleration, desired acceleration, desired velocity, minimum distance, and desired time gap can be considered. The task of the probabilistic graphical model is to generate an intention estimation with maximum probability, given observed information. Individual Gaussian processes are coupled through an interaction potential that models cooperation between different agents' trajectories. Terms for affordance, for progress, and to penalize close distances to other agents can also be included in their joint cost function.

Data being handled by low-cost-sensors, data will be able to flow from information blind spots to augment and improve decision making. With focus on sensor networks, especially wireless sensor networks in which an object having a sensor on it comprises of heterogeneous computing environment. Within the ecosystem, the system is integrated with hardware, software, connectivity, and information flows linked with decision making capability. Objects in a SOA architecture can consist of Internet Protocol address and sends data about its state and immediate environment and also can receive data linked to actions. The individual tasks become end-to-end process consisting of a workflow managed in real-time data environment. Trustable data is the primary advantage of Blockchain technology, can be used in applications that can seek to improve the situations where low levels of trust exist. The strategic advantage of IOT strategy is that to handle emerging changes and integrate IT innovations such as Big Data and Artificial Intelligence based on which new skills will emerge for making jobs to be digitally displaceable as well as new jobs arising.

In comparison to research & development work done at NVIDIA, the organization's project trained a deep convolutional neural network to map raw images from a front-facing camera directly to steering commands and were able to handle challenging scenarios such as driving on a gravel road, passing through roadwork, and driving during the night in poorly lit environments. During training, random shifts and rotations are applied to the original input image and virtual human interventions are simulated to artificially increase the number of training samples that require corrective control actions. By observing which regions of the input image contributed most to the output of the network. A large-scale driving video data set to train an end-to-end fully convolutional long short-term memory network to predict both multimodal discrete behaviors on a task-based level and continuous driving behaviors. The architecture for time-series prediction essentially fuses a long short-term memory temporal encoder with a fully convolutional visual encoder. Once the information quantity of various experience become large, he or she may possess human's big data thinking, which is hierarchical as deep learning. One differences between big data analysis and cognitive computing is data size. There are various degrees of processes such as cognition, memory, learning, thinking and problem solving. Cloud computing virtualizes the computing, storage and band-width. Information related to the literal information and the pictorial information correspond to natural language processing and machine vision. Cloud computing and IoT provide cognitive computing with software and hardware basis, while big data analysis provides methods and thinking for discovering and recognizing new opportunity and new value in data. Traditional supervised learning and unsupervised learning are based on closed training with data input.

The benefits of using the implementations of the modern self-driving cars can be seen in the implementations of feedforward and feedback neural networks modeling the throttling and braking, speed and steering, lateral and longitudinal controllers designed to handle the dynamic and kinematic movements of the car. Also, are the implementations of the least squares for parameter and state estimations by applying the Kalman Filter algorithms which provides the motion and measurement models, bias and consistency using the prediction and correction procedures for estimating the state of the vehicle. Implementations of reference frames are also visible wihin the navigation systems using vectors for coordinate rotations and rotation matrix, euler angles which are visible in the actions performed in the sensor frames. The drawbacks are mostly related to having augmented reality in combination with autonomous vehicles which would provide the benefit of monitoring the sensor data while the car processes it, also the car would be able to overcome physical obstacles and virtual vehicles, also the rider would be able to get more glimpse into the surrounding areas as well as able to monitor road conditions and slowdowns. So, there is more research and development needed in this area of combining augmented reality with autonomous driving.

We also need to see new tasks being undertaken such as monitoring the state and health of embedded sensors within the system on a construction site and beyond. Internet Transport Protocols including TCP/IP, UDP, OSI model of packaging the messages as well as sending and receiving the packets of data. The data from user-requests on end-user devices could be brought in by encapsulating data from sensors which are involved in sending more information-rich pages back to the client. The other infrastructure related components are related to cloud and virtualization. SOA architecture is being evolving into DevOps, Virtualization, Serverless Architecture, Operational Technology, Information Technology convergence. Process control systems consisting of equipment, process flows, sensors and actuators. IoT solution is consisting of network of computing resources example processors, volatile and persistent memory/storage, networking software, applications, analytics algorithms and more. Embedded Sensors, Smart Sensors, embedded and autonomous computing Machine Learning model similar to Linear regression model can be used for predicting the temperature of radiation waves present with the components in the platform that can include integration of hardware, operating system, virtualization, IoT enablement related to MQTT, DDS, Kafka, Cassandra, Tensorflow tools. Data running through an API as well as data virtualization layer should be monitored for security analysis. Machine Learning and Neural Networks techniques related to Convolutional Neural Network, Recursive Neural Network Security and Privacy Preserving algorithms including man-in-the-middle attack, Public-Private keys, RSA algorithm, Format Preserving Encryption, Blockchain are all the security methods through which the data in the pipeline can be preserved.

4 Conclusions

The current automation industry that uses the Big Data technologies has a gap in neural network algorithm development. The current implementation and development shows the advantages of overcoming the shortcoming within the self-driving car model and its benefits to the industry. The paper has been involved in identifying the challenges associated by implementing the self-driving car model in order to handle the driving conditions safely while inculcating driving modes by having additional layers of security encompassed into the model to prevent accidents. Also, future research in this area can be conducted to include additional metrics of security, privacy, safety, decision-making, behavioral-driven, networking layers to handle the movement of objects based on the principles of virtual reality and being able to control it.

References

1.Alsamhi, S. H., Ma, O., & Ansari, M. S. (2018). Predictive Estimation of the Optimal Signal Strength from Unmanned Aerial Vehicle over Internet of Things Using ANN. arXiv preprint arXiv:1805.07614.

2.Kuutti, S., Fallah, S., Katsaros, K., Dianati, M., Mccullough, F., & Mouzakitis, A. (2018). A Survey of the State-of-the-Art Localization Techniques and Their Potentials for Autonomous Vehicle Applications. IEEE Internet of Things Journal, 5(2), 829-846.

3.Perez, J. A., Deligianni, F., Ravi, D., & Yang, G. Z. (2018). Artificial Intelligence and Robotics. arXiv preprint arXiv:1803.10813.

4.Schwarting, W., Alonso-Mora, J., & Rus, D. (2018). Planning and decision-making for autonomous vehicles. Annual Review of Control, Robotics, and Autonomous Systems.

5.Uhlemann, E. (2016). Connected-vehicles applications areemerging[connected vehicles]. IEEE Vehicular Technology Magazine, 11(1), 25-96.

6.Wulfmeier, M. (2018). On Machine Learning and Structure for Mobile Robots. arXiv preprint arXiv:1806.06003.

7.Yang, J., & Coughlin, J. F. (2014). In-vehicle technology for self-driving cars: Advantages and challenges for aging drivers. International Journal of Automotive Technology, 15(2), 333-340.

8.Yin, C. (2018). Policy learning for task-oriented dialogue systems via reinforcement learning techniques.

Text Classification and Sentiment Analysis in Social Media for the Marketing Domain

Yaakov HaCohen-Kerner

Dept. of Computer Science, Jerusalem College of Technology - Lev Academic Center, 9116001 Jerusalem, Israel
kerner@jct.ac.il

Abstract. The increase in online social media provides an excellent platform for companies, on the one hand, to read and learn from customers and improve their marketing policies and on the other hand, to perform various analysis and classification tasks. In this short paper, we present basic statistics of the domains of text classification, sentiment analysis, social media, and marketing over the last nine years. The three main findings derived from these statistics are: (1) the sentiment analysis, text classification, and social media topics are increasing; (2) the marketing topic is declining; and (3) marketing combined with (sentiment analysis or text classification or social media) are constantly increasing. We also reviewed a few studies relevant to these domains. We can see that in many of these studies: (1) relatively simple tasks have been performed such as simple sentiment classification (only to positive, negative or neutral without predicting the degree of the sentiment and finding the underlying causes of positive or negative sentiments); (2) relatively simple features have been applied; and (3) only SVM methods have been applied.

Keywords: Data Mining, Marketing, Sentiment Analysis, Supervised Machine Learning, Text Classification.

1 Introduction

The constant and impressive increase in online social media (e.g., Facebook, Flickr, Twitter, blogs, forums, and websites) provides an excellent platform for organizations and companies to read and learn from customers [8]. Traditional marketing methods such as face-to-face interviewing and focus groups are both costly and time-consuming, and sometimes even biased. In contrast, huge social media, such as the millions of blogs, and tweets are available for free.

Customer satisfaction and consumer complaint behavior have both been recognized in the academic and the practical world as important phenomena, which impact an organization's success [10]. The marketing policies of organizations and companies can be greatly influenced by text analysis in general, and sentiment analysis, in particular based on various natural language processing (NLP) tools and text classification, using supervised machine learning (ML) methods.

In this short paper, we present, on the one hand, basic and preliminary statistics of the domains of text classification, sentiment analysis, social media, and marketing, and on the other hand, summaries of a number of articles relevant to these domains.

The structure of this paper is as follows. Section 2 introduces some general trends of the discussed domains. Section 3 provides summaries of several relevant articles. Finally, Section 4 summarizes and offers some suggestions for future research.

2 General Trends in the Discussed Domains

In this section, we show a number of trends in the scientific research conducted in the domains of text classification, sentiment analysis, social media, and marketing. At the beginning, we decide to check these trends by the following simple heuristic method that counts the number of publications having these domains in the publications' titles, over the last nine years (2010-2018), retrieved by Google scholar's engine. Google scholar was chosen because it is a freely accessible bibliographic database, which enables web search of most online academic journals and books, conference papers, theses and dissertations, preprints, abstracts, technical reports, and other scholarly literature, including court opinions and patents[1].

Table 1 presents the number of publications having the various discussed domains in the publications' titles.

Table 1. Number of publications having the domains in the publications' titles.

Year	keywords			
	marketing	**sentiment analysis**	**text classification**	**social media**
2010	16,600	201	341	3,410
2011	20,600	301	319	6,000
2012	20,000	486	355	7,780
2013	20,200	672	337	8,650
2014	19,200	890	335	9,320
2015	20,700	1,070	381	9,940
2016	17,200	1,280	414	10,400
2017	17,000	1,500	445	10,500
2018	14,100	1,540	550	10,500

In Table 1[2], we see two main trends. The first trend is the decline of the number of publications having "marketing" in their titles over the last nine years. The second trend is the increase of the number of publications having "sentiment analysis", "text classification", and "social media" in their titles over the last nine years.

Fig. 1 presents the first trend, using a polynomial of degree five (this function was found to be most suitable for describing the trend shown in the graph from a wide range of functions of different degrees). The second trend is presented in Figures 2-4 (in these

[1] "Search Tips: Content Coverage". *Google Scholar*. Retrieved 27 April 2016.

[2] According to Google Scholar on 20-MAR-19.

figures as well, each graph was described using the function that was found to be most suitable from a wide range of functions of different degrees).

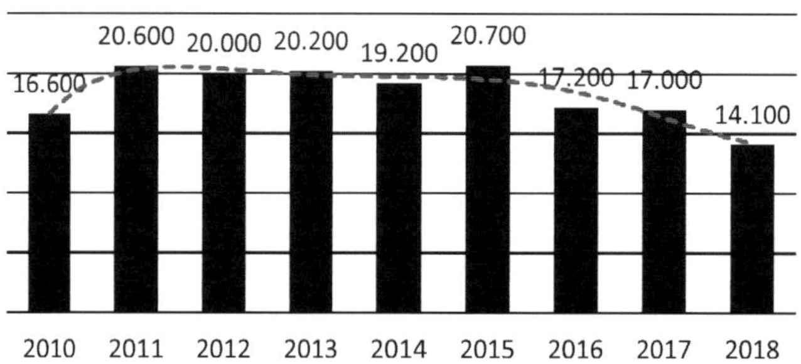

Fig. 1. # of publications in Google Scholar having "marketing" in their title for the last 9 years.

Fig. 2 presents an increase of the results over the years using a rising linear line.

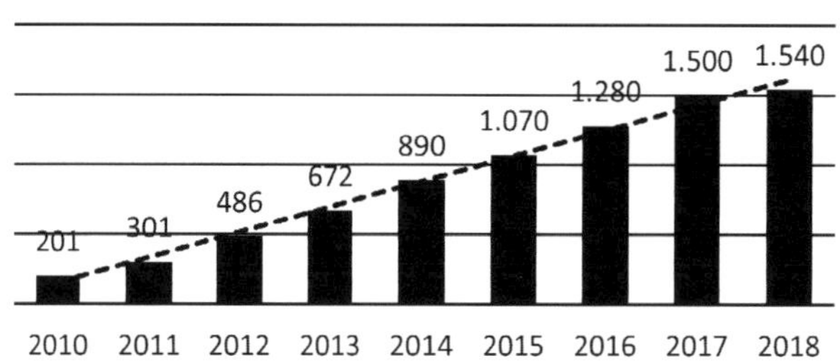

Fig. 2. # of publications in Google Scholar having "sentiment analysis" in their title for the last 9 years.

Fig. 3 presents an increase of the results over the years using a polynomial of degree six.

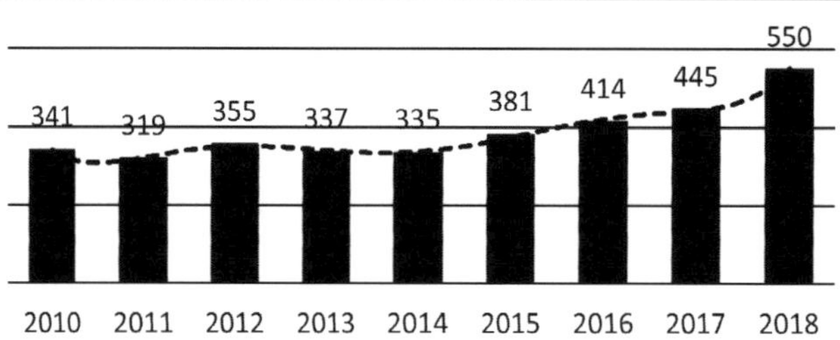

Fig. 3. # of publications in Google Scholar having "text classification" in their title for the last 9 years.

Fig. 4 presents an increase of the results over the years using a polynomial of degree two.

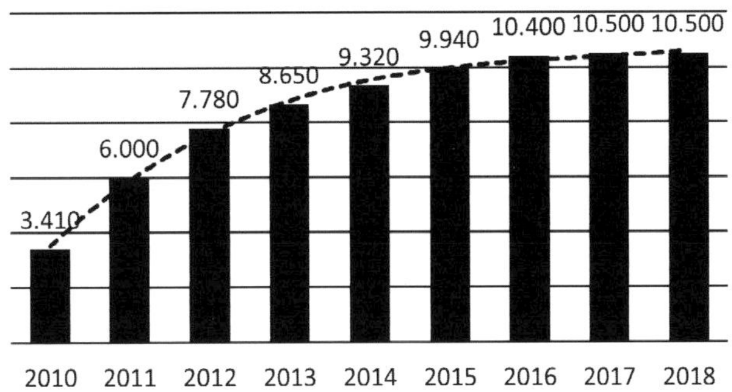

Fig. 4. # of publications in Google Scholar having "social media" in their title for the last 9 years.

On the one hand, the general trend introduced in Figure 1 shows a decline in the number of publications having "marketing" in their titles over the last nine years.

On the other hand, there is an increase of research in text classification, sentiment analysis, and social media according to Table 1 and Figures 2-4, where we see the number of publications in Google Scholar having "text classification", "sentiment analysis", and "social media" in their title for the last nine years. The overall trend in Figures 2-4 is an increase in the number of publications having "marketing" in their titles over the last nine years.

We then decided to generate a new table (Table 2) that presents the number of articles containing (anywhere in the paper) at least one appearance of "marketing" with at least one appearance of each of the other keywords, as well as creating appropriate Figures (Figures 5-7).

Table 2. Number of publications containing marketing with each of the other keywords.

Year	Concept		
	marketing & sentiment analysis	marketing & text classification	marketing & social media
2010	693	433	13,600
2011	1,180	499	22,600
2012	1,850	642	34,300
2013	2,610	680	46,700
2014	3,500	755	56,600
2015	4,550	951	56,900
2016	5,310	1,010	57,700
2017	6,480	1,160	59,000
2018	7,280	1,180	45,000

Fig. 5 presents an increase of the results over the years using a rising linear line.

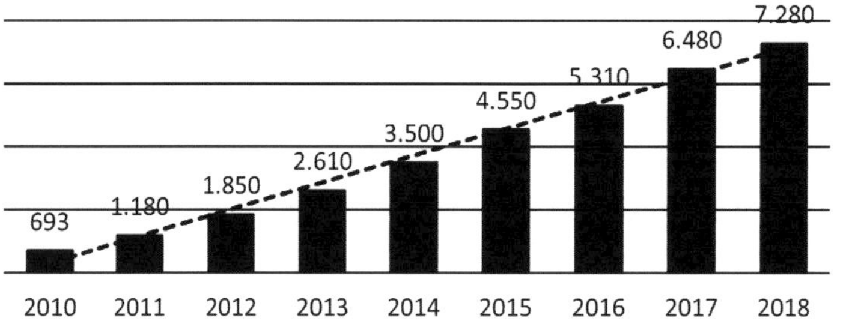

Fig. 5. # of publications in Google Scholar having "marketing" & "sentiment analysis" for the last 9 years.

Fig. 6 presents a decline of the results over the years using a rising linear line.

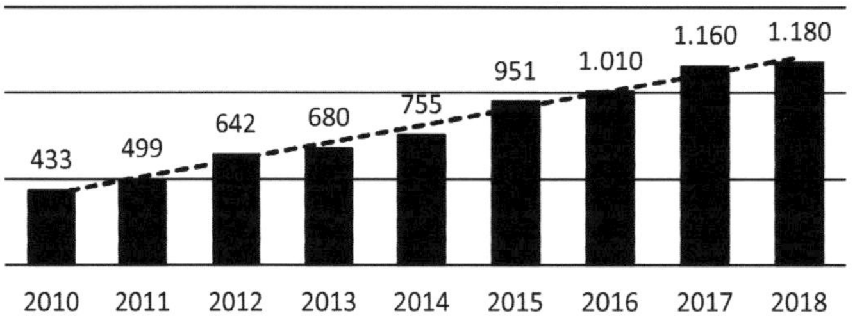

Fig. 6. # of publications in Google Scholar having "marketing" & "text classification" for the last 9 years.

Fig. 7 presents a decline of the results over the years using a polynomial of degree two.

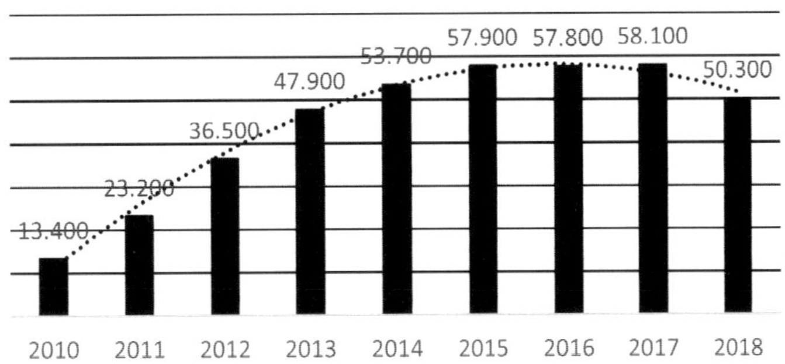

Fig. 7. # of publications in Google Scholar having "marketing" & "social media" for the last 9 years.

Figures 5 and 6 present a similar overall trend, which is a linear increase in the number of publications having "marketing" & "sentiment analysis" or "text classification" over the last nine years. Figure 7 presents the number of publications having "marketing" & "social media" over the last nine years. The general trend is a clear increase trend until 2015. During 2015-2017, the number is rather steady.

These findings show that the study of marketing combined with the other keywords is in general increasing until at least 2018. In 2018, there is an increase for two first combinations ("marketing" & "sentiment analysis", "marketing" & "text classification") and only one puzzling and unexplained decline for the "marketing" & "social media" combination. The overall picture of the increase in the number of publications of these three combinations over the years is particularly noteworthy, given the fact that "marketing" itself is declining, at least according to its frequency in the headlines of articles.

3 Previous Studies

In this section, we present a summary of a number of articles relevant to the discussed domains. Each summary contains a description of the presented research and its results. In addition, each summary will contain, as much as possible, shortcomings and/or future work that is offered for the discussed study.

Glance et al. [4] described an end-to-end system that is used to support a number of marketing intelligence and business intelligence applications, e.g., early alerting – informing subscribers when a rare but critical, or even fatal, condition occurs; buzz tracking – following trends in topics of discussion and understanding what new topics are forming; and sentiment mining – extracting aggregate measures of positive vs. negative opinion. Their system collects specific types of online content and provides analytics based on classification, NLP tools (e.g., a part-of-speech (POS) tagger and a shallow parser), phrase finding, and other mining technologies in a marketing intelligence application. The analysis system allows a user to rapidly characterize the data, to and drill down to discover and validate specific issues. The system delivers both qualitative and quantitative accounts of features derived from online messages. The authors of this article neither mentioned shortcomings of their system nor offered any suggestions for future work.

Engin and Can [2] investigated the semantic classification of Turkish Web documents in the marketing domain. They constructed various feature extraction methods, based on characteristics of the Turkish language, structures of Web documents, and online content in the marketing domain. They constructed a labeled marketing dataset in Turkish. They applied and compared various support vector machine (SVM) configurations, using the TFIDF scheme, considering the performance needs of practical context-sensitive systems. Their results show that linear kernel classifiers achieve the best performance in terms of accuracy and speed on text documents expressed as keyword root features. The authors suggest extension of their research study in two main areas. The first is to improve the feature extraction and classification phases using NLP tools such as a Turkish WordNet, Named entity recognizers, part of speech taggers and other language processing methods. The second is the design and development of the ad distribution system as a practical mechanism. Their dataset can be generalized with new labeled web documents that have different page structures and contents, and their labeling and keyword extracting procedures should be improved and made more efficient.

Cho and Kang [1] proposed a method of text sentiment classification for social network service (SNS)-based marketing for tweets written in Korean in five different datasets (Consumer Products, Persons, Travel, Food, and Movies), where each dataset contains a few hundred tweets. In contrast to previous methods that used only formal vocabulary, the authors use also informal vocabulary such as emoticons and newly coined words. They built five special sentiment-based domain dictionaries, in which each vocabulary is associated with a sentiment and its weight. The sentiment is labeled as one of three sentiments (positive, negative or neutral) if at least 7 of 10 students agreed on the label. Each tweet is decomposed into morphemes using an existing morpheme analyzer. They create a feature vector for each morpheme, using the sentiment-based domain dictionaries. They applied 10 cross-validation. The sentiment of each tweet is classified by a SVM classifier. Their method presents better performance in almost all type of measures (precision, recall, and F1-Measure) in all five examined tasks. In this research paper too, the authors neither mentioned shortcomings of their system nor offered any suggestions for future work.

Mostafa in his research [9], attempted to answer the following research questions: (1) Can social networks' opinion mining methods be used to successfully detect hidden patterns in consumers' sentiments towards global brands? and (2) Can companies effectively use the blogosphere to redesign their advertising and marketing campaigns? He used a random sample of 3,516 tweets to evaluate consumers' sentiment towards sixteen global brands, e.g., DHL, IBM, KLM, Nokia, and T-Mobile. He used an expert-predefined lexicon including about 6,800 seed adjectives with known orientation (2,006 positive words and 4,783 negative words) to perform the analysis. To conduct the qualitative part of this study, the author used the QDA Miner 4.0 software package (Provalis Research [11]). The results indicate a generally positive consumer sentiment towards several famous brands. The author noted three drawbacks of their system and proposed future research ideas to solve these drawbacks, as follows: (1) Their sentiment analysis component does not reveal the underlying reason behind the consumers' opinions. Future research using sentiment topic recognition should be conducted to determine the most representative topics discussed behind each sentiment, and by that way it should be possible to gain overall knowledge regarding the underlying causes of positive or negative sentiments. (2) Their lexicon-based approach can detect only basic sentiments, and might fail to recognize expressions used in situations such as sarcasm, irony or provocation. A possible solution might be the use of a large corpus containing such idiomatic expressions. (3) Consumers' opinions might in fact be posted by online vendors who pretend to be as real consumers. Such opinions might distort sentiments of real consumers. Future research should try to distinguish between opinions of real consumers, and opinions that reflect the position of vendors interested in selling more products or services.

Howells and Ertugan [7] proposed a model for sentiment analysis of social media network data. Their model applies fuzzy logic methods to design, create and build social bots that can analyze consumer comments in social media networks. Their model is specifically aimed at applications in consumer relationship management, customer retention, and other aspects of marketing. The social bots of this experiment were successful as follows. 27% of the user population decided to follow one of the social bot accounts. 12% of the user population mentioned at least one of the social bots in a tweet. An idea for future research is to build a highly efficient tool that will not only find a target population, but will communicate and prompt the target for more information. Such a tool can be an extremely useful in customer relationship management, as the marketer would be able to probe the user for more feedback on a particular subject.

Giatsoglou et al. [3] proposed a generic methodology for sentiment detection out of textual snippets that express people's opinions in English and Greek. Their methodology uses a SVM method and textual documents are represented by vectors that are used for training a polarity classification model. Several documents' vector representation approaches have been explored and compared, including word embedding-based, lexicon-based, and hybrid vectorizations. The competence of these feature representations for the sentiment classification task was evaluated by experiments on four datasets containing online user reviews in both English and Greek, in order to represent high and weak inflection language groups. Possible future research are, on the one hand, to conduct experiments to showcase the flexibility and the computational efficiency of their methodology and to improve the model's performance and, on the other hand, to: (a) explore new topics beyond online customer reviews, (b) consider another high inflection language and also other language specific phenomena, (c) consider other emotional lexicons for the English language, and (d) apply the methodology to big data sentiment datasets (e.g., large tweet datasets).

4 Summary and Future Work

In this short paper, we present basic statistics of the studies in the domains of text classification, sentiment analysis, social media, and marketing over the last nine years. The three main findings derived from these statistics are: (1) the sentiment analysis, text classification, and social media topics are increasing; (2) the marketing topic is declining; and (3) marketing combined with (sentiment analysis or text classification or and social media) are increasing all over the years (except marketing combined with social media for the last few years).

In addition, we provide summaries of a few relevant articles. Each summary contains not only a description of the presented research and its results, but also as much as possible, shortcomings and/or ideas for future work that are suggested for the discussed study. The summaries show some of the potential of text classification and sentiment analysis in social media to improve marketing.

We see in many of the studies that have been surveyed above: (1) relatively simple tasks have been performed, e.g., simple sentiment classification (only to positive, negative or neutral, without predicting the degree of the sentiment and finding the underlying causes of positive or negative sentiments); (2) relatively simple features have been applied; and (3) only SVM methods have been applied. Additional advanced machine learning (ML) methods such as deep learning models should be applied at least on large datasets.

The major achievements in text classification and sentiment analysis have not yet been absorbed into many of the studies in marketing intelligence and business intelligence applications.

Possible future research proposals include (1) applying more advanced sentiment methods in the domain of marketing (e.g., automatic extraction of positive and negative words using seed lists [5]); (2); applying classification tasks using not only n-gram features and lexicons, but also stylistic features such as function words, quantitative features, orthographic features, part of speech (POS) features, and lexical features [6]; and (3) applying the most advanced supervised ML methods such as various deep learning models to match the vast amount of knowledge available in social media.

Acknowledgments. The author thanks three anonymous reviewers for their reviews and fruitful comments. Thanks also to Shalom Mashbaum for his English editing.

References

1. Cho, S. H., Kang, H. B.: Text sentiment classification for SNS-based marketing using domain sentiment dictionary. In Proceedings of the 2012 IEEE International Conference on Consumer Electronics (ICCE) (pp. 717-718). IEEE (2012).
2. Engin, M., Can, T.: Text classification in the Turkish marketing domain for context sensitive ad distribution. In Proceedings of the 24th International Symposium on Computer and Information Sciences (pp. 105-110). IEEE (2009).

3. Giatsoglou, M., Vozalis, M. G., Diamantaras, K., Vakali, A., Sarigiannidis, G., Chatzisavvas, K. C.: Sentiment analysis leveraging emotions and word embeddings. Expert Systems with Applications, 69, 214-224 (2017).
4. Glance, N., Hurst, M., Nigam, K., Siegler, M., Stockton, R., Tomokiyo, T.: Deriving marketing intelligence from online discussion. In Proceedings of the eleventh ACM SIGKDD international conference on Knowledge discovery in data mining (pp. 419-428)ACM (2005).
5. HaCohen-Kerner, Y., Badash, H.: Positive and negative sentiment words in a blog corpus written in hebrew. Procedia Computer Science, 96, 733-743 (2016).
6. HaCohen-Kerner, Y., Beck, H., Yehudai, E., Mughaz, D.: Stylistic feature sets as classifiers of documents according to their historical period and ethnic origin. Applied Artificial Intelligence, 24(9), 847-862 (2010).
7. Howells, K., Ertugan, A.: Applying fuzzy logic for sentiment analysis of social media network data in marketing. Procedia computer science, 120, 664-670 (2017).
8. Jin, J., Yan, X., Yu, Y., Li, Y.: Service failure complaints identification in social media: A text classification approach, In the Proc. of the Thirty Fourth International Conference on Information Systems (2013).
9. Mostafa, M. M.: More than words: Social networks' text mining for consumer brand sentiments. Expert Systems with Applications, 40(10), 4241-4251 (2013).
10. Pinto, M. B., Mansfield, P.: Facebook as a complaint mechanism: An investigation of millennials. Journal of Behavioral Studies in Business, 5, 1-12 (2012).
11. Provalis Research.: QDA Miner version 4.0 User Manual. Montreal, QC, Canada (2011).

Feature Impact for Prediction Explanation

Mohammad Bataineh✉ [0000-0003-0030-5827], David Steenhard, Harpreet Singh

Humana Inc., Louisville KY, USA
mbataineh649@humana.com

Abstract. Companies across the globe have been adapting complex Machine Learning (ML) techniques to build advanced predictive models to improve their operations and services and help in decision making. While these ML techniques are extremely powerful and have found success in different industries for helping with decision making, a common feedback heard across many industries worldwide is that too often these techniques are opaque in nature with no details as to why a particular prediction probability was reached. This work presents an innovative algorithm that addresses this limitation by providing a ranked list of all features according to their contribution to a model's prediction. This new algorithm, Feature Impact for Prediction Explanation (FIPE), incorporates individual feature variations and correlations to calculate feature impact for a prediction. The true power of FIPE lies in its computationally-efficient ability to provide feature impact irrespective of the base ML technique used.

Keywords: black box · model interpretation · prediction explanation

1 Introduction

Machine learning (ML) algorithms provide new milestones for a company's success by providing future prediction and forecasting for various metrics and events for better and optimized outcomes. Simple algorithms, like logistic regression and decision trees, have architectures that make it easy to interpret and explain the reasons behind the algorithms predictions. On the other hand, with the technological advancement in computing power and big-data sources, more complex ML algorithms have become dominant over these simple algorithms in practical applications. Techniques like multi-perceptron neural network, deep learning tools, random forest, and gradient-boosted trees usually outperform the simple ML algorithms. The downside is that these more complex algorithms are not interpretable when it comes to explaining individual predictions. This in turn makes it difficult for the users of these models to take personalized actions based on the individual predictions. For example, a model might be used to predict patients who might be non-compliant with their medications. While the model can provide a list of these patients, it cannot provide any indication of why these individuals are non-compliant with their medications. Being non-compliant could be due to a variety of reasons, financial difficulties to pay for expensive medications or lacking transportation to pick up the medications, for example. These different burdens require alternative actions to be taken by the model users.

Through examination of the literature, a clear gap is apparent in that there is a critical need to have some efficient tool to interpret these complex model predictions in important fields like healthcare and finance, among others [1-2]. The effort in model interpretation, however, has been recent and limited. One of earliest proposed methods to solve this challenging problem is the permutation-based interpretation method called individual conditional expectation (ICE) [3]. ICE creates variants of an instance by replacing the feature's value with values from a grid and makes new predictions using the original model. Lundberg [4] proposed another approach that calculates marginal contribution of a feature value across all possible options; then all contributions are averaged using Shapley values. Both the ICE and Shapely values require expensive run times when you have many features. In addition, both techniques can produce invalid local interpretations when features are correlated.

Other approaches for black box model interpretation are the local surrogate models like local interpretable model-agnostic explanations (LIME), which builds logistic regression to represent each observation predictive value [5]. Another derivation of the surrogate models uses decision trees to represent the predictive values [6]. These surrogate methods experience serious limitations that include: computationally expensive since each observation should be represented in new model, over simplification assumption for the model by assuming all features have simple relationships at local level, and instability of the explanations due to heuristic settings and variable sampling process [1, 7-8]. Evaluation of majority of these and other similar methods along with their limitations are detailed in Guidotti [9]. There are other approaches that are designed for global model interpretation [10-13], but those are beyond the scope of this work since they are not capable of providing individual explanation for each observation.

Besides the fact that use of these model interpretation algorithms burdens the user with severe limitations, the algorithms are neither mature nor widely used in industrial applications. In real world situations where the model has thousands of features to be evaluated, some algorithms like ICE and LIME run into memory and run time issues. Moreover, other algorithms are designed for scenarios that are too specific and crafted with simplistic assumptions. Therefore, this work was motivated by the fact that there are still tremendous areas of improvement needed in regards to model interpretation. This is especially the case when it comes to real world applications with flexible settings, and ML models with large numbers of features.

To address these issues, we introduce in this work a novel algorithm that can be used to interpret ML modeling by providing the top predictors that are driving the model prediction for each observation. The new algorithm is called Feature Impact for Prediction Explanation (FIPE). The FIPE algorithms can be used with any ML model with superior credibility because: (1) it preserves and uses the original built model to rank top predictors and interpret the predictions; (2) it runs relatively fast without running in memory issues or implementation obstacles, which makes it scalable to any application; (3) it produces local prediction interpretation for each observation; and (4) it's proven to have broad representation of all predictors in the model without any biases or in-advanced assumptions and settings that might limit or change the number of represented predictors.

2 Feature Impact for Prediction Explanation (FIPE)

The hypothesis for the FIPE algorithm is built around the fact that an informative feature in a model is the one that has varying values and is correlated to the target (i.e., output) so that the variation in the model predictions are caused by these informative features. The greatest impact on a model prediction is produced by the features with extreme values relative to each other. Essentially, the features with extreme low or high values from their median/mode drives the resulting score along with their importance/weight in the model architecture. The feature impact on a model prediction can actually be estimated by evaluating the prediction changes when that impact is removed. The most straightforward way to do this is to set the feature value back to its normal value, like the median for numeric features and the mode for categorical features. In most practical ML problems, features are somewhat correlated to each other. They all contribute cohesively to the model predictions. Thus, whenever a feature impact is evaluated the correlated impact with other features should also be considered.

The FIPE algorithm was developed to calculate the feature impact using two aspects: the impact of the individual feature on the model, and the correlated impact resulting from being associated with other features. Eventually, FIPE algorithm calculates the total feature impact as the resulting sum of both impacts based on the changes they cause on the model prediction. We have summarized the FIPE algorithm in the following steps:

Step 1: Each input (i.e., each observation, which is called ID in this context) is scored using the original ML predictive model. The resulting predicted score is called (S_o)

Step 2: Calculate feature statistics. The median value is calculated for each numeric feature. The mode value is calculated for each categorical feature

Step 3: Within each observation, each input feature x is used to create two new scores using the original model as follows:

S_x: Predicted score when only feature x is set to its median/mode value while all other input features are kept at their original values

S_c: Predicted score when all input features except x are set to their median/mode values. Feature x is kept at its original value

Step 4: Repeat step 3 for all features within the same observation. Then, repeat the process for all observations.

Step 5: Create one additional score that is a result of setting all features to their median/mode values (called S_m). This single score is a common score that will be used for all observations.

Step 6: Calculate feature x net impact (Y_x) using Equation 1. The impact Y_x consists of the impact sign (U_x) (Equation 2) multiplied by the absolute impact value. The impact value comes from the feature x individual impact and its correlated impact with all other features.

$$Y_x = U_x \times \left| \frac{|S_x - S_o| + |(S_m - S_o) - (S_c - S_o)|}{S_m} \right| = U_x \times \left| \frac{|S_x - S_o| + |S_m - S_c|}{S_m} \right| \quad (1)$$

$$U_x = \begin{Bmatrix} -1, \text{ if } (|S_x - S_o| \geq |S_m - S_c|) \text{ and } (S_x \geq S_o) \\ -1, \text{ if } (|S_m - S_c| \geq |S_x - S_o|) \text{ and } (S_m \geq S_c) \\ 1, \text{ Otherwise} \end{Bmatrix} \quad (2)$$

In order to communicate the underlying mathematical logic for the FIPE algorithm that was presented in the above steps, we demonstrate how the feature x impact is calculated in Equation 1, as follows. Figure 1 represents the scores distribution for a hypothetical ML predictive model. In Figure 1, the individual impact for feature x is obtained in (A), which explains the first part of Equation 1. The correlated impact for feature x is obtained in (B), which explains the second part in Equation 1. Then, the final net impact is normalized by dividing it by S_m, which is the result of setting all features to their median/model values, allowing for all features impacts to be evaluated relative to each other. Both impacts A and B represent isolating the entire effect of feature x on the original predicted score S_o by eliminating the features' extreme values through adjusting them to their mean/median.

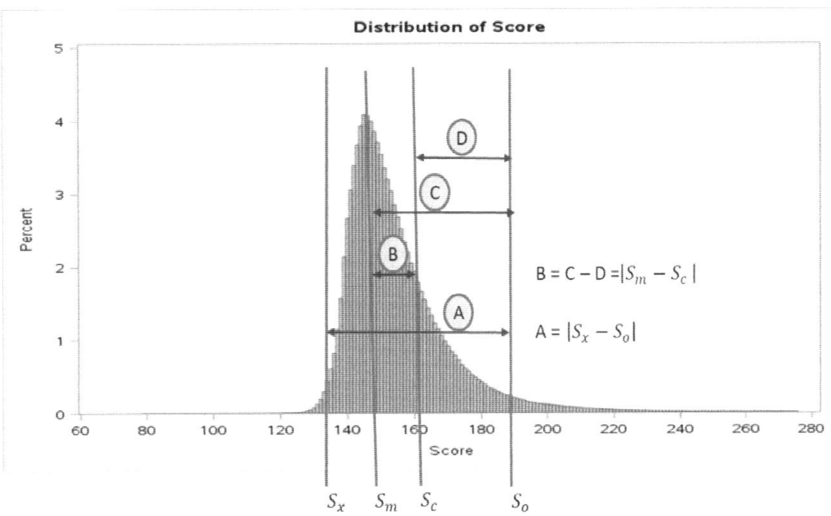

Fig. 1. Score distribution for hypothetical predictive model along with representation for the FIPE feature impact portions and their associated scores

With respect to the impact sign U_x that is presented in Equation 2, the larger impact portion between A and B determines the final sign of the net impact. If A > B, then feature x has a negative impact only when $S_x \geq S_o$. This means that removing feature x impact, which is represented by the score S_x, leads to a higher score compared to the original score S_o. This in turn indicates that having feature x with its current value reduces the score S_o from what it should be when x has a normal value (i.e., set to median/mode value). Using the same logic, when B > A, then feature x impact is negative when $S_m \geq S_c$.

The feature impact calculations are repeated over all features for the same observation. Therefore, each feature will have its own normalized impact that can be compared relative to other features for the same observation. Features then can be ranked by positive, negative, or absolute impact. To make the features impact values more interpretable to end users, the features impacts are normalized by dividing each feature impact Y_x by the maximum feature impact for the same observation. In the next section we provide a few examples on the FIPE implementation, and calculate the feature impacts.

3 Examples

Like many other fields, the healthcare field is full of ML applications – from disease or diagnosis prediction to identifying members with a high risk of an emergency department (ED) visit or inpatient admission. Regardless of the application, it becomes critical to know why the model produced a high prediction for someone enabling those making use of the model (care manager, nurse, social worker, etc.) to provide impactful interventions and obtain better engagement with patients. In this section, we provide a simplified example using healthcare data to examine the FIPE implementation. In this example, we have a hypothetical model with 3 inputs and single classification output. The model inputs are the person's age, ED visits in past 1 year, and utilization count in past 1 year (doctors' visits). The model output is simply a raw prediction between 0 and 1 for a classification output (i.e., target).

Table 1 presents sample predicted results (S_o) for 3 patients, which have been anonymized to patient identifications (ID). For the remainder of this section, we will calculate and rank the 3 features impact for ID number 1 only.

Table 1. Sample of three IDs with their input values along with their model predictions

ID	Age	ED Visits	Utilization count	Model Prediction (S_o)
1	62	4	7	0.95
2	66	1	2	0.93
3	66	4	7	0.92

ED = Emergency department

From the FIPE steps detailed in the previous section, the next step is to get the resulting score from setting all inputs to their median/mode values. In this case, the median values for the entire evaluated population is provided in Table 2, which also provides the result score (S_m).

Table 2. The median values for the model three inputs and the resulting prediction

Age	ED Visits	Utilization count	Model Prediction (S_m)
66	1	2	0.2

ED = Emergency department

Now, each individual feature will be used to create 2 additional scores derived from new settings for the features values. The new observations along with their scores are provided in Table 3. The table includes additional columns: (1) the column "feature Name" is to flag the feature used to create the new score, and (2) the column "Score Tag" is to provide the type of resulting score for the evaluated feature. As noted, all evaluated features in Table 3 are for the same single ID.

Table 3. The new observations for the three features and their resulting scores

ID	Age	ED Visits	Utilization count	Model Prediction	Feature Name	Score Tag
1	66	4	7	0.91	Age	S_x
1	62	1	2	0.12	Age	S_c
1	62	1	7	0.27	ED Visits	S_x
1	66	4	2	0.73	ED Visits	S_c
1	62	4	2	0.55	Utilization count	S_x
1	66	1	7	0.61	Utilization count	S_c

ED = Emergency department

Based on the different resulting scores, the feature impacts are estimated using Equations 1 and 2. The detailed calculations for each of the three features are provided below:

$$Y_x(\text{Age}) = -1 \times \left| \frac{|0.91 - 0.95| + |0.2 - 0.12|}{0.2} \right| = -1 \times \left| \frac{0.04 + 0.08}{0.2} \right| = -0.6$$

$$Y_x(\text{ED Visits}) = 1 \times \left| \frac{|0.27 - 0.95| + |0.2 - 0.73|}{0.2} \right| = 1 \times \left| \frac{0.68 + 0.53}{0.2} \right| = 6.05$$

$$Y_x(\text{Utilization count}) = 1 \times \left| \frac{|0.55 - 0.95| + |0.2 - 0.61|}{0.2} \right| = 1 \times \left| \frac{0.4 + 0.41}{0.2} \right| = 4.05$$

From the calculated impacts, it is clear the "ED visits" feature has the largest absolute impact. In order to produce more interpretable impact values, the impacts are all normalized by dividing each feature impact by the maximum impact value (i.e., in this case "ED visits" has the maximum impact equal 6.05). The resulting normalized impacts and their absolute ranking are presented in Table 4.

Table 4. Summary of features impacts, normalized impacts, and their absolute ranks.

ID	Feature Name	Impact (Y_x)	Normalized Impact	Absolute Rank
1	Age	-0.6	-0.1	3
1	ED Visits	6.05	1	1
1	Utilization count	4.05	0.7	2

ED = Emergency department

The examples presented in this section can be populated for each input ID among the entire dataset. In the result, the features impacts and ranking that are similar to those produced in Table 4 will be available for each ID. Depending on the user preference and needs it is necessary to choose the appropriate ranking. In this case, we were interested in the absolute ranking of all three features; however, other applications of this tool may be of interest for features with positive or negative impacts only.

It is important to emphasize that the FIPE algorithm runs relatively quickly, and the program should not undergo memory or implementation issues once expanded to a large real-world model in an industrial setting. That is because, along with one fixed score S_m that is used for all features, FIPE algorithm creates only two new scores S_x and S_c for each feature to calculate the impact. As opposed to other algorithms with expensive calculations and computation time increases exponentially with the number of features, FIPE always calculates new observations equal to twice the number of features.

4 Discussion

The model prediction explanation for any ML algorithm has been generating concern due to the use of advanced predictive models in applications in a diverse variety of fields. This work provides a new algorithm called FIPE for prediction explanation that can be applied on any ML model. Besides the importance ranking of all model features for an individual prediction, the new FIPE algorithm is easy to implement for any ML technique and runs very quickly. The FIPE algorithm makes what is usually known as a black box ML model to an open and transparent tool. This will essentially open new areas of research not just useful for advancing the ML algorithms and its usage, but also for future effort in trying to understand the behaviors of the underlying complex problems.

FIPE algorithm provides a new tipping point for practical and realistic implementation of a personalized model explanation. Future effort will be focused around identifying a standard methodology to evaluate FIPE and other similar algorithms in applied settings. Moreover, the algorithm should be subjectively evaluated on a full ML model with a large number of features and concise validation.

References

1. Alvarez-Melis D, Jaakkola T.S.: On the robustness of interpretability methods. arXiv preprint arXiv:1806.08049. 2018 Jun 21.
2. Interpretable machine learning. A Guide for Making Black Box Models Explainable, https://christophm.github.io/interpretable-ml-book/, last accessed 2019/03/20.
3. Goldstein A, Kapelner A, Bleich J, Pitkin E.: Peeking inside the black box: Visualizing statistical learning with plots of individual conditional expectation. Journal of Computational and Graphical Statistics. 2015 Jan 2;24(1):44-65.
4. Lundberg S, Lee SI.: An unexpected unity among methods for interpreting model predictions. arXiv preprint arXiv:1611.07478. 2016 Nov 22.

5. Ribeiro MT, Singh S, Guestrin C.: Why should i trust you?: Explaining the predictions of any classifier. InProceedings of the 22nd ACM SIGKDD international conference on knowledge discovery and data mining 2016 Aug 13 (pp. 1135-1144). ACM.
6. Bastani O, Kim C, Bastani H.: Interpreting blackbox models via model extraction. arXiv preprint arXiv:1705.08504. 2017 May 23.
7. Fong RC, Vedaldi A.: Interpretable explanations of black boxes by meaningful perturbation. InProceedings of the IEEE International Conference on Computer Vision 2017 (pp. 3429-3437).
8. Ithapu VK.: Decoding the Deep: Exploring class hierarchies of deep representations using multiresolution matrix factorization. InProceedings of the IEEE Conference on Computer Vision and Pattern Recognition Workshops 2017 (pp. 45-54).
9. Guidotti R, Monreale A, Ruggieri S, Turini F, Giannotti F, Pedreschi D.: A survey of methods for explaining black box models. ACM computing surveys (CSUR). 2018 Aug 22;51(5):93.
10. Friedman JH, Popescu BE.: Predictive learning via rule ensembles. The Annals of Applied Statistics. 2008;2(3):916-54.
11. Apley DW.: Visualizing the effects of predictor variables in black box supervised learning models. arXiv preprint arXiv:1612.08468. 2016 Dec 27.
12. Lakkaraju H, Kamar E, Caruana R, Leskovec J.: Interpretable & explorable approximations of black box models. arXiv preprint arXiv:1707.01154. 2017 Jul 4.
13. Fisher A, Rudin C, Dominici F.: All Models are Wrong but many are Useful: Variable Importance for Black-Box, Proprietary, or Misspecified Prediction Models, using Model Class Reliance. arXiv preprint arXiv:1801.01489. 2018 Jan 4.

Data-driven American Option Pricing using Artificial Neural Networks

Hanen Borchani[1], Wojciech Michal Pawlak[1], Steffen Holmslykke[1], and Allan Peter Engsig-Karup[1]

Simcorp Technology Labs, SimCorp A/S, Copenhagen, Denmark
{hnbh,wmpk,snh,aptk}@simcorp.com

Abstract. Many widely used numerical algorithms for option pricing and instrument valuation in finance are computationally expensive. In this work, we explore a means to lower this computational cost by considering a data-driven option pricing approach based on artificial neural networks (ANNs). We consider ANNs for both creating a function approximation of the instrument valuation and improving significantly the efficiency of the predictions of instrument pricing. To serve as an example, the training of our neural option pricing network is performed by supervised learning with data sets synthetically generated using the classical least-squares Monte Carlo (LSMC) algorithm, due to Longstaff & Schwartz, considered here as a reference high-fidelity model. The trained ANN is then useful for a fast and inexpensive estimation of the option valuations, subject to the uncertainty assumed in the model parameters. We empirically report on the speedup and the error rates achieved. Our experimental results show that ANNs have the potential to provide a means for a significant speedup with an accuracy close to the high-fidelity runs using LSMC. Note that, we restrict our experiments to American option pricing, but as a data-driven approach, ANNs are also well-suited for a general-purpose function approximation of other instrument types.

Keywords: Option Pricing · Monte Carlo Simulations · Artificial Neural Networks · Machine Learning · American Options.

1 Introduction

In finance, performing instrument valuations requires different and changing inputs for analysis. This usually implies that, if the cost of one pricing valuation is computationally expensive, then it may be intractable to perform a large number of pricing valuations ad hoc. An alternative approach to lower the computational cost is to use *surrogate modelling*. The objective in this case is to find a *surrogate model*, denoted $\hat{f}(\mathbf{x})$, that approximates well a high-fidelity model, denoted $f(\mathbf{x})$, such that $f(\mathbf{x}) = \hat{f}(\mathbf{x}) + \varepsilon(\mathbf{x})$, where the errors $\varepsilon(\mathbf{x})$ can be uniformly bounded below an acceptable user-defined error tolerance ϵ such that $\varepsilon(\mathbf{x}) \leq \epsilon$. As a potential surrogate model that can meet these requirements, we consider artificial neural networks (ANNs) [1] and apply them to a particular problem of financial instrument valuation – option pricing.

To our knowledge the first use of ANNs for option pricing was proposed by [2], where the ANNs predictive performance to estimate closing prices has been proved and compared to Black-Scholes model. Similar studies have been later conducted by [3] for the case of S&P 500 index call options, and by [4] for pricing European style call options on the FTSE 100 index, both proving that the ANNs predictive performance is either superior or comparable to Black-Scholes. More recently, Shuaiqiang et al. [5] also showed empirically that ANNs can estimate option prices and implied volatilities efficiently and accurately.

In this work, similarly to the mentioned existing works, we investigate how useful ANNs can be for estimating option pricing. However, we consider a different type of options, namely, the pricing of *American call options*. The focus is not only on the ANNs predictive performance but also on their computational efficiency. We examine this accuracy-speed trade-off by carrying out empirical experiments with computationally expensive Monte Carlo based path simulations with different parameters.

The remainder of this paper is organized as follows: In Section 2 we briefly present American option pricing. In Section 3 we introduce our application of ANNs to estimate American option pricing. In Section 4 we present the experimental setup and discuss the results obtained from our synthetically generated data sets. Finally, we conclude in Section 5.

2 American Option Pricing

An American option is a financial derivative that grants its holder a right to select the date at which to exercise the option at any time before maturity. We consider a *Vanilla put option* on a single underlying share of non-dividend-paying stock and use Least-Squares Monte Carlo (LSMC) algorithm due to Longstaff and Schwartz [6] for the valuation. The approximation quality of a Monte Carlo simulation depends on the number of paths (usually from 100.000 to 1.000.000) and the number of time steps that depends on the option maturity that might be daily, weekly or monthly, cf. [7].

In this work, we choose model parameters to simulate a case, where we price a basket of *put options* on a different underlying equities. We consider an option with a fixed strike price and maturity. The risk-free interest rate is also fixed. For each option, we then draw different values for spot price and volatility of the underlying. Parameter values are summarized in Table 1.

Table 1. Parameter value ranges for the LSMC model.

Parameter	Value range
Spot price (S) [$]	$S \in [60, 100]$
Strike price (K) [$]	90
Time to maturity (T) [years]	0.4167
Risk-free interest rate (r) [%]	0.05
Volatility (σ) [%]	$\sigma \in [0.06, 0.5397]$

3 Data-driven Option Pricing using ANNs

The valuation of an option can be seen as a supervised learning problem that consists of finding a function approximation $f : \mathbf{x} = (x_1, x_2, ..., x_n) \mapsto y$ that predicts for each input instance $\mathbf{x}$ an option price y. In our case, each instance $\mathbf{x}$ corresponds to the aforementioned LSMC model parameter values, and $n = 5$ denotes the number of these parameters. In order to solve this regression task, we resort to the use of ANNs [1]. ANNs are biologically inspired models that become increasingly popular. They consist of interconnected artificial neurons, grouped into layers, according to different architectures. Typically, as shown in Figure 1, an ANN consists of: 1) an input layer including n_{input} neurons: one for each input variable; 2) one or more hidden layers each including n_{hidden} neurons; and 3) an output layer including n_{output} neurons: one for each output variable. We adopt a heuristic by [8] for setting the number of neurons in each hidden layer as $n_{hidden} = n_{input} + n_{output} + 1$. Thus, for our option pricing case, we consider an ANN including an input layer with $n = 5$ neurons, an output layer with 1 neuron, and 2 hidden layers with $5 + 1 + 1 = 7$ neurons each.

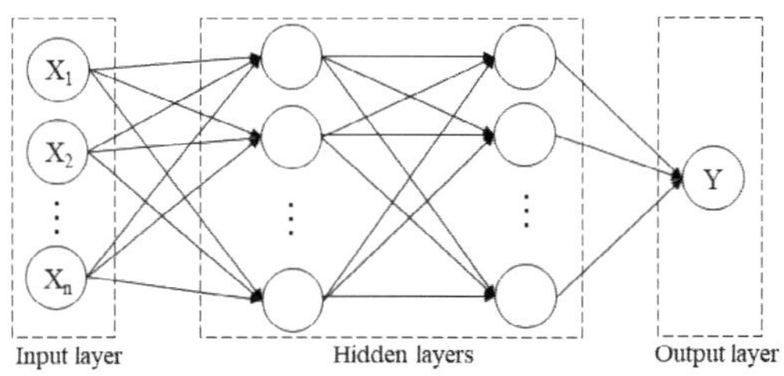

Fig. 1. Illustration of an ANN with two hidden layers.

The training of our neural option pricing network is performed using synthetically sampled data sets using the LSMC algorithm [6], considered here as a reference high-fidelity model. For the network training, we used the TensorFlow platform [9], where the back-propagation algorithm [10] is employed to find the ANN hyperparameters (i.e., weights) that minimize the error of the output, measured by a loss function as the discrepancy between the predicted output $\hat{y}$ and the actual one y. As a loss function, we used here the mean squared error MSE; as activation function, we used the Leaky Rectified Linear Units (Leaky ReLU); and as optimizer, we used the Adam optimization algorithm, cf. [9].

The ANN training phase can be computationally intensive, however, may be done *offline* only once or in an incremental way by resuming the training process and updating the hyperparameters as needed, e.g, when significant changes occur in the data. The trained ANN is then useful for a fast and inexpensive estimation of the option valuations. This price estimation (also known as ANN testing or prediction phase) can be done *online* at a low computational cost and comes with a minimal memory footprint through a single forward pass.

4 Experiments

In order to evaluate the ANN performance for option pricing, three synthetic data sets are defined by samples based on simulations with LSMC parameters in Table 1, 100 time steps and three different path numbers: 10.000, 100.000, and 1.000.000. Data sets are comprised of scattered data across the parameter ranges obtained using random sampling. Each data set includes 100.000 samples. We consider a feed-forward fully connected ANN with 2 hidden layers having 7 neurons each. The ANN training is performed using 80% of the data sets, while the evaluation of how well the ANN performs on new data is carried out with the remaining 20%. Two different publicly available settings for LSMC implementation are used, *sequential* LSMC using QuantLib[1] and an accelerated *parallel* LSMC-mGPU using NVIDIA's CUDA LSMC implementation[2]. LSMC is not parallelized and therefore runs sequentially on one core of a 20-core Intel Xeon CPU. LSMC-mGPU is improved to run as a massively parallel multi-device implementation that is executed on 8 NVIDIA Tesla V100 GPUs.

Table 2 shows the results comparing LSMC, LSMC-mGPU and ANN models. Offline time refers to ANN sequential training time, while online time refers to the option price estimation time. To assess the ANN performance, we report three error rates: the mean squared error MSE $= \frac{1}{n}\sum_{i=1}^{n}(y_i - \hat{y}_i)^2$, the mean absolute error MAE $= \frac{1}{n}\sum_{i=1}^{n} \mid y_i - \hat{y}_i \mid$ and the mean absolute percent error MAPE $= \frac{1}{n}\sum_{i=1}^{n} \mid \frac{y_i - \hat{y}_i}{y_i} \mid$.

Table 2. Performance comparison. Offline and online times are reported in seconds.

Model	Paths	Online time[s]	Offline time[s]	MSE	MAE	MAPE [%]
LSMC		0.97	-	-	-	-
LSMC-mGPU	10.000	3.39×10^{-3}	-	-	-	-
ANN		15×10^{-6}	160	1.31×10^{-3}	2.65×10^{-2}	4.59
LSMC		7.26	-	-	-	-
LSMC-mGPU	100.000	3.31×10^{-3}	-	-	-	-
ANN		15×10^{-6}	206	2.29×10^{-3}	3.85×10^{-2}	2.14
LSMC		31.39	-	-	-	-
LSMC-mGPU	1.000.000	3.09×10^{-3}	-	-	-	-
ANN		18×10^{-6}	213	1.24×10^{-3}	2.99×10^{-2}	4.69

From Table 2, it is clear that the online running time of the ANN model when used for inference runs sequentially and outperforms the LSMC algorithms especially when a higher number of paths is considered. In fact, with 1.000.000 that is often recommended as a default setting, the ANN achieves an impressive estimated ×172 online speedup compared to the state-of-the-art LSMC-mGPU implementation. The offline running time related to the training of the ANN model is also quite fast with less than 4 minutes for all cases. In addition, ANNs

[1] QuantLib library for quantitative finance. `http://www.quantlib.org`
[2] NVIDIA's CUDA LSMC implementation. `https://github.com/NVIDIA-developer-blog/code-samples/tree/master/posts/american-options`

predictive performance measured using MSE/MAE shows small loss. The relative average error MAPE is below 5% compared to the values obtained in the high-fidelity runs. These results show that it is possible to achieve high-performance and good accuracy at a low computational cost, since LSMC requires access to GPU hardware, whereas the ANN can be easily deployed for fast repetitive executions on available system setups.

5 Conclusion

In this paper, we have studied how to improve numerical efficiency by reducing the need for expensive pricing evaluations through using ANNs that are inexpensive to evaluate, however, may be influenced by approximation errors. The ANN training cost is dependent on the data generation process using the LSMC algorithm, which comes with a computational cost that can be significantly lowered using high-performance computing.

In ongoing work, we intend to carry out additional experiments with extracting the relevant information from real data sets, investigate further the use of surrogate models such as ANNs for accelerated pricing valuations, and compare their performance against ANN models in the context of practical work flows.

Acknowledgment

The research presented contributes to the research project "Accelerated Financial Algorithms" (2017-2020) that is supported by Innovation Fund Denmark.

References

1. Bishop, C. M.: Neural networks for pattern recognition. Oxford University Press, Inc., New York, USA (1995)
2. Malliaris, M., Salchenberger, L.: A neural network model for estimating option prices. Applied Intelligence **3**, 193–206 (1993)
3. Qi, M., Maddala, G.S: Option pricing using artificial neural networks: The case of S&P 500 index call options. Proceedings of Third International Conference on Neural Networks in the Capital Markets, 78–91 (1996)
4. Amilon, H.: A neural network versus Black-Scholes: A comparison of pricing and hedging performances. Journal of Forecasting **22(4)**, 317–335 (2003)
5. Shuaiqiang, L., Oosterlee, C., Bohte, S.: Pricing options and computing implied volatilities using neural networks. Risks **7**, 16 (2019)
6. Longstaff, F. A., Schwartz, E. S.: Valuing American options by simulation: A simple least-squares approach. The Review of Financial Studies **14**(1), 113–147 (2001)
7. Hull, J., White, A.: Options, futures and other derivatives. Prentice Hall, Tenth Edition (2018)
8. Hanin, B., Sellke, M.: Approximating continuous functions by ReLU nets of minimal width. ArXiv:1710.11278v2 (2017)
9. Abadi, M., Agarwal, A., et al.: TensorFlow: Large-scale machine learning on heterogeneous systems. (2015) Software available from `tensorflow.org`
10. Rumelhart, D. E., Geoffrey, E. H., Williams, R. J.: Learning representations by back-propagating errors. Nature **323**, 533–536 (1986)

CLUES: Detection of User Intent through Interactive Comparison

Chitra Phadke[1][0000-0003-3853-2451], Paishun Ting[2][0000-0002-5675-3816], Jin Cao[1][0000-0002-5685-8706], and Huseyin Uzunalionglu[1][0000-0003-2065-8697]

[1] Nokia Bell Labs, Murray Hill, NJ, USA,
firstname.lastname@nokia-bell-labs.com,
[2] University of Michigan, Ann Arbor, MI, USA
paishun@umich.edu

Abstract. Many tasks in data analytics require finding data instances that are similar to each other in some way. However, similarity is often an inexact and subjective concept which can vastly depend on one's opinions and intent. Such intent can often be mapped to a set of prominent object features or attributes that dominantly quantify the between-object similarity. Uncovering such intent therefore translates to identifying these important object attributes where the user's intent is embedded. Prior work in this area either resorts to domain experts to manually identify key attributes or requires carefully estimating an accurate distance value between objects, both of which are noticeably difficult to put in practice. In this work, we propose an intent-identification framework called *Comparative Lookup and User-intent Extraction System* (CLUES), which, through a series of interactive comparisons, extracts the weights that describe the importance of features and reflect the user's intent. This in turn enables quantification of object similarity. CLUES is straightforward to use, as it only asks as inputs for object comparisons, which are usually easier to perform than specifying an accurate between-object distance. Experimental results demonstrated for both a synthetic dataset and a real-world dataset confirmed that intent-reflecting feature weights can be recovered accurately with reasonable numbers of object comparisons. We also discuss promising future directions for the present work in progress.

Keywords: similarity quantification · feature importance detection · interactive visualization · intent discovery.

1 Introduction

Measuring or quantifying similarity among data instances plays an important role in many tasks in data analytics, including information retrieval, object clustering, data visualization, anomaly detection, among others. For example, in the task of clustering, similarity between data instances or objects is used to divide the set of objects into homogeneous groups in a way that each group contains objects that are more similar to each other than to objects in a different group.

This allows properties of objects in the same group to be inferred by their similarity. Also, recommendations can be made based on the group membership. Another important use of similarity detection is root-cause analysis of failure events, in which past events that are similar to the current failure event must be quickly retrieved to aid the identification of the failure cause and recommend potential solutions.

Despite its prominent role in data analytics, similarity quantification remains a challenging task, as it is usually an inexact concept that can heavily depend on subjective opinions. To illustrate this, consider classifying a set of different foods based on their similarity. Different people may deliver different classification results, as their judgment on food similarity can vary widely. For example, Jane may classify the foods based on their color, so that an apple and a hot pepper fall in the same group. James, on the other hand, may classify the fruits based on their sweetness, and now an apple and a hot pepper belong to different groups. This illustrative example identifies the fact that a person's opinions and intent, while being highly subjective, are often an indispensable part in quantifying similarity. This hints at the need to uncover the intent of a user to better quantify similarity for data analytics tasks, which in turn can deliver results that better suits the user's needs.

This paper presents an interactive system called *Comparative Lookup and User-intent Extraction System* (CLUES) to tackle the preceding problem. It does so by actively asking for inputs from a user which hint at his/her intent. It then updates its definition of object similarity in a way that best reflects the latent user intent. The type of inputs that the user provides are answers to a series of comparative questions, in which some sampled objects are presented for similarity comparison. The process is iterative, and can continue until satisfactory outcomes have been obtained.

The rest of this paper is organized as follows. Section 2 provides some background and describes related work, which further motivates our work. Section 3 details CLUES, our proposed framework for similarity quantification based on user intent. Experimental results on both synthetic data and real-world data are given in Section 4, which also provides promising future directions for this work in progress. Finally, Section 5 summarizes the paper and draws some conclusions.

2 Background and Motivation

The basis of our work is quantifying the similarity in multivariable objects. For example, consider the simple case where we are presented with a set of geometric objects, each being described by three features: color, shape and size. If we are to cluster these objects based on their similarity, there could be multiple reasonable ways to perform this task, as we have briefly discussed in Section 1. For instance, one can group objects that are similar in color, in which case the clustering outcome is given in Fig. 1*a*. Similarly, it is also reasonable to group these objects based on size or shape; see Fig. 1*b*-*c*. The foregoing example highlights the fact that there is inherent ambiguity embedded in tasks that require

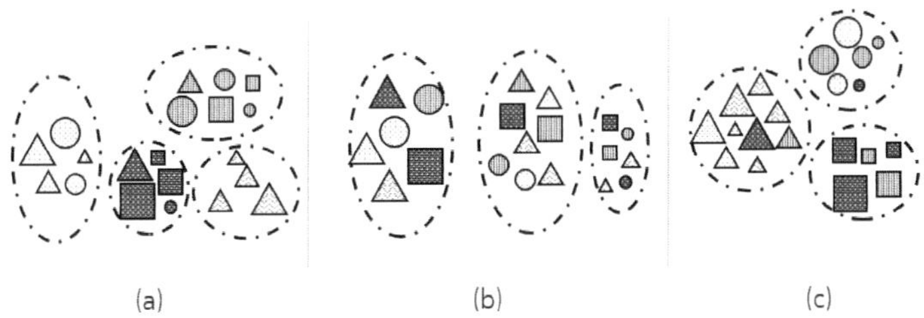

Fig. 1. Geometric objects grouped by (a) color, by (b) size, and by (c) shape, respectively.

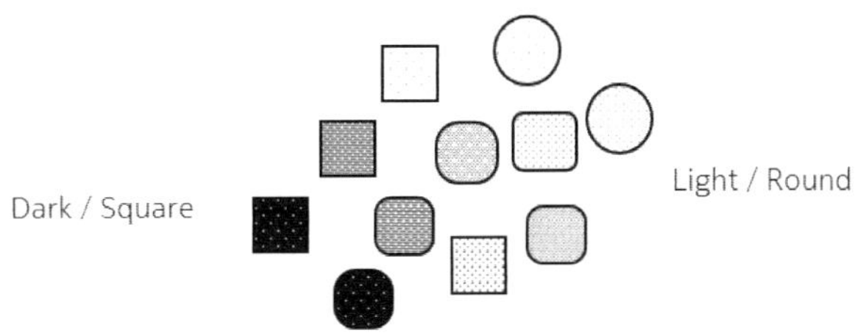

Fig. 2. 2D visualization of geometric objects based on their color and shape.

similarity measure, which can depend on a user's intent. The key to addressing such ambiguity is to inquire information from the user to help quantify similarity. Although similarity quantification looks trivial for this simple example, this task can be far more complex for real-world applications, as each data instance can be high dimensional with attributes that interact with each other via the user's latent intent in an unexpected way.

It is important to note that similarity between a pair of objects is a direct reflection of the distance between their feature representations and identification of important features. Objects that are similar can be thought as "close" in distance. Thus, the problem of quantifying object similarity can be easily translated to defining a reasonable distance function. In practice, however, defining an appropriate distance function is a vexing problem. This is mainly because many candidate distance functions, including linear and non-linear ones, are available, and each of them can have a very different performance implication depending on the target task and the nature of data features, e.g. whether they are categorical or numerical. In this work, we assume that the distance between a pair of objects takes the form of a weighted sum of difference in individual features. This allows us to formulate the problem of finding a user's intent as a task of recovering the weights for each feature; a large weight implies that the associated feature is deemed important.

Several prior works have attempted to incorporate user's intent to define the distance between objects. Visual to Parametric Interaction (V2PI) [1] provides a generic framework for data analytics that explicitly incorporates a user as part of the pipeline. A user can observe a visualized outcome, and actively provides feedback which the system can account for when regenerating a new visualization. This makes data analytics an iterative process with the interaction between the system and the user being bidirectional. Andromeda, described in [2], is also an interactive system in which a user can manipulate objects visualized on a 2D plane enabled by multi-dimensional scaling (MDS)[6], so to provide feedback to the data analysis system. Specifically, the user can not only manage the parameters of the system, but also directly move the objects on the plane to a new place, based on which the system will adjust the parameters to best accommodate the objects' new locations. However, an applicability limitation of this methodology is that the absolute distance between a pair of objects is not always apparent. For example, it can be very hard for a user to determine the exact numerical distance between an apple and a banana in the food example. In other words, using Andromeda to adjust object distances can sometimes bear the challenging requirement of knowing the exact values of the distances. Another promising method called CHISSL, described in [3], is an interactive clustering system that allows a user to reassign an object to an appropriate cluster based on the user's intent. The system can then adjust its parameters to accommodate for the new clustering results enforced by the user. However, this method only applies to clustering tasks in which objects can be explicitly assigned to some groups. It does not apply to other scenarios such as the data visualization task shown in Fig. 2, in which objects do not have an apparent cluster membership, and their location distribution on the plane is widely dispersed.

In this paper, we aim at overcoming the limitations posed by the preceding methods. We propose an interactive framework called CLUES for data analysis that can draw conclusions on object similarity that best reflects the user's intent. It does so by presenting a series of sets of objects to the user, who is then asked to compare the relative distance among these objects. This avoids the need of providing an exact numerical distance or cluster membership for these objects. One of the major advantages that CLUES has is that it is easy to use, as it is usually far easier to make comparisons than to draw precise conclusions.

3 Framework for Intent Discovery

This section describes CLUES, the proposed framework for uncovering the user's intent on similarity measure.

3.1 Framework Setup

CLUES is a metric-incubating method that actively asks a user to compare the similarity of a chosen set of object instances, based on which the distance between a pair of objects will adjust. Specifically, CLUES considers a dataset comprised of n objects o_1, o_2, ..., o_n, each of which is characterized by a p-dimensional feature vector $o_i = [o_i^{(1)}, o_i^{(2)}, ..., o_i^{(p)}]^T$. Each feature can be either numerical or

Algorithm 1 Pseudo-algorithm for CLUES

Input: dataset $\mathcal{D}$; LASSO coefficient λ; time budget t_{max}
Initialization: randomize weights $\mathbf{w}$; compared set $\mathcal{C} \leftarrow \emptyset$; $t \leftarrow 0$
while $t < t_{max}$ and satisfactory results not achieved **do**
  $t \leftarrow t + 1$
  Draw a tuple $\{i, j, h\} \notin \mathcal{C}$; Here o_i, o_j, $o_h \in \mathcal{D}$.
  $r \leftarrow$ user's response to the inquiry formed by $\{i, j, h\}$
  if $r =$ SKIP **then**
    continue
  else if $r =$ " o_i is closer to o_h than o_j is" **then**
    Add $\{i, j, h\}$ to $\mathcal{C}$; Associate $\{i, j, h\}$ with attenuation factor $\beta_{i,j,h,t}$
  else
    Add $\{j, i, h\}$ to $\mathcal{C}$; Associate $\{j, i, h\}$ with attenuation factor $\beta_{j,i,h,t}$
  end if
  update $\mathbf{w}$ as a solution to Optimization Problem (2)
end while
Output: weight vector $\mathbf{w}$

categorical. Pairwise similarity between two objects is defined by the distance function

$$D_{i,j} = \mathbf{w} \cdot \mathbf{d_{i,j}} = \sum_{k=1}^{p} w_k d_{i,j}^{(k)} \tag{1}$$

where each $w_k \in [0, 1]$ is a numerical weight that hints at how important the feature $o_i^{(k)}$ is in defining the distance between objects. $d_{i,j}^{(k)} = d(o_i^{(k)}, o_j^{(k)})$ is a user-chosen distance metric defined on a pair of features of a certain type. For illustration purposes, this work uses ℓ_2 norm $d_{i,j}^{(k)} = \|o_i^{(k)} - o_j^{(k)}\|_2$ for numerical features and categorical difference $d_{i,j}^{(k)} = \mathbb{1}_{\{o_i^{(k)} \neq o_j^{(k)}\}}(o_i^{(k)}, o_j^{(k)})$ for categorical features.

The distance between a pair of objects defined in Eq. (1) is in essence a weighted sum of these objects' individual feature distances. As mentioned previously, the weights can be used to rank the importance of the features. In other words, weights implicitly reflect the user's intent.

3.2 User-supplied Comparative Information

CLUES works interactively with the user to find the set of weights for Eq. (1). It does so by first presenting a comparative question which the user can answer or skip. Based on the user's response, CLUES then updates the weights and presents another comparative question. This iterative process continues until the user is satisfied with the findings or the time budget is exhausted.

Each user response to a comparative question provides partial information about the value of the weights. Specifically, a comparative question asks the user to input new information by comparing three objects: an anchor object o_h and two comparative objects o_i and o_j. The user compares by indicating whether o_i

is closer to o_h or o_j is closer to o_h. If o_i is closer, then this comparative input translates to the constraint $\mathbf{w} \cdot \mathbf{d}_{j,h} \geq \mathbf{w} \cdot \mathbf{d}_{i,h}$. Otherwise, this constraint will be $\mathbf{w} \cdot \mathbf{d}_{i,h} \geq \mathbf{w} \cdot \mathbf{d}_{j,h}$. The constraints collected over multiple iterations will jointly form an optimization objective, whose solution can be used to identify possible values for the weights w_k, and hence the user's intent. Specifically, each constraint of "o_i being closer to o_h" is associated with a penalty term $\beta_{i,j,h,t_0} \cdot \max\{0, \mathbf{w} \cdot \mathbf{d}_{i,h} - \mathbf{w} \cdot \mathbf{d}_{j,h}\}$, where β_{i,j,h,t_0} is an attenuation factor that decreases over iterations t. We will discuss the rationale and more details about attenuation later in Section3.3. The term $\max\{0, \mathbf{w} \cdot \mathbf{d}_{i,h} - \mathbf{w} \cdot \mathbf{d}_{j,h}\}$ produces a positive penalty value, if the current weights suggest that "o_j is closer to o_h" which goes against the user's input. Otherwise, this term will be 0. We denote a set of compared objects collected so far as $\mathcal{C}$, so that the tuple $\{i, j, h\} \in \mathcal{C}$, if the constraint "$o_i$ is closer to o_h than o_j" has been provided by the user. The overall objective function can then formulated as:

$$\arg\min_{\mathbf{w}} \sum_{i,j,h:\{i,j,h\} \in \mathcal{C}} \beta_{i,j,h,t_0} \cdot \max\{0, \mathbf{w} \cdot \mathbf{d}_{i,h} - \mathbf{w} \cdot \mathbf{d}_{j,h}\} + \lambda \|\mathbf{w}\|_1 \tag{2}$$

$$s.t. \|\mathbf{w}\|_2 = 1, \ \mathbf{w}_k \geq 0 \ \forall \ k$$

where a non-negative constraint and a unity constraint are explicitly imposed on each weight and the weight vector, respectively. The objective function also optionally includes a LASSO penalty placed on the weights to enforce sparsity for better understanding the user's intent. Intuitively, the optimization objective Eq. (2) is intended to find such weights that, when used to induce the pairwise distance for objects, satisfy the distance constraints provided by the user. Finally, the objective Eq. (2) is solved by subgradient methods, as it is not differentiable at all points. Algorithm 1 summarizes CLUES.

3.3 Conflict Handling

A close look at the comparative questions reveals that in some cases, it can be very challenging or impossible for a user to compare without going against his/her intent. In this section, we examine some of these "difficult" cases, and provide solutions to them.

Anchor Switching: Consider the scenario where the user is presented with a comparative question where, in the user's mind, the two comparative objects o_i and o_j are much more similar than anyone of them and the anchor object o_h are; see Fig. 3. Further, the distance between o_i and o_h and the distance between o_j and o_h can both be relatively large, making them difficult to compare. In this case, the user can opt to replace the anchor object with one of the comparative object. As shown in the figure, this may ease the comparison decision for the user.

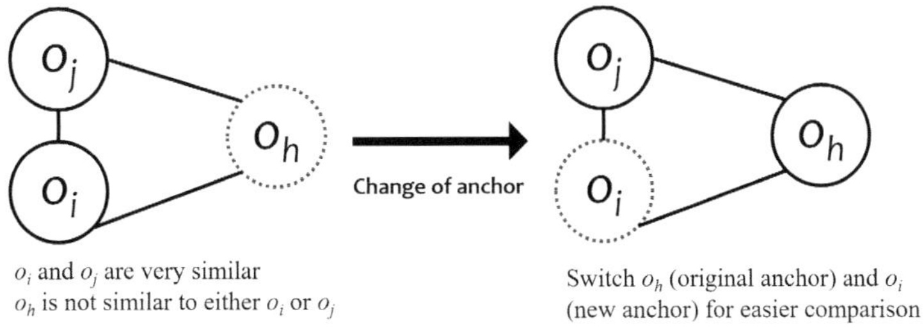

Fig. 3. Switching the anchor to ease the comparison process.

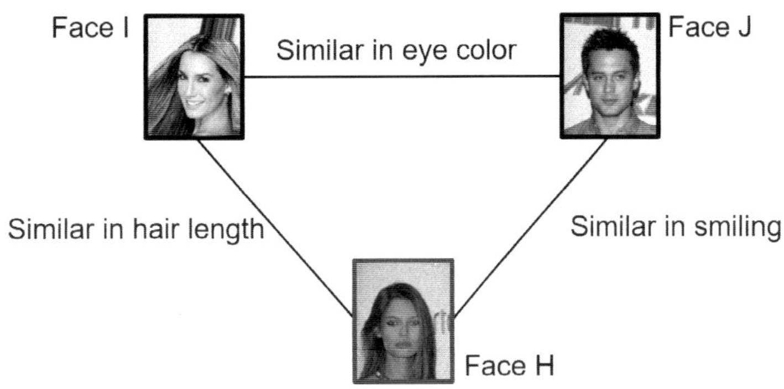

Fig. 4. Difficult comparison scenario that anchor switching does not resolve. Here, the user is interested in hair length, eye color and whether smiling or not, but not interested in other features like gender, face angle, hair color, age, etc.

Skipping: Another scenario of comparative question that is hard to respond is given in Fig. 4. Here, for illustration purposes, we assume the user's latent intent is to find faces that are similar in hair length, eye color and whether the person is smiling or not. The user is not interested in other facial features such as gender, hair color, facial angle, age, etc. However, the objects presented are pairwise similar in a specific feature. Specifically, Face I and Face H are similar in hair length, Face I and Face J are similar in eye color, while Face J and Face H are similar in whether the person is smiling or not. Setting Face H to be the anchor object result in the dilemma that it has both similarities and dissimilarities with both of the comparative objects, making the comparison hard. This problem, unfortunately, cannot be solved simply by anchor switching. In this case, the user may choose to skip the comparison. It is noteworthy that skipping also applies to those cases where anchor switching can be used, as the user may not always be aware of the opportunities for anchor switching.

Constraint Attenuation: Recall that in Eq. (2), each user-supplied constraint is associated with an attenuation factor β_{i,j,h,t_0} that decreases over time. The user is human and can be prone to making mistakes. The attenuation factor allows mistakes made previously to have a lesser impact, and eventually be forgotten. It also prevents the solution from being unstable as mistakes tend to produce conflicting constraints that can lead to slow finding of weights. While in general, any positive but decreasing sequence can serve the purpose of attenuation, in this work we adopt a constant attenuation factor, i.e. $\beta_{i,j,h,t_0}(t) = {\alpha_{i,j,h}}^{t-t_0}$, where $\alpha_{i,j,h} \in (0, 1]$.

4 Experimentation

We assessed the performance of CLUES using both a synthetic dataset and a real-world dataset. Specifically, the synthetic dataset comprises objects whose features are each generated according to a Gaussian-mixture distribution. The real-world dataset is a subset of a data repository, PubFig [4], containing facial images of public figures.

4.1 Datasets

Synthetic Gaussian-mixture Dataset: This dataset contains 500 synthetic objects, each characterized by 10 features. Each of these features is generated according to a Gaussian mixture model.

PubFig Data: The PubFig dataset [4] contains 140 public figures with over 57K images collected from various internet sources. Each image has 73 descriptors, with most of them being visually related and labeled using Amazon Mechanical Turks [5], a popular crowd-sourcing platform that allows users to get paid by completing labeling work. The labeled visual descriptors are mostly binary, e.g. long hair versus short hair. Subsequent to the label collection, a Support Vector Machine (SVM)[7] classifier was constructed for each descriptor. The final attribute value for each descriptor is the distance from the corresponding object to the SVM boundary. Consequently, the attribute values are continuous and can be either negative or positive depending on which side of the SVM boundary the object lies. For illustration purposes, we chose 128 random images and ten prominent and visually identifiable attributes for assessing CLUES. These attributes include gender, skin and hair color, and facial expressions like whether smiling or not and whether the teeth are visible or not.

4.2 Evaluating CLUES via Emulation

To facilitate the performance assessment, we emulated a human user that responds to CLUES's inquiry based on some predefined standard. Specifically, the emulator first randomly determines a set of ground-truth weights that indicate the importance of object features. This way, when presented with a comparative inquiry, the emulator can compare and respond in a consistent manner. It

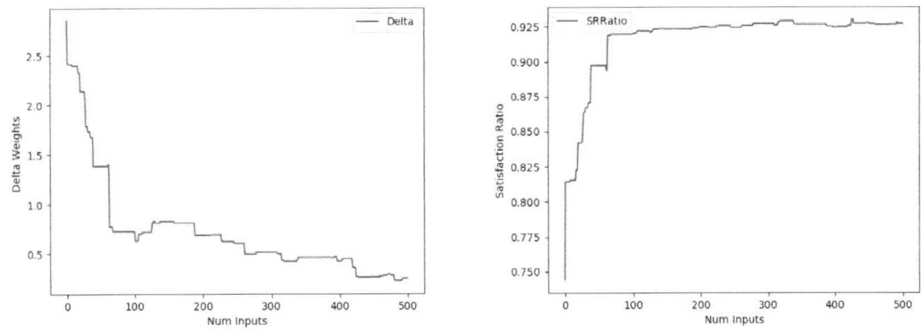

(a) (b)

Fig. 5. Performance evaluation against numbers of user responses for a single trial on the synthetic dataset using the metrics (a) delta weight, and (b) satisfaction ratio, respectively.

does so by using the hidden ground-truth weights to compute the ground-truth distances between the objects presented to it. CLUES, on the other hand, randomly initializes the weights it stores that are later to be recovered. CLUES then keeps asking new comparative questions without replacement, and records the responses it receives from the emulator. The weights stored in CLUES system will then be updated according to the optimization objective given in Eq. (2). The performance of CLUES is then assessed based on the quality of the recovered weights. This can be done either by comparing the weights recovered by CLUES against the ground-truth weights predefined by the emulator, or by using the proposed *Satisfaction Ratio* score, which we discuss next.

4.3 Performance Assessment Using Satisfaction Ratios

In fact, it can be shown that it is not possible in general to recover the ground-truth weights exactly simply based on user responses to comparative inquiries, as there may exist several different weight vectors that satisfy the constraints formed by the user responses to the comparative inquiries. To avoid the preceding issue in evaluating CLUES, we proposed to use a devised measure score called *Satisfaction Ratio* (SR) alongside with the weight difference. In a nutshell, SR is the percentage of satisfied distance constraints, where distances are induced by the recovered weights. More specifically, recall that the emulator introduced previously assumes a ground-truth weight vector. For any $\{o_i, o_j, o_h\}$ with o_h being an anchor object and o_i, o_j being a pair of comparative objects, the ground-truth weights can be used to dictate the comparison result made on $\{o_i, o_j, o_h\}$. Also, using the recovered weights, one can also obtain a comparison result predicted by CLUES on $\{o_i, o_j, o_h\}$. SR is simply the percentage of all possible object sets $\{o_i, o_j, o_h\}$ where the comparison results provided by the emulator and that predicted by CLUES's recovered weights match. Fig. 5 plots

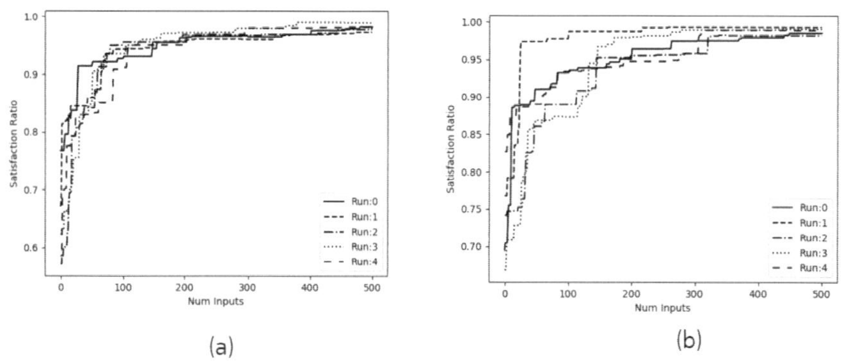

Fig. 6. Satisfaction Ratio achieved by CLUES in multiple trials on (a) Gaussian-mixture dataset, and (b) PubFig dataset, respectively.

the two evaluation metrics, namely delta weight and SR, against the number of inquiries for a single trial on the synthetic dataset. Here, delta weight is the metric we used for weight difference, which is the sum of the absolute difference between the ground-truth weight vector and the recovered weight vector. Obviously, as the user responds to more comparative inquiries, CLUES accumulates more information which improves the quality of the recovered weights. This is reflected on both delta weight and SR, as the former decreases and the latter increases with the number of user responses. Similar results were obtained by applying the emulator to both the Gaussian-mixture dataset and the PubFig dataset for multiple trials; see Fig. 6. Specifically, in both datasets, each object was characterized by a selected set of ten features, with two of them randomly chosen to be deemed as important by the emulator. As suggested by Fig. 6, high SRs were achieved for both datasets in all trial runs within hundreds of user responses to randomly generated comparative inquiries, whereas the total possible comparative inquires can be more than thousands.

4.4 Observations and Next Steps

From the plots in Fig. 5 and Fig. 6, we note that there are obvious jumps and flat regions in the curves. This suggests that sometimes a response provides no additional information at all as the distance constraints formed by some user responses may have already been asserted by previously formed constraints. Also, among those useful responses, some are more informative than others, as can be seen from the sudden jumps appearing in the curves of both Fig. 5 and Fig. 6. This can be attributed to the fact that comparisons made on objects that are more distinctive tend to provide more hints on the user's intent, resulting in a boost in the SR score. We also note that while CLUES usually achieves good SR eventually, it may require an excessive number of user responses to do so. This is because the objects chosen for comparison were randomly selected.

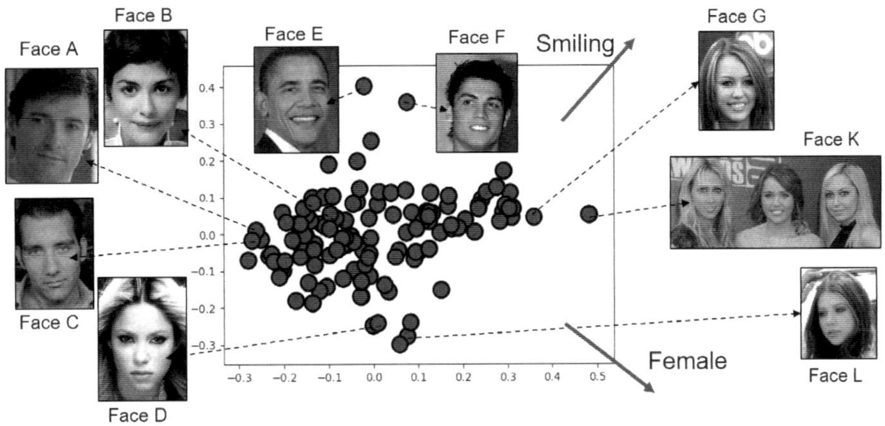

Fig. 7. Face Similarity visualisation using MDS representation

The preceding observations strongly suggest that if we carefully choose the objects to compare, one can achieve a good SR score with a relatively small number of user responses. In fact, for the PubFig dataset, we handpicked three representative comparative inquiries and found that they were sufficient for CLUES to achieve an SR score of 93% . This convinced us that further investigation is needed on how to sample objects to compare wisely so that good SR scores can be achieved with a very few number of user responses.

To further assess the quality of the weights recovered based on only those three user responses, we visualized the 128 images from the PubFig dataset on a 2D plane via MDS, which attempts to preserve the pairwise distances induced by the recovered weights; see Fig. 7. Here, the ground-truth weights dictate that "gender" and "whether smiling or not" are the two important features that reflect the user's intent. As can be seen from Fig. 7, the visualization enabled by the recovered weights clearly identifies "gender" and "whether smiling or not" as the focused features. Specifically, the directions highlighted by the two solid-line arrows correspond to the axes for attribute values of "gender" and "whether smiling or not," respectively. Fig. 7 also provides some sample face images, which confirm the fact that these image objects are distributed based on their similarity in the two features. For instance, Face E and Face F are both male/smiling faces, and are located close to each other. Face A and Face C, both male with a neutral expression of smiling, also appear close to each other, but they are further away from Face E and Face F.

5 Summary and Conclusions

Finding similar objects in a large corpus of data is often an important task in data analytics. This task vastly depends on quantification of object similarity, which however, is very difficult and highly subjective to a user's intent. Finding a suitable between-object distance function and an intuitive way to translate and encode users' intent to the distance function also presents huge challenges. This paper proposed a framework called CLUES to address the preceding issues. Specifically, it assumes a distance function formed by a weighted sum of individual feature differences, where the weights are intended to reflect a user's intent. It then incorporates the user's intent by asking the user to compare sampled objects, whose results can be used to recover the weights. Our prelimary results showed that CLUES is able to recover feature weights with satisfactory accuracy and high SR scores. This paper also suggests that wisely sampling what to compare can greatly reduce the number of user responses required for a high SR score; this provides a promising direction for future research. CLUES is general and can be applied to a wide range of datasets for intent-aware similarity quantification, an important task that improves data analytics applications like clustering and analysis of failure root cause.

References

1. Leman, S.C. et al. "Visual to Parametric Interaction (V2PI)." *PloS one*, 8(3), p.e50474, 2013.
2. Self, J.Z. et al. *Andromeda : Observation-Level and Parametric Interaction for Exploratory Data Analysis.* in Technical report, Department of Computer Science, Virginia Tech, Blacksburg, Virginia, 2015.
3. Arendt, D. et al. "CHISSL: A Human-Machine Collaboration Space for Unsupervised Learning." *Proc. International Conference on Augmented Cognition*, pp.429-448, 2017.
4. Kumar, N. et al. "Attribute and simile classifiers for face verification." *Proc. International Conference on Computer Vision (ICCV)*, pp.365-372, 2009.
5. Amazon Mechanical Turk, https://www.mturk.com/. Last accessed 14 March 2019
6. Cox, M.A. and Cox, T.F. *Multidimensional Scaling.* in Handbook of Data Visualization, pp. 315-347, Springer, Berlin, Heidelberg, 2008.
7. Cortes, C., Vapnik V. "Support-Vector Networks." *Proc. Journal of Machine Learning* 20(3), pp.273-297, 1995.

A Common Gene Expression Signature Analysis Method for Multiple Types of Cancer

Yingcheng Sun, Xiangru Liang and Kenneth Loparo

Case Western Reserve University, Cleveland OH 44106, USA
{yxs489, xxl487, kal4}@case.edu

Abstract. Mining gene expression profiles has proven valuable for identifying signatures serving as surrogates of cancer phenotypes. However, the similarities of such signatures across different cancer types have not been strong enough to conclude that they represent a universal biological mechanism shared among multiple cancer types. Here we describe a network-based approach that explores gene-to-gene connections in multiple cancer datasets while maximizing the overall association of the subnetwork with clinical outcomes. With the dataset of The Cancer Genome Atlas (TCGA), we studied the characteristics of common gene expression of three types of cancers: Rectum adenocarcinoma (READ), Breast invasive carcinoma (BRCA) and Colon adenocarcinoma (COAD). By analyzing several pairs of highly correlated genes after filtering and clustering work, we found that the co-expressed genes across multiple types of cancers point to particular biological mechanisms related to cancer cell progression, suggesting that they represent important attributes of cancer in need of being elucidated for potential applications in diagnostic, prognostic and therapeutic products applicable to multiple cancer types.

Keywords: Gene Expression Signature, Gene Network, Cancer.

1 Introduction

Cancer is known to be not just one disease, but many diseases, as evidenced by the diversity of its pathological manifestations. With the goal of clinically stratifying samples into risk groups, several gene expression biomarkers have been proposed for a large variety of cancer types [1, 2]. Most biomarkers have been identified and designed for a specific type of cancer, but it has been appreciated that there exist some unifying capabilities or "hallmarks" that can be used as tumor markers, characterizing all cancers because they exhibit similar biomolecular phenotypes [3]. Furthermore, it has been recognized that gene expression signatures resulting from analysis of cancer datasets can serve as surrogates of cancer phenotypes [4]. Therefore, it is reasonable to hypothesize that computational analysis of rich biomolecular cancer datasets may reveal signatures that are shared across many cancer types and are associated with specific cancer phenotypes, and are related to sustaining proliferative, insensitivity to anti-growth signals, metastasis, and etc [3].

Gene expression signatures that can be applied for a broad range of cancers could be highly useful in research and clinical settings. In clinics, such signatures may serve as a standard assessment for facilitating the interpretation and broad application of laboratory test results, simplifying laboratory protocols, and reducing costs. In research, these signatures may help to elucidate broadly observed biological mechanisms and possible drug targets [8].

With the availability of rich data sets from many different cancer types provides an opportunity for thorough computational data mining in search of such common patterns. Distinct algorithms and strategies have been used to identify common gene expression signatures: regulatory network [5], clustering approaches [6] and other related techniques. In this paper, we use gene co-expression network and develop a statistical method of common gene expression signature analysis for multiple types of cancer.

Previous research evaluates such common patterns within a couple of cancer types [7, 8], but never explore the following three cancer types together: Colon adenocarcinoma (COAD), Rectum adenocarcinoma (READ) and Breast invasive carcinoma (BRCA). In this paper, we use the above three types of cancer for experiment. Our purpose is to identify gene expression pattern across multi-cancers, and reveal hallmarks of cancer, and thus helps to find bio-markers associated with different types of cancer, and contributes to the prognosis of cancer.

2 Method

A co-expression network identifies which genes have a tendency to show a coordinated expression pattern across a group of samples. This co-expression network can be represented as a gene–gene similarity matrix, which can be used in downstream analyses [9]. Canonical co-expression network construction and analyses can be described with the following three steps.

To begin with, one needs to define a measure of similarity between the gene expression profiles. This similarity measures the level of concordance between gene expression profiles across the experiments. Individual relationships between genes are defined based on correlation measures [29] or mutual information [10] between each pair of genes. Different measures of correlation have been used to construct networks, including Pearson's or Spearman's correlations [11]. Alternatively, least absolute error regression [12] or a Bayesian approach [13] can be used to construct a co-expression network [14]. In this paper, we use the commonly used Pearson's correlation as follows:

$$\tau = \frac{1}{n}\sum_{i=1}^{n}(\frac{x_i - \bar{x}}{\sigma_x})(\frac{y_i - \bar{y}}{\sigma_y})$$

where σ_x is the standard deviation of x and $\sigma_y$is the standard deviation of y.

In the second step, co-expression associations are used to construct a network where each node represents a gene and each edge represents the presence and the strength of the co-expression relationship [15]. In order to filter out the genes that are not related to cancer, we select genes expressed differently between cancer samples and normal samples with T-test. To get the common gene expression signatures, we choose the genes existed in all the types of cancer samples.

In the third step, modules (groups of co-expressed genes) are identified using one of several available clustering techniques. Clustering in co-expression analyses is used to group genes with similar expression patterns across multiple samples to produce groups of co-expressed genes rather than only pairs. The clustering method needs to be chosen with consideration because it can greatly influence the outcome and meaning of the analysis. Many clustering methods are available, such as k-means, self-organizing maps (SOM) and etc. In this paper, we use k-means as our clustering algorithm because it is faster and produce tighter clusters than other clustering methods [23, 24, 25]. Modules can subsequently be interpreted by functional enrichment analysis, a method to identify and rank overrepresented functional categories in a list of genes [16, 17].

3 Experiment

The datasets we used in our experiments are the level 3 data of three types of cancer from The Cancer Genome Atlas (TCGA): Rectum adenocarcinoma (READ), Breast invasive carcinoma (BRCA) and Colon adenocarcinoma (COAD). For each type of cancer, cancer samples and normal samples are randomly picked up from the same batch. Table 1 lists the number of selected genes and samples.

Table 1. Number of genes and samples selected

No	Cancer	Gene Number	Caner Sample	Normal Sample
1	BCRA	17814	10	10
2	COAD	17814	10	10
3	READ	17814	10	3
Total		53442	30	23

The database does not supply enough number of normal samples for READ, so we only use three normal samples as the comparison with cancer samples. Besides, all the gene expression data are detected by Agilent microarrays with the same processing and normalization way by the following formula shows, so they are comparable.

$$log_2\left(\frac{Cy5}{Cy3}\right) = log_2\left(\frac{sample}{control}\right)$$

3.1 Find Genes Expressed Differently between Cancer and Normal Samples

Firstly, we want to find the genes expressed differently between cancer and normal samples since these genes are more possible to be the target genes than those with the similar expressions between cancer samples and normal samples.

T-test can be used here to determine if two sets of data are significantly different from each other. Before doing T-test, we need to use F-test to examine the homogeneity of variance between two data sets. We select the data with p value larger than 0.05 after T-test. Table 2 shows the number of genes left.

Table 2. Number of genes left after t-test

No	Gene	Original	After F-test	After T-test
1	BCRA	17814	12208	4535
2	COAD	17814	12721	6635
3	READ	17814	16349	4939
Total		53442	41278	**16109**

3.2 Select Common Genes among Different Cancers

Next, we select the genes appeared in all the three gene sets and called them "common genes", because we are interested in finding the common patterns across multiple cancer types. 878 common genes are then selected from 16109 genes obtained in last step after T-test. Table 3 lists the results.

Table 3. Number of genes appeared in different cancer sets

Genes	Number
Appear in Only One Cancers	6676
Appear in Only Two Cancers	3398
Appear in All Three Cancers	**878**

We then list the cancer samples expressed by each gene of the three types of cancers, and obtain a gene-expression matrix with 878 rows and 30 columns, where the gene expression data of each type of cancer are represented by 10 columns of values.

3.3 Cluster Common Genes

With the common gene expression matrix, we can find the closely related genes with similar gene expression through clustering, which might give us clues of seeking bio-events for cancers. We use Pearson Correlation as the gene similarity metric and k-means as the clustering algorithm with the number of clusters set to 20. We use the SPSS Statistics software package (version 22) to process the data and export the analysis results. After clustering, we have 814 genes valid (92.7 %) and 64 genes missing

(7.3%). It shows that most of the genes have high correlation and can be clustered into multiple groups. Fig. 1 shows the gene network.

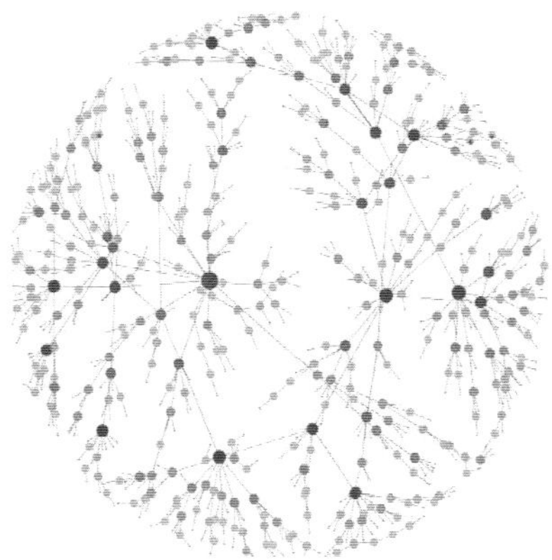

Fig. 1. Common gene network of selected 878 genes

In each cluster, we chose the pair of genes with highest coefficient as Table 4 shows. These genes may be related to the cancer specific bio-events, and we will discuss the significance of them in next section.

Table 4. Pair of genes with highest coefficient in each cluster

Cluster	Pair of Genes		Coefficient
Cluster1	MT1H	MT1B	0.984
Cluster2	PTTG3	PTTG1	0.982
Cluster3	PDGFD	APOD	0.941
…	…	…	…
Cluster20	FBLN5	RBMS3	0.935

3.4 Cluster Samples

Besides clustering genes, we also try to find whether there are some interesting results by clustering samples. We first transpose gene-expression matrix, and then use the Pearson Correlation as the similarity metric and Between-Groups Linkage as the clustering algorithm. We only have 1 case missing and obtained a valid rate of 96.7 % for all the 30 samples. Figure 2 shows the dendrogram of clustering result. We can see that there are basically two groups of samples after clustering.

The significance of the clustering is evaluated by its statistical results. The results are basically classified into two classes: "between groups" and "within groups" values. We want the clusters with short "within group" linkage and long "between group" linkage. There are only one sample out of thirty with p value larger than 0.05:

READ-TCGA-AF-3400-01A-01R-0821-07 with 0.8. The p values of the all rest samples are less than 0.05, making the clustering significance to be 96.7%.

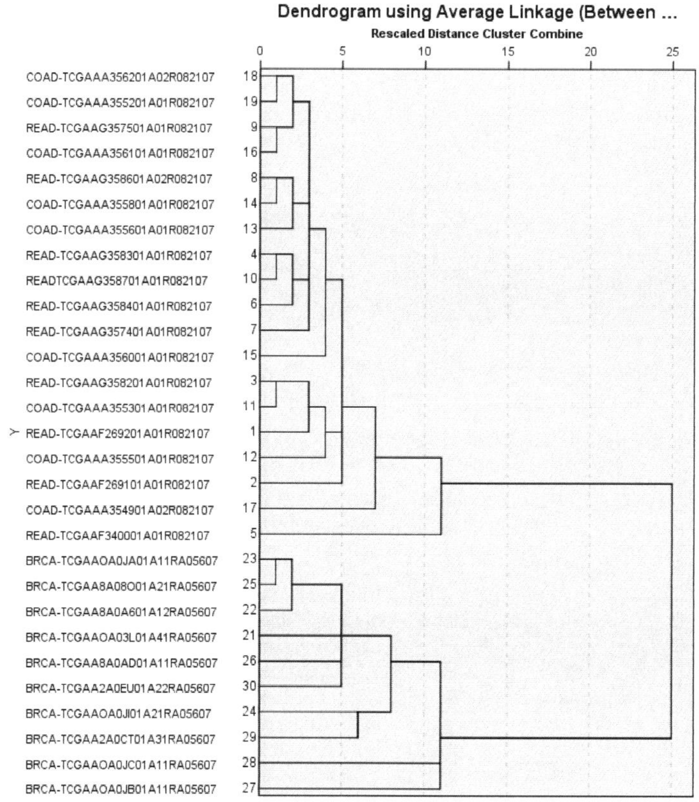

Fig. 2. Dendrogram of the clustering result

4 Analysis

We respectively choose three pairs of genes from three clusters: APOD and PDGFD, RBMS3 and FBLN5, TUBB6 and DDR2. Genes in each pair are highly related to each other, meaning their expression patterns are similar in all cases. As shown in Fig 3, each pair of genes is positively related under each type of cancer. Additionally, the values and relationships of gene expressions are closer in cancer COAD and READ, and separated from BRCA. It corresponds to the fact that rectum is a part of colon, so the origins of COAD and READ are closer, and they may share lots of commons.

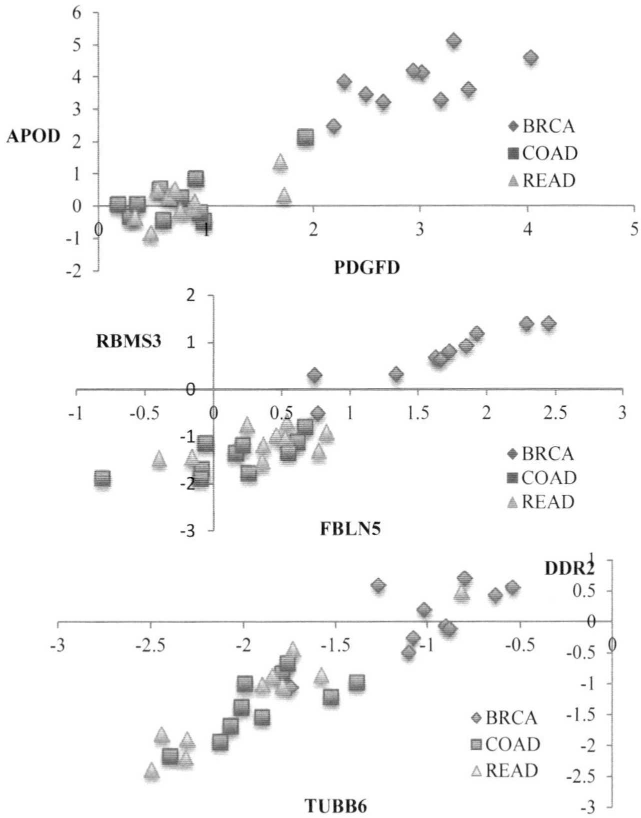

Fig. 3. Gene co-expression in three types of cancers

Let's focus on each pair of genes separately. In the first pair, PDGFD encodes platelet derived growth factor D, which promotes cancer progression [19]. Compared to normal samples, PDGFD is down regulated in the cancer samples. However, it makes no sense because cancer cells tend to grow rapidly and uncontrolledly, so it may up-regulate the gene expression of growth factors. APOD – apolipoprotein D is a good prognostic marker, and it is expressed differently in COAD and READ cancer samples, which may represent different patient prognosis conditions. Other genes such as FBLN5 – fibulin 5, plays a role in proliferation, migration and invasion [20], TUBB6 – tubulin beta 6, malignant transformation and drug resistance and DDR2 – discoidin domain receptor try kinase 2, which promotes matastasis. According to the other research, all these genes should contribute to cancer cells progression, but they are down regulated in the cancer samples. It may be explained by fact that patients are receiving treatments and they are turning good, so the genes promoting cancer progression are down regulated. In terms of RBMS3 – single stranded interacting protein 3 that inhibits cell proliferation is also down regulated, but it makes sense because this protein is encoded by the gene serve as a tumor suppressor. Figure 4 shows the difference of these gene expressed in normal and cancer samples.

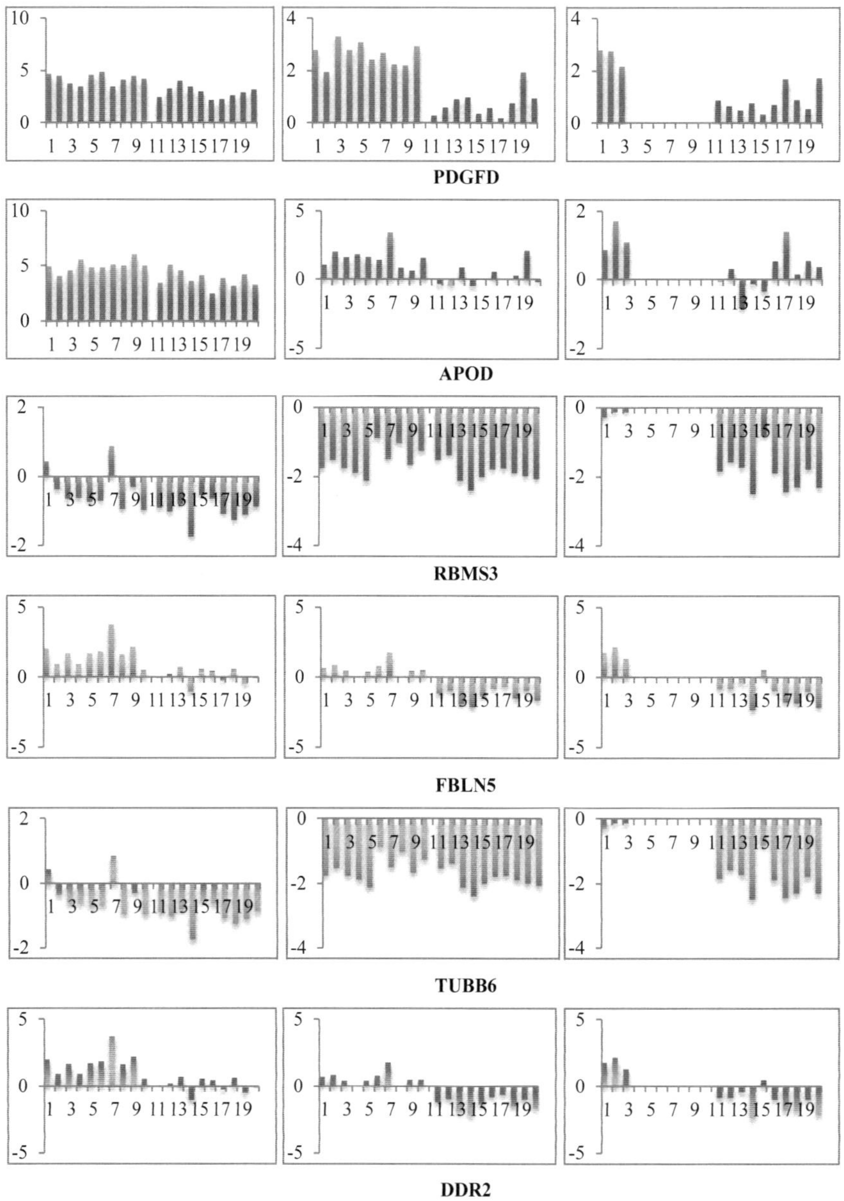

Fig. 4. Gene expression in normal (blue color) and cancer samples (red color) for three types of cancer: COAD, READ and BRCA

From the clustering result of sample in Figure 2, we can see that COAD and READ have closer relationships, and the patients of these two cancers mix together, while BRCA forms a separate cluster as Table 5 shows, that is an evidence of the above analysis.

Table 5. Clustering results of samples

Cluster	Number of Cancer Samples		
	COAD	READ	BRCA
Cluster1	10	9	0
Cluster2	0	0	10

5 Discussion

We study the real functions of the genes selected from each cluster by searching the National Center for Biotechnology Information (NCBI) database, and pay more attention to the genes that are cell essential or related to disease. In one cluster, two genes are found related to tumor suppression and migration. FLNA encodes filamin A, alpha, that is involved in remodeling the cytoskeleton to effect changes in cell shape and migration. Previous research shows that FLNA plays an important role in cancer proliferation and metastasis [18]. FLNA also interacts with oncogenesis and metastasis related proteins, meaning that it is essential for cancer progression. GAS1 is growth arrest-specific 1 which encodes GAS1 protein to blocks cells to enter S phase, so it is considered as a tumor suppress gene, and previous research suggests that GAS1 expression significantly reduce the colony-forming ability of gastric cancer cells in vitro and cell growth in vivo [21]. In Figure 5, we can see that in BRCA cancer, FLNA and GAS1 are positive related. In COAD and READ, it seems that FLNA and GAS1 do not have any relevance but their expression values are close to each other according to the dataset.

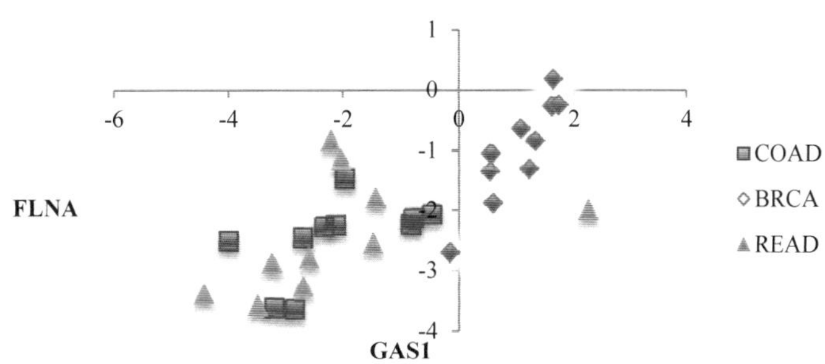

Fig. 5. Expression of gene FLNA and GAS1 in three types of cancers

In the future, we are interested in using machine learning methods [22, 26, 27, 31] to find more possible gene signatures, and combine the medical knowledge to explain them [28, 30].

Acknowledgment

This work was supported by the Ohio Department of Higher Education, the Ohio Federal Research Network and the Wright State Applied Research Corporation under award WSARC-16-00530 (C4ISR: Human-Centered Big Data).

References

1. Chen, R., Khatri, P., Mazur, P.K., Polin, M., Zheng, Y., Vaka, D., Hoang, C.D., Shrager, J., Xu, Y., Vicent, S. and Butte, A.J.: A meta-analysis of lung cancer gene expression identifies PTK7 as a survival gene in lung adenocarcinoma. Cancer research 74(10), 2892-2902 (2014)
2. Peng, Z., Skoog, L., Hellborg, H., Jonstam, G., Wingmo, I.L., Hjälm-Eriksson, M., Harmenberg, U., Cedermark, G.C., Andersson, K., Ährlund-Richter, L. and Pramana, S.: An expression signature at diagnosis to estimate prostate cancer patients' overall survival. Prostate cancer and prostatic diseases 17(1), 81 (2014).
3. Hanahan, D. and Weinberg, R.A.: Hallmarks of cancer: the next generation. cell, 144(5), 646-674 (2011)
4. Nevins, J.R. and Potti, A.: Mining gene expression profiles: expression signatures as cancer phenotypes. Nature Reviews Genetics 8(8), 601 (2007)
5. Segal, E., Friedman, N., Kaminski, N., Regev, A. and Koller, D.: From signatures to models: understanding cancer using microarrays. Nature genetics 37(6s), S38 (2005)
6. Collisson, E.A., Sadanandam, A., Olson, P., Gibb, W.J., Truitt, M., Gu, S., Cooc, J., Weinkle, J., Kim, G.E., Jakkula, L. and Feiler, H.S.: Subtypes of pancreatic ductal adenocarcinoma and their differing responses to therapy. Nature medicine 17(4), 500 (2011)
7. Cheng, W.Y., Yang, T.H.O. and Anastassiou, D.: Biomolecular events in cancer revealed by attractor metagenes. PLoS computational biology, 9(2), p.e1002920 (2013)
8. Martinez-Ledesma, E., Verhaak, R.G. and Treviño, V.: Identification of a multi-cancer gene expression biomarker for cancer clinical outcomes using a network-based algorithm. Scientific reports, 5, p.11966 (2015)
9. Van Dam, S., Vosa, U., van der Graaf, A., Franke, L. and de Magalhaes, J.P.: Gene co-expression analysis for functional classification and gene–disease predictions. Briefings in bioinformatics, 19(4), 575-592 (2017)
10. Margolin, A.A., Nemenman, I., Basso, K., Wiggins, C., Stolovitzky, G., Dalla Favera, R. and Califano, A.: ARACNE: an algorithm for the reconstruction of gene regulatory networks in a mammalian cellular context. BMC bioinformatics, Vol. 7, No. 1, p. S7 (2006)
11. Ala, U., Piro, R.M., Grassi, E., Damasco, C., Silengo, L., Oti, M., Provero, P. and Di Cunto, F.: Prediction of human disease genes by human-mouse conserved coexpression analysis. PLoS computational biology, 4(3), p.e1000043 (2008)
12. van Someren, E.P., Vaes, B.L., Steegenga, W.T., Sijbers, A.M., Dechering, K.J. and Reinders, M.J.: Least absolute regression network analysis of the murine osteoblast differentiation network. Bioinformatics, 22(4), 477-484 (2005)

13. Friedman, N., Linial, M., Nachman, I. and Pe'er, D.: Using Bayesian networks to analyze expression data. Journal of computational biology, 7(3-4), 601-620 (2000)
14. D'haeseleer, P., Liang, S. and Somogyi, R.: Genetic network inference: from co-expression clustering to reverse engineering. Bioinformatics, 16(8), 707-726 (2000)
15. Albert, R. and Barabási, A.L.: Statistical mechanics of complex networks. Reviews of modern physics, 74(1), p.47 (2002)
16. Gupta, S., Ellis, S.E., Ashar, F.N., Moes, A., Bader, J.S., Zhan, J., West, A.B. and Arking, D.E.: Transcriptome analysis reveals dysregulation of innate immune response genes and neuronal activity-dependent genes in autism. Nature communications, 5, p.5748 (2014)
17. De Magalhães, J.P., Finch, C.E. and Janssens, G.: Next-generation sequencing in aging research: emerging applications, problems, pitfalls and possible solutions. Ageing research reviews, 9(3), 315-323 (2010)
18. Zhang, K., Zhu, T., Gao, D., Zhang, Y., Zhao, Q., Liu, S., Su, T., Bernier, M. and Zhao, R.: Filamin A expression correlates with proliferation and invasive properties of human metastatic melanoma tumors: implications for survival in patients. Journal of cancer research and clinical oncology, 140(11), 1913-1926 (2014)
19. Wang, Y., Qiu, H., Hu, W., Li, S. and Yu, J.: Over-expression of platelet-derived growth factor-D promotes tumor growth and invasion in endometrial cancer. International journal of molecular sciences, 15(3), 4780-4794 (2014)
20. Hwang, C.F., Shiu, L.Y., Su, L.J., Yin, Y.F., Wang, W.S., Huang, S.C., Chiu, T.J., Huang, C.C., Zhen, Y.Y., Tsai, H.T. and Fang, F.M.: Oncogenic fibulin-5 promotes nasopharyngeal carcinoma cell metastasis through the FLJ10540/AKT pathway and correlates with poor prognosis. PloS one, 8(12), p.e84218 (2013)
21. Wang, H., Zhou, X., Zhang, Y., Zhu, H., Zhao, L., Fan, L., Wang, Y., Gang, Y., Wu, K., Liu, Z. and Fan, D.: Growth arrest-specific gene 1 is downregulated and inhibits tumor growth in gastric cancer. The FEBS journal, 279(19), 3652-3664 (2012)
22. Sun, Y., Li, Q.: The research situation and prospect analysis of meta-search engines. In: 2nd International Conference on Uncertainty Reasoning and Knowledge Engineering, pp. 224-229. IEEE, Jalarta, Indonesia (2012).
23. Li, Q., Zou, Y., Sun, Y.: Ontology based user personalization mechanism in meta search engine. In: 2nd International Conference on Uncertainty Reasoning and Knowledge Engineering, pp. 230-234. IEEE, Jalarta, Indonesia (2012).
24. Li, Q., Sun, Y., Xue, B.: Complex query recognition based on dynamic learning mechanism. Journal of Computational Information Systems 8(20), 8333-8340 (2012).
25. Li, Q., Zou, Y., Sun, Y.: User Personalization Mechanism in Agent-based Meta Search Engine. Journal of Computational Information Systems 8(20), 1-8 (2012).
26. Li, Q., Sun, Y.: An agent based intelligent meta search engine. In: International Conference on Web Information Systems and Mining, pp. 572-579. Springer, Berlin, Heidelberg (2012).
27. Sun, Y., Loparo, K.: Context Aware Image Annotation in Active Learning with Batch Mode. In: 43rd Annual Computer Software and Applications Conference (COMPSAC), vol. 1, pp. 952-953. IEEE (2019).
28. Sun, Y., Loparo, K.: A Clicked-URL Feature for Transactional Query Identification. In 2019 IEEE 43rd Annual Computer Software and Applications Conference (COMPSAC), vol. 1, pp. 950-951. IEEE (2019).
29. Sun, Y., Loparo, K.: Topic Shift Detection in Online Discussions using Structural Context. In 2019 IEEE 43rd Annual Computer Software and Applications Conference (COMPSAC) , vol. 1, pp. 948-949. IEEE (2019).

30. Sun, Y., Loparo, K.: Information Extraction from Free Text in Clinical Trials with Knowledge-Based Distant Supervision. In: IEEE 43rd Annual Computer Software and Applications Conference (COMPSAC), vol. 1, pp. 954-955. IEEE (2019).
31. Sun, Y., Loparo, K.: Learning - based Adaptation Framework for Elastic Software Systems. In: Proceedings of 31st International Conference on Software Engineering & Knowledge Engineering, pp. 281-286. IEEE, Lisbon, Portugal (2019).

A Deep Learning Framework for Classification of *in vitro* Multi-Electrode Array Recordings

Yun Zhao[1], Elmer Guzman[2,3], Morgane Audouard[2,3], Zhuowei Cheng[1], Paul K. Hansma[2], Kenneth S. Kosik[2,3], and Linda Petzold[1]

[1] Department of Computer Science, University of California, Santa Barbara
[2] Neuroscience Research Institute, University of California, Santa Barbara
[3] Department of Molecular Cellular and Developmental Biology, University of California, Santa Barbara
yunzhao@cs.ucsb.edu

Abstract. Multi-Electrode Arrays (MEAs) have been widely used to record neuronal activities, which could be used in the diagnosis of gene defects and drug effects. In this paper, we address the problem of classifying *in vitro* MEA recordings of mouse and human neuronal cultures from different genotypes, where there is no easy way to directly utilize raw sequences as inputs to train an end-to-end classification model. While carefully extracting some features by hand could partially solve the problem, this approach suffers from obvious drawbacks such as difficulty of generalizing. We propose a deep learning framework to address this challenge. Our approach correctly classifies neuronal culture data prepared from two different genotypes — a mouse Knockout of the delta-catenin gene and human induced Pluripotent Stem Cell-derived neurons from Williams syndrome. By splitting the long recordings into short slices for training, and applying Consensus Prediction during testing, our deep learning approach improves the prediction accuracy by 16.69% compared with feature based Logistic Regression for mouse MEA recordings. We further achieve an accuracy of 95.91% using Consensus Prediction in one subset of mouse MEA recording data, which were all recorded at six days *in vitro*. As high-density MEA recordings become more widely available, this approach could be generalized for classification of neurons carrying different mutations and classification of drug responses.

Keywords: Deep learning · Convolutional neural network · Classification · MEAs.

1 Introduction

Deep learning models have achieved remarkable success in computer vision [1], speech recognition [2], natural language processing [3] and the game of Go [4]. Recently there has been increasing interest in using deep learning in end-to-end neuroscience data analysis [6, 5, 7]. Inspired by biology, deep learning models share many common properties with neuron functions. Deep learning models enable the extraction of information from action potential recordings of neuron activity, playing a vital role in several important neuron-based research and application areas [8].

Convolutional neural networks (CNN) can learn local patterns in data by using convolution filters as their key components [9]. Originally developed for computer vision, CNN models have recently been shown to be effective for neuroscience data analysis. Deep learning has recently been used to identify abnormal EEG signals [5]. In [6], researchers designed an end-to-end EEG decoding for movement-related information using deep CNNs. With the latest development in fabrication of MEAs, a CNN was used to classify different neuronal cell types using simulated in-vivo extracellular recordings [10]. However, most of the work in this area has focused on simulated data [10, 11] since the experimental *in vitro* recordings are too noisy and there are not sufficient training samples for deep learning models. Researchers have also manually extracted features for deep learning training [10, 11]. However, this does not fully exploit the deep learning model's ability of end-to-end learning, which learns from the raw data without any prior feature selection.

MEAs with advanced neural probes have been widely utilized to measure neuronal activity by recording local field potential [12]. Since the same units are measured on multiple recording sites, MEA recordings provide rich spatial information, which could be used to help diagnose diseases and genetic abnormalities. Our objective in this work has been to develop a deep learning framework which can distinguish MEA recordings of different genotypes. For example, delta-catenin is a crucial brain-specific protein of the adherens junction complex that localizes to the postsynaptic and dendritic compartments. It is enriched in dendrites and can be localized to the post-synaptic compartment. Recent studies indicate that delta-catenin is required for the maintenance of neural structure and function in the mature cortex [13–15]. Williams syndrome (WS) is a neurodevelopmental disorder caused by a genomic deletion of about 28 genes [16, 17]. As a result of this hemideletion, the subjects display a characteristic phenotype with mild to moderate intellectual disability as well as behavioral features such as an outgoing personality and conserved communication skills. Studying those genes is of particular interest in order to decipher the social behaviors in humans [18].

In the present work, we propose an end-to-end CNN architecture to classify *in vitro* MEA recordings with different genotypes. We test our framework on mouse recordings to classify Wild Type and delta-catenin Knockout. We also attempt to classify human derived induced Pluripotent Stem Cell (iPSC) neuron cultures from Williams syndrome versus Control cultures. We split the long recordings into smaller slices for training to provide more training samples, and then apply Consensus Prediction during testing.

The key contributions of this paper include:

1) We propose a CNN based model to classify the genotype of *in vitro* MEA recordings, which outperforms Logistic Regression by 16.69%. To the best of our knowledge, this is the first paper using deep leaning to classify *in vitro* MEA recordings.

2) We split the long recordings into smaller slices for training, which not only eases the burden on GPU memory but also provides many training samples for deep learning models.

3) We define Consensus Prediction as the majority voting result of the sampled short slices for testing, since not all of the short slices can be expected to contain enough useful information. We achieve an accuracy of 95.91% using Consensus Prediction in one subset of MEA recording data, which were all recorded at 6 days *in vitro* (DIV).

The rest of this paper is organized as follows. Section 2 describes how our MEAs are recorded and introduces the classification problem. We delineate the deep learning model in Section 3 and describe the experimental setup in Section 4. Evaluation and discussion are provided in Sections 5 and 6, respectively.

2 Data Collection and Classification

2.1 Mouse neuron culture

Commercial MEAs (MultiChannel Systems) were sterilized with UV irradiation for > 30 minutes, incubated with poly-L-lysine(0.1 mg/ml) solution for at least one hour at $37°C$, rinsed several times with sterile deionized water and allowed to dry before cell plating. Wild-type mice were in a C57BL/6 background and littermate controls were obtained by breeding heterozygote male and female delta-catenin transgenic mice. For the delta-catenin transgenic mice, a targeted mutation in the delta-catenin gene is located within axon 9 of the delta-catenin locus and consists of a GFP reporter fused to a PGK-hyygro-pA cassette followed by a stop condon, which results in the prevention of transcription of the rest of the delta-catenin gene. Mouse pups were decapitated at P0 or P1, the brains were removed from the skulls and the hippocampi were dissected from the brain followed by manual dissociation and plating of 250,000 cells in the MEA chamber [19]. After one week, cultures were treated with 200 μM glutamate to kill any remaining neurons, followed by a new batch of cells added at the same density as before. Cultures were grown in a tissue culture incubator ($37°C$, 5% CO_2), in a medium made with Minimum Essential Media with 2 mM Glutamax (Life Technologies), 5% heat-inactivated fetal calf serum (Life Technologies), 1 ml/L of Mito+ Serum Extender (BD Bioscience) and supplemented with glucose to an added concentration of 21 mM. All animals were treated in accordance with University of California and NIH policies on animal care and use.

2.2 Culture of iPSCs neurons

iPSCs were cultured in mTeSR1 media (Stem Cell Technologies) and routinely passaged with ReleSR (Stem Cell Technologies). The cells were subsequently infected with TetO-hNgn2-UBC-puro (plasmid from Addgene # 61474) and rtTA (plasmid from Addgene # 20342) lentiviruses. Briefly, the cells were passaged as single cells into 4 wells with accutase (Life Technologies) and Y-27632 dihydrochloride (Tocris) at a final concentration of 10 M. On day 2 the cells were infected with hNgn2 in fresh mTeSR1 media. On day 3, the infected iPSCs were selected by adding puromycin at 2 ug/ml for a 2 day period. The cells were infected with rtTA virus on day 5 and incubated overnight. The neurons were differentiated by adding doxycycline at a final concentration of 2 ug/ml. Two days after addition of doxycycline, the neurons were replated on poly-l-lysine coated MEAs at a density of 180,000 cells concentrated in a 15 ul droplet. iPSCs-derived neurons were cocultured with mouse primary astrocytes in BrainPhys complete medium (Stem Cell Technologies). Doxycycline was kept in the media for 14 days total.

2.3 Electrophysiology

We used 120 electrode MEAs (120MEA100/30iR-ITO arrays; MultiChannel Systems) for recording as is shown in Fig. 1. All recordings were performed in cell culture medium so as to minimally disturb the neurons. The osmolality of the culture medium was adjusted to 320 mosmol. Recordings were performed using MultiChannel Systems MEA 2100 acquisition system. Data were sampled at 20 kHz. Recordings were performed at 30°C. All recordings were performed on neurons at 2-30 DIV. Data recordings were typically 3 minutes long. The recording duration was controlled to minimize the effects of removing MEAs from the incubator.

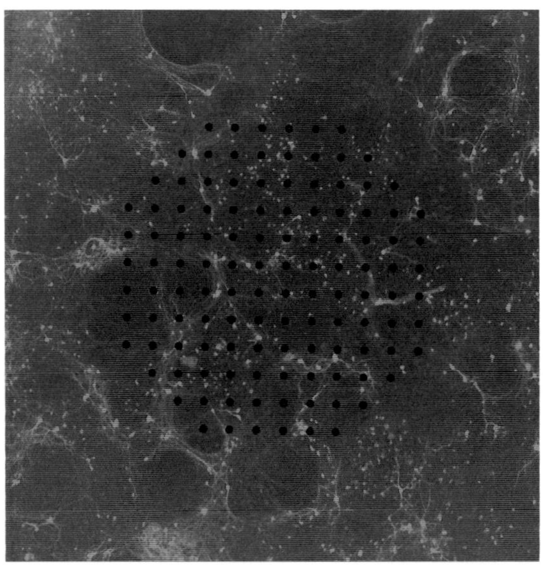

Fig. 1. Neural networks were grown on arrays of 120 electrodes. The purpose of this research was to determine whether neural cultures derived from genetically different neurons could be distinguished by analysis of their electrical activity.

2.4 Spike Detection

For each MEA recording, we performed spike detection [21]. Extracellular signals were band pass filtered using a digital 2nd order Butterworth filter with cutoff frequencies of 0.2 and 4 kHz. Spikes were then detected using a threshold of 5 times the standard deviation of the median noise level. Since there are 120 electrodes in our MultiChannel Systems, the spike detection result of a 3 min recording is a 120×180000 shape matrix made up of 1s and 0s, where 1 represents neuron firing and 0 represents not firing.

2.5 Classification

For the remainder of this paper, Wild Type (WT) means that there is no gene mutation. Knockout (KO) means that the gene delta-catenin is knocked out or not expressed in the mouse neurons. WS is Williams syndrome neurons, compared with Control. Fig. 2 shows Raster Plots for some sample mouse MEA recordings from WT and KO. From the figure, the recording patterns vary drastically according to different mice, different DIV and even different recording numbers. However, recordings of different genotypes sometimes perform similarly. It is challenging for human eyes to distinguish KO from WT. There are several reasons: 1. The recordings are noisy due to the errors in measuring potentials and spike detection. 2. The firing pattern will change drastically according to many factors like different DIV, different mice and even different recordings. A deep learning classification framework is therefore introduced to automatically predict the genotype, given an MEA recording.

We use two separate sets of MEA recordings in our classification: one dataset consists of mouse neuron recordings to classify KO and WT, while the other dataset consists of human iPSC neuron recordings to distinguish WS and Control human cells. Our mouse recordings consist of 5 separate experiments (Exp1, Exp2, Exp3, Exp4, Exp5) and 331 180000 ms recordings in total, of which 198 recordings are WT and the remainder are delta-catenin KO. Our iPSC recording data are made up of 12 WS recordings and 8 Control recordings. Considering the size of the two datasets, we randomly shuffle and split the mouse MEA data into training, validation and testing by 70%, 10% and 20%, while we apply 5-fold cross-validation for human iPSC recordings.

3 Deep Learning Model

The model architecture, shown in Fig. 3, consists of convolution-pooling layers followed by fully connected layers. To learn temporal and spatial invariant features, the convolution is performed on both time and space dimensions. We split the long recordings into smaller slices with length of seq_length. Detected spikes with shape of (120, seq_length) serve as input x for the neural network. A convolution operation involves a filter $w \in \mathbb{R}^{st}$, which is applied to a window of s electrodes and t ms to produce a new feature. For example, a feature

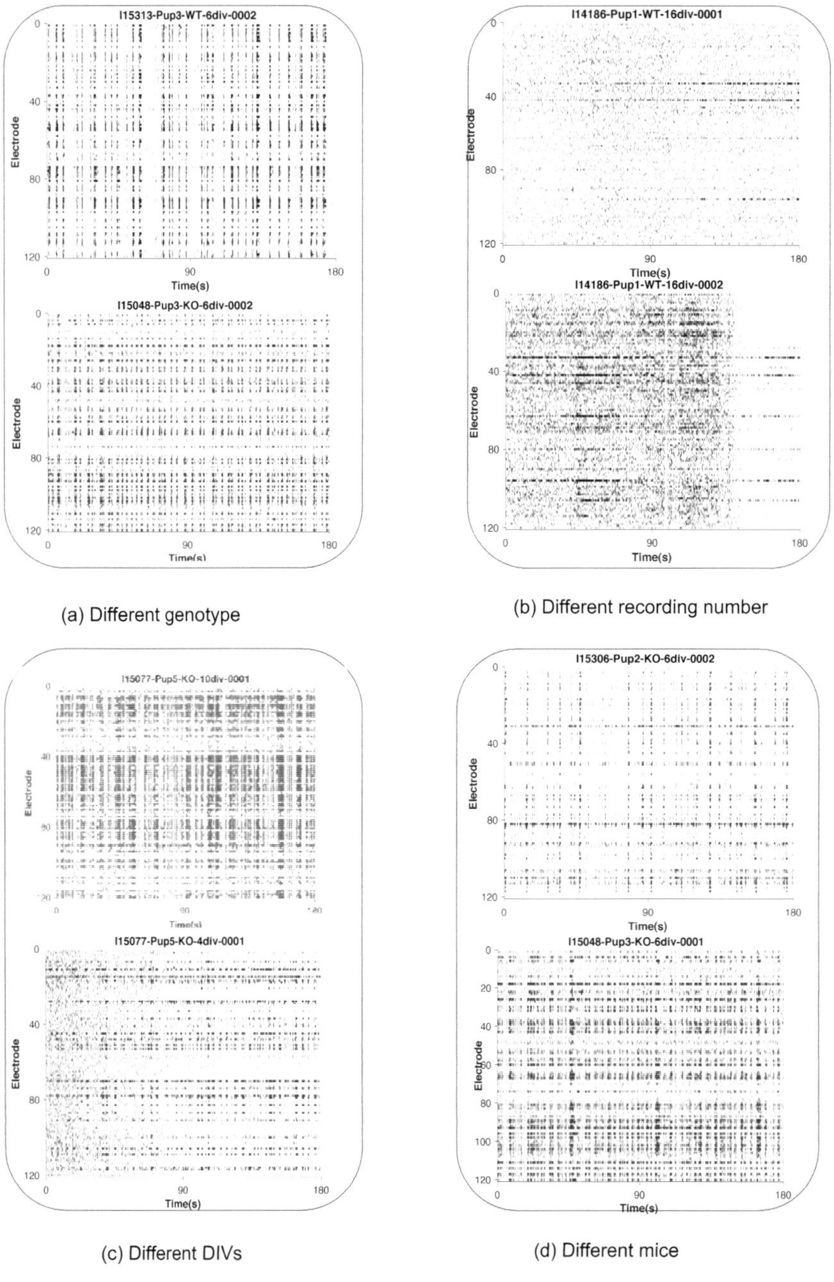

(a) Different genotype

(b) Different recording number

(c) Different DIVs

(d) Different mice

Fig. 2. Raster Plots of WT and delta-catenin KO. Blue represents WT and red indicates delta-catenin KO. The title of each raster plot is formatted as "MEA device-Mouse-Gene type-DIV-Record Number". (a) KO and WT share some common firing patterns. (b) Different recordings with the same gene type, as well as the same DIV look different. (c) Recordings with the same mouse, the same gene type but different DIV look different. (d) Recordings with the same gene type, the same DIV, but different mouse look different.

$f_{i,j}, (0 \leq i \leq 120 - s + 1, 0 \leq j \leq seq\_length - t + 1)$ is generated from a window size (s, t) of the spike train:

$$f_{i,j} = ReLU(wx_{i:i+s-1,j:j+t-1} + b), \quad (1)$$

where $b \in \mathbb{R}$ is a bias term. This filter is applied to each possible window of the spike trains to produce a feature map:

$$f = \begin{bmatrix} f_{1,1} & f_{1,2} & \cdots & f_{1,seq\_length-t+1} \\ f_{2,1} & f_{2,2} & \cdots & f_{2,seq\_length-t+1} \\ \cdots & \cdots & \cdots & \cdots \\ f_{120-s+1,1} & f_{120-s+1,2} & \cdots & f_{120-s+1,seq\_length-t+1} \end{bmatrix}, \quad (2)$$

with $f \in \mathbb{R}^{120-s+1,seq\_length-t+1}$. We then apply a max-pooling operation over the feature map and take the maximum value $m = \max f$ as the feature corresponding to this particular filter. The idea is to capture the most important feature, the one with the highest value, for each feature map. Our model uses multiple filters to obtain multiple features. These features form the penultimate layer and are passed to a fully connected softmax layer whose output is the probability distribution over two different genotypes. We adjust the number of convolutional ReLU layers from 2 to 5, based on the choice of seq_length.

We use Batch Normalization [25] to accelerate training. For regulaization, dropout [23] and early stopping methods [24] are implemented to avoid overfitting. Dropout prevents co-adaptation of hidden units by randomly dropping out a proportion of the hidden units during backpropagation. Model training is ended when no improvement is seen during the last 100 validations. Softmax cross entropy loss is minimized with the Adam optimizer [26] for training.

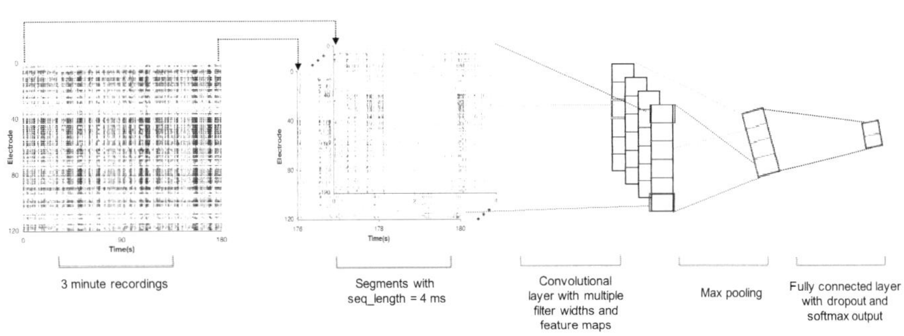

Fig. 3. Model architecture: 3 minute recordings of the electrical potentials measured on the 120 electrodes are collected form the neuron cultures. Segments with seq_length = 4 ms of these recordings are individually classified. These individual classifications are conducted for Consensus Prediction in mouse MEA recordings.

4 Experimental Setup

4.1 Training and Hyperparameters

We use 1 ms time bins for our spike train data, thus the dimensionality of time is extremely high. For example, a slice of 10 seconds has 10,000 data points along the time dimension. Thus, the CNN model has a very high demand for memory, while the memory for the graphics processing unit (GPU) is limited. In practice, we randomly sample segments from each recording for training, which not only decreases the GPU memory usage by reducing the dimensionality of time but also increases the number of training samples. For example, if we use seq_length of 1000ms, then a 180000ms recording can provide 180 independent samples.

We implement the deep learning framework using Tensorflow [22] with the following configurations. The (120, seq_length) spike detected matrices (see Fig. 3) are input to convolutional ReLU layers which filter the input spike train with 2×5 kernels and stride of (1, 1). It is interesting to note several biologically inspired hyperparameters in Table 1. Seq_length is the slice length that we use to split the recordings. Kernel_size and stride in CNN correspond to propagation signals, synaptic coupling and correlation between channels. Short latency, monosynaptic, interactions are in a range of 2-4 ms. Propagation signals occurring between nearby electrodes have an average latency of 0.3 ms to 0.7 ms. We choose a kernel size of 2×5 and stride of (1, 1) to capture propagation signals and synaptic coupling. Hyperparameters are described in Table 2. Max pooling is then applied after each convolutional ReLU layer. The feature maps are input for fully connected layers with 2 output nodes for the binary classification.

4.2 Testing

For testing, we define Consensus Prediction to measure the performance of predictions for the whole recordings. Consensus Prediction synthesizes results from odd numbers of short slices by majority voting, which can significantly improve the prediction accuracy for a long recording. This is because not all of the short time-slices can be expected to contain useful information. The results of mouse MEA recordings in Section 5 are reported with Consensus Prediction.

4.3 Implementation

We implement a framework that can distribute the convolutional neural network into multiple (N) GPUs to ease the burden on GPU memory. Each GPU contains an entire copy of the deep learning model. We first split the training batch evenly into N sub-batches. Each GPU only processes one of the sub-batches. Then we collect gradients from each replicate of the deep learning model, aggregate them together and update all the replicates. With 3 NVIDIA GeForce GTX 1080s, each of which has a memory of 11178 MB, we can handle spike train segments of 14 seconds with batch size of 24.

Table 1. Bio-inspired parameters

Para	Biological Justification	value
Seq_length	The appropriate slice length which can represent a recording	4000 ms
Kernel_size	Propogation signals	(2,5)
Stride	Synaptic coupling, correlation between channels	(1,1)

Table 2. Hyperparameters

Hyperparameters	Value
Batch size	24
Epoch	5000
Dropout rate	0.5

5 Empirical Evaluation

We focus our evaluation mainly on the accuracy of predicting genotype. We use Consensus Prediction, which is the majority voting result of the sampled short slices, for the mouse recordings. We report the initial prediction accuracy of short slices for human iPSC recordings without Consensus Prediction, since the recording experiments are better controlled.

5.1 Performance Analysis

Results of our framework compared against other machine learning models on mouse recordings and human iPSC recordings are shown in Table 3 and Table 4 respectively. We compare our CNN model with Multilayer Perceptron(MLP) and feature based Logistic Regression. We use a two layer MLP, which shares the same hyperparameters with our model's fully connected layers. For Logistic Regression, we first extract features of firing rate and Pearson correlation coefficient between different electrodes for each recording, and then classify neuron genotypes based on these two features. For the mouse recordings, our CNN based deep learning approach improves the Consensus Prediction accuracy by 16.69% compared with feature based Logistic Regression. Fig 4 shows the Consensus Prediction accuracy. The accuracy improves by 5.92% using Consensus Prediction. Although not all of the short slices can be expected to contain enough useful spike patterns, we can overcome that when we synthesize multiple individual classification results from these short slices. For the human iPSC recordings, we report the prediction accuracy of short recording slices. Our model achieves accuracy of 96.18% even without Consensus Prediction, which is a 15.59% improvement over feature based Logistic Regression. Our CNN based deep learning model also outperforms MLP on both of the two sets of recordings by 7.00% and

7.81% respectively, which shows CNN's advantage of local feature extraction using convolutional kernels over MLP.

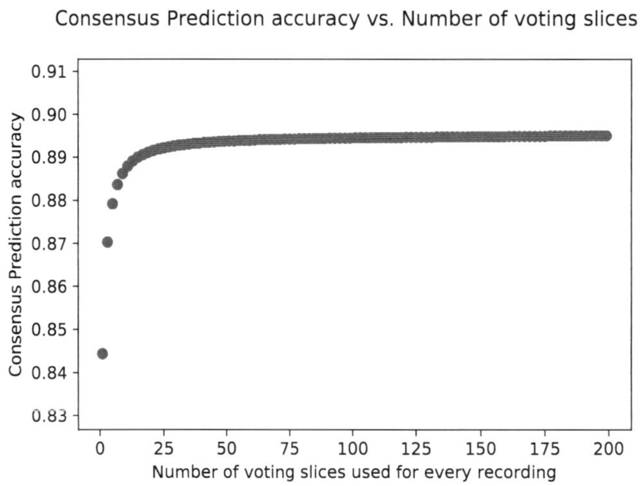

Fig. 4. Consensus Prediction accuracy vs. number of short slices used for mouse recordings.

Fig 5 shows the trend of accuracy versus the choice of seq_length for human iPSC. For the effect of seq_length on accuracy, there exists a trade off between number of training samples and representation of a whole recording. The short slices contain less information but can provide more independent training samples. For deep learning models, larger numbers of training slices help more than a larger sample. However, we still cannot choose too small of a seq_length, since a too short slice is not representative for a recording. Given the data we currently have, we use a seq_length of 4000 ms.

Dropout proved to be such a good regularizer that it was fine to use a larger than necessary network or train too many epochs and simply let dropout regularize it [27]. Dropout consistently added 2% - 4% relative performance. Our model converged best with Adam optimizer compared with Vanilla gradient descent, Adagrad [28], Adadelta [29] and RMSprop [30].

5.2 Case Study

It is challenging to classify the genotype of mouse MEA recordings due to the differences in recordings taken from neurons of different DIV, different mice and different recordings. Considering that the neuron firing patterns change drastically with different DIV, we use two subsets of mouse recording data (Exp1 and Exp2), recorded at 6 DIV and 10 DIV respectively, to study the effect of Consensus Prediction. Fig. 6 shows the prediction accuracy versus number

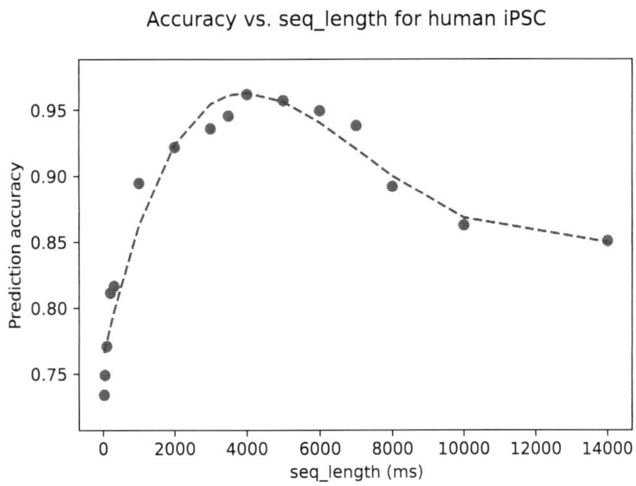

Fig. 5. Accuracy vs. seq_length trend for human iPSC recordings.

Table 3. Consensus Prediction performance comparison of our deep learning model with Multilayer Perceptrons and Logistic Regression on mouse recordings.

Model	Accuracy on Testing
Convolutional Neural Network	**0.8951**
Multilayer Perceptron	0.8366
Logistic Regression	0.7671

Table 4. Performance comparison of our deep learning model with Multilayer Perceptrons and Logistic Regression on iPSC recordings.

Model	Accuracy on Testing
Convolutional Neural Network	**0.9618**
Multilayer Perceptron	0.8921
Logistic Regression	0.8321

of voting slices in Consensus Prediction. By taking one subset of experiments all recorded at 6 DIV, we achieve a Consensus Prediction accuracy of 95.91% for Exp1. Similarly, we achieve a Consensus Prediction accuracy of 94.12% for recordings in Exp2, which are all at 10 DIV. Using Consensus Prediction, we improve the prediction accuracy by 12.70% and 11.68% for Exp1 and Exp2 respectively, which indicates that combining information from different parts of one recording significantly helps improve the performance.

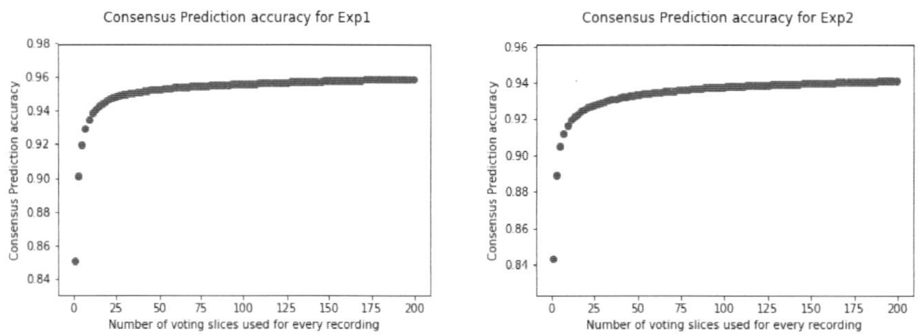

Fig. 6. Consensus Prediction accuracy for Exp1 and Exp2.

6 Discussion

We have addressed the issue of classifying different genotype MEA recordings by proposing a deep learning framework. We split the long recordings into smaller slices, which not only eases the burden on GPU memory but also provides more training samples for the deep learning model. We use Consensus Prediction during testing, to predict the genotype for a recording. This paper is a proof of principle for classification via deep learning of in-virtro MEA recordings. Clearly, however, more work is needed before it can be known if deep learning will be a generally useful technique for classification of neural cell genotypes or drug effects from *in vitro* MEA recordings. For example, one can use more recordings and MEAs with larger numbers of probes in future work.

7 Acknowledgement

This research was sponsored by the U.S. Army Research Laboratory and Defense Advanced Research Projects Agency under Cooperative Agreement Number W911NF-15-2-0056, Cohen Veterans Biosciences and the Larry L. Hillblom Foundation. We acknowledge helpful comments from Ken Tovar.

References

1. Krizhevsky, A., Sutskever, I., and Hinton, G. E.: Imagenet classification with deep convolutional neural networks. In: Advances in Neural Information Processing Systems, pp. 1097-1105. (2012)
2. Graves, A., Mohamed, A. R., and Hinton, G.: Speech recognition with deep recurrent neural networks. In: 2013 IEEE International Conference on Acoustics, Speech and Signal Processing, pp. 6645-6649. (2013)
3. Collobert, R., Weston, J.: A unified architecture for natural language processing: Deep neural networks with multitask learning. In: Proceedings of the 25th international conference on Machine learning, pp. 160167. ACM (2008)
4. Silver, D., Schrittwieser, J., Simonyan, K., Antonoglou, I., Huang, A., Guez, A., Hubert, T., Baker, L., Lai, M., Bolton, A. and Chen, Y.: Mastering the game of go without human knowledge. Nature, 550(7676), pp. 354. (2017)
5. Van Leeuwen, K. G., H. Sun, M. Tabaeizadeh, A. F. Struck, M. J. A. M. Van Putten, and M. B. Westover.: Detecting abnormal electroencephalograms using deep convolutional networks. Clinical Neurophysiology 130 (1), pp. 77-84. (2019)
6. Schirrmeister, R.T., Springenberg, J.T., Fiederer, L.D.J., Glasstetter, M., Eggensperger, K., Tangermann, M., Hutter, F., Burgard, W. and Ball, T.: Deep learning with convolutional neural networks for EEG decoding and visualization. Human Brain Mapping 38(11), pp. 5391-5420. (2017)
7. Kell, A.J., Yamins, D.L., Shook, E.N., Norman-Haignere, S.V. and McDermott, J.H.: A task-optimized neural network replicates human auditory behavior, predicts brain responses, and reveals a cortical processing hierarchy. Neuron, 98(3), pp. 630-644. (2018)
8. Buccino, A.P., Ness, T.V., Einevoll, G.T., Cauwenberghs, G. and Hfliger, P.D.: Localizing neuronal somata from multi-electrode array in-vivo recordings using deep learning. In: 39th Annual International Conference of the IEEE Engineering in Medicine and Biology Society (EMBC), pp. 974-977. IEEE (2017)
9. LeCun, Y., Bottou, L., Bengio, Y. and Haffner, P.: Gradient-based learning applied to document recognition. In: Proceedings of the IEEE, 86(11), pp. 2278-2324. (1998)
10. Buccino, A.P., Kordovan, M., Ness, T.V.B., Merkt, B., Hfliger, P.D., Fyhn, M., Cauwenberghs, G., Rotter, S. and Einevoll, G.T.: Combining biophysical modeling and deep learning for multi-electrode array neuron localization and classification. Journal of neurophysiology. (2018)
11. Buccino, A.P., Ness, T.V., Einevoll, G.T., Cauwenberghs, G. and Hfliger, P.D.: A Deep Learning Approach for the Classification of Neuronal Cell Types. In: 2018 40th Annual International Conference of the IEEE Engineering in Medicine and Biology Society (EMBC), pp. 999-1002. IEEE (2018)
12. Obien, M.E.J., Deligkaris, K., Bullmann, T., Bakkum, D.J. and Frey, U.: Revealing neuronal function through microelectrode array recordings. Frontiers in neuroscience 8, pp. 423. (2015)
13. Turner, T.N., Sharma, K., Oh, E.C., Liu, Y.P., Collins, R.L., Sosa, M.X., Auer, D.R., Brand, H., Sanders, S.J., Moreno-De-Luca, D. and Pihur, V.: Loss of -catenin function in severe autism. Nature 520(7545), pp. 51. (2015)
14. Matter, C., Pribadi, M., Liu, X. and Trachtenberg, J.T.: Delta-Catenin is required for the maintenance of neural structure and function in mature cortex in vivo. Neuron 64(3), pp. 320-327. (2009)
15. Kosik, K.S., Donahue, C.P., Israely, I., Liu, X. and Ochiishi, T.: Delta-Catenin at the synapticadherens junction. Trends in cell biology, 15(3), pp. 172-178. (2015)

16. Lalli, M.A., Jang, J., Park, J.H.C., Wang, Y., Guzman, E., Zhou, H., Audouard, M., Bridges, D., Tovar, K.R., Papuc, S.M. and Tutulan-Cunita, A.C.: Haploinsufficiency of BAZ1B contributes to Williams syndrome through transcriptional dysregulation of neurodevelopmental pathways. Human molecular genetics 25(7), pp. 1294-1306. (2016)
17. Bays, M., Magano, L.F., Rivera, N., Flores, R. and Jurado, L.A.P.: Mutational mechanisms of Williams-Beuren syndrome deletions. The American Journal of Human Genetics 73(1), pp. 131-151. (2003)
18. Morris, C.A., Lenhoff, H.M. and Wang, P.P. eds.: Williams-Beuren syndrome: Research, evaluation, and treatment. JHU Press. (2016)
19. Tovar, K.R. and Westbrook, G.L.: Amino-terminal ligands prolong NMDA receptor-mediated EPSCs. Journal of Neuroscience 32(23), pp. 8065-8073. (2012)
20. Tovar, K.R., Bridges, D.C., Wu, B., Randall, C., Audouard, M., Jang, J., Hansma, P.K. and Kosik, K.S.: Recording action potential propagation in single axons using multi-electrode arrays. bioRxiv, pp. 126425. (2017)
21. Quiroga, R.Q., Nadasdy, Z. and Ben-Shaul, Y.: Unsupervised spike detection and sorting with wavelets and superparamagnetic clustering. Neural Computation 16(8), pp. 1661-1687. (2014)
22. Abadi, M., Agarwal, A., Barham, P., Brevdo, E., Chen, Z., Citro, C., Corrado, G.S., Davis, A., Dean, J., Devin, M. and Ghemawat, S.: TensorFlow: Large-scale machine learning on heterogeneous systems, 2015. Software available from tensorflow. org, 1(2). (2015)
23. Srivastava, N., Hinton, G., Krizhevsky, A., Sutskever, I. and Salakhutdinov, R.: Dropout: a simple way to prevent neural networks from overfitting. The Journal of Machine Learning Research 15(1), pp. 1929-1958. (2014)
24. Prechelt, L.: Early stopping-but when?. In: Neural Networks: Tricks of the trade, pp. 55-69. Springer, Berlin, Heidelberg. (1998)
25. Ioffe, S. and Szegedy, C.: Batch normalization: Accelerating deep network training by reducing internal covariate shift. arXiv preprint arXiv:1502.03167. (2015)
26. Kingma, D.P. and Ba, J.: Adam: A method for stochastic optimization. arXiv preprint arXiv:1412.6980. (2014)
27. Wu, H. and Gu, X.: Towards dropout training for convolutional neural networks. Neural Networks 71, pp. 1-10. (2015)
28. Duchi, J., Hazan, E. and Singer, Y.: Adaptive subgradient methods for online learning and stochastic optimization. Journal of Machine Learning Research, pp.2121-2159. (2011)
29. Zeiler, M.D.: ADADELTA: an adaptive learning rate method. arXiv preprint arXiv:1212.5701. (2012)
30. Tieleman, T. and Hinton, G.: Lecture 6.5-RMSProp, COURSERA: Neural networks for machine learning. University of Toronto, Technical Report. (2012)

Knowledge-guided Text Structuring in Clinical Trials

Yingcheng Sun and Kenneth Loparo

Case Western Reserve University, Cleveland OH 44106, USA
{yxs489,kal4}@case.edu

Abstract. Clinical trial records are variable resources or the analysis of patients and diseases. Information extraction from free text such as eligibility criteria and summary of results and conclusions in clinical trials would better support computer-based eligibility query formulation and electronic patient screening. Previous research has focused on extracting information from eligibility criteria, with usually a single pair of medical entity and attribute, but seldom considering other kinds of free text with multiple entities, attributes and relations that are more complex for parsing. In this paper, we propose a knowledge-guided text structuring framework with an automatically generated knowledge base as training corpus and word dependency relations as context information to transfer free text into formal, computer-interpretable representations. Experimental results show that our method can achieve overall high precision and recall, demonstrating the effectiveness and efficiency of the proposed method.

Keywords: Information Extraction, Natural Language Processing, Distant Supervision Machine Learning, Clinical Trials.

1 Introduction

The growing volume of clinical trial records are one of the most valuable sources of evidence on the efficacy of treatments in humans. In clinical trial records, many items like eligibility criteria and summary of results and conclusions are usually written in unstructured free text. The free – text format and lack of standardization have inhibited the effective use for automatic identification of eligible patients from electronic health records (EHRs), and makes extracting the target data for evidence - based synthesis burdensome.

To structure the free text in clinical trial records, three major elements need to be extracted: entity, attribute and the relations between them. Figure 1 shows an example of eligibility criteria with three types of elements.

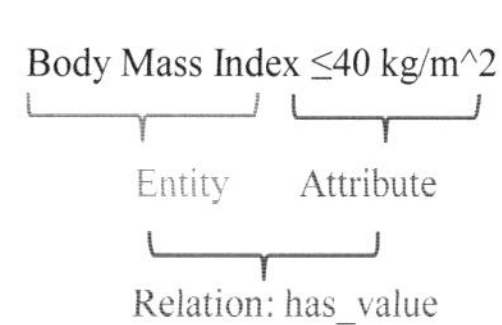

Fig. 1. Example of free text annotated by entity, attribute and relation between them

"Body Mass Index" is the medical entity, often identified as Unified Medical Language System (UMLS) concept with an unique identifier (CUI). "≤40 kg/m^2" is the attribute of "Body Mass Index" with value 40, unit "kg/m^2" and comparison "≤", and "has_value" is the relationship between the entity and its corresponding attribute. Most previous work has focused on structuring eligibility criteria that usually only contains a single pair of entity and attribute in one sentence like the example in Figure 1, while information extraction in other types of free text has received little attention. The free text of a clinical trial like summary of results and conclusions may contain more than one medical entity and associated attributes, with multiple mappings needing to be inferred. Figure 2 shows examples of two long paragraphs of free text with multiple entities and attributes.

Patients who are taking any concomitant medications that might confound assessments of pain relief, such as psychotropic drugs, antidepressants, sedative hypnotics or any analgesics taken within three days or five times of their elimination half-lives, whichever is longer. Selective serotonin reuptake inhibitors (SSRIs) and selective noradrenaline reuptake inhibitors (SNRIs) are permitted if the patient has been on a stable dose for at least 30 days prior to screening. [NCT04018612]

M/F ages 21-45 with a history of smoked cocaine use at least twice a week for the past six months. A normal resting 12-lead electrocardiograph (ECG) and blood pressure of less than 140/90 mmHg. [NCT01640873]

Fig. 2. Examples of long paragraphs with multiple entities and attributes. They is acquired from ClinicalTrials.gov

The possible entities in the first paragraph are: medications, pain, psychotropic drugs, antidepressants, sedative hypnotics, analgesics, elimination half-lives, screening, Selective serotonin reuptake inhibitors (SSRIs) and selective noradrenaline reuptake inhibitors (SNRIs). The possible attributes are concomitant, within three days, five times, at least 30 days prior. After comparing all the information extraction tools, especially those for eligibility criteria such as cTAKES, MetaMap and Criteria2query, we find that there are no tools so far that can extract all the entities and attributes correctly, and neither do their relations after our experiments. For the second paragraph, we found the same issues: entity and attributes are missing, and relations extracted are not accurate. Therefore, extracting all the possible candidates and detecting the correct relations among all candidates becomes an important concern.

Because of the complexities of inferring "many-to-many" relationships, simple text parsing methods, such as regular expressions, may not be an effective way to extract and structure the elements in the target text [15, 19]. Machine learning models are adopted in some systems for the relation extraction task, such as support vector machine and convolutional neural networks [23]. However, traditional machine learning models rely on human annotation for training data generation, which is time and labor consuming. Moreover, the reliance on human annotation further limits the systems to certain pre-specified relational types and makes it unable to further extend the systems to new relational types.

Each medical entity has its own value range and unit format that can be easily obtained from an online knowledge base such as Wikipedia and Observational Health Data Sciences and Informatics (OHDSI), so those formats can be used as attribute constraints when inferring the relations [13, 14, 16, 17]. In this paper, we present a novel distant supervision approach that generates training data automatically by aligning texts and a knowledge base, and learns to automatically extract relations between a medical entity and its corresponding attribute. We also use the syntactical structure of a sentence to assign the mapping direction because all relations are directional, pointing from the entity to its attribute. Experimental results show that our method achieves overall high precision and recall, demonstrating the effectiveness and efficiency of the proposed method.

The rest of the paper is organized as follows. In Section 2, we present related work. In Section 3, we propose the knowledge-based distant supervision approach. In Section 4, we introduce the datasets, comparison methods and evaluation metrics, as well as experimental results. We conclude our work in Section 5.

2 Related Work

Parsing clinical text is important to leverage the reuse of clinical information for automatic decision support. Following this assumption, various methods and techniques have been recently developed to transform clinical trial protocol text into computable representations that can be used to facilitate automated tasks.

2.1 Ontology-based and rule-based approaches

Riccardo et al. [1] proposed a clinical trial search framework eTACTS that combines tag mining of free-text eligibility criteria and interactive retrieval based on dynamic tag clouds to reduce the number of resulting trials returned by a simple search. Tu et al. [2] designed the Eligibility Rule Grammar and Ontology for clinical eligibility criteria and used it to transform free-text eligibility criteria into computable criteria [3]. Bhattacharya and Cantor [4] proposed a template-based representation of eligibility criteria for standardizing criteria statements. Weng et al. [5] leveraged text mining to develop a Unified Medical Language System – a semantic like network-based representation for clinical trial eligibility criteria called EliXR.

2.2 Machine learning based approaches

Methods based on machine learning models for standardizing categorical eligibility criteria were developed, such as EliXRTIME [6] for temporal knowledge representation and Valx [7] for numeric expression extraction and normalization. Much of the more recent work on distant supervision since has been focused on the task of relation extraction [8, 9] and classification of Twitter/microblog texts [10]. Supervised distant supervision is used to automatically extract Population/Problem, Intervention, Comparator, and Outcome (PICO criteria) in clinical trial records [11].

Despite these efforts, there is still a need to develop a solution for directly transforming all kinds of free text in clinical trial records to structured information, with a computational output data format. We explored the method of information extraction from free text in clinical trials with knowledge-based distant supervision in our previous research [18, 20, 21, 22], and provide more details in this paper.

3 Knowledge-Based Distant Supervision Framework

In this section, we propose a probabilistic linking model to deal with the task of entity linking with its corresponding attribute. The overall framework is shown in Fig. 2.

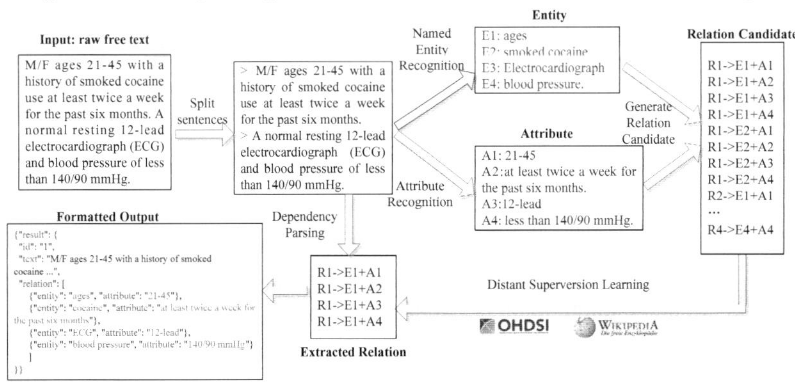

Fig. 3. The overview of the knowledge-based distant supervision framework

The inputs are text paragraphs from a clinical trial corpus. Generally, eligibility criteria are organized by lines, but other types of clinical records are written in paragraphs, so the first step is to split the input text into sentences. After separating the input text into sentences, medical entities need to be annotated as UMLS concept and attributes need to be recognized as temporal expressions or value expressions. We use part of speech(POS) pattern mining to build the knowledge base from the knowledge sources medical dictionary, Wikipedia and OHDSI as Fig. 4 shows.

We use a small training dataset to train the random forest classifier, and refine the results manually. In the knowledge base table, the first column is "term", which lists medical concepts. They can be used to improve the entity recognition. The second and third columns are value and units that can be used to improve the relation extractions. For example, suppose we identified two concepts: "blood pressure" and "body weights", and have two values as their attributes. It is highly possible that the value ending with "mmHg" will be blood pressure's attribute and the value ending with "kg" will be body weight's attribute because they are their usually used units. We found that unit is more useful than value in the relations recognition because in clinical trials, the values from patients are usually not in a normal range.

Knowledge Base

Term	Value	Unit
Electrocardiography	12	lead
Heart rate	40 to 60	beats/min
blood pressure	120/80	mmHg
Body weight	20	kg
hormone	0.8	x
Body mass index	95th	percentile
age	40	years
Hematocrit	0.36	

Fig. 4. Knowledge sources and a snippet of the knowledge base

We updated the algorithms in Criteria2Query by introducing the knowledge base for named entity recognition [12]. After this step, M entities and N attributes are extracted from the free-text record automatically, and then we have M*N relational candidates. Next, we use the Stanford dependency parser CoreNLP to discover the syntactical structure of a sentence.

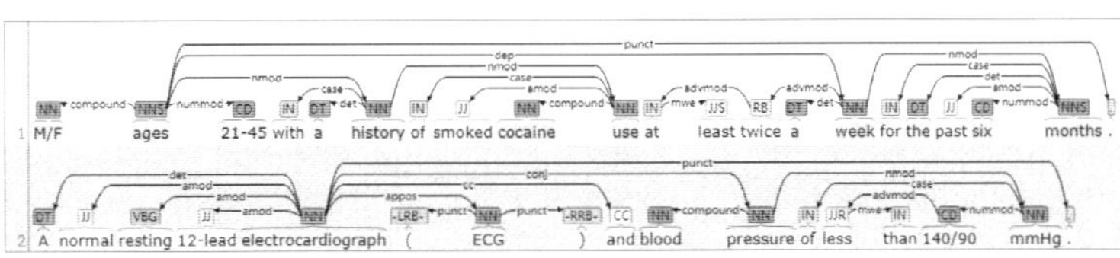

Fig. 5. Word dependency extracted by CoreNLP for of the second paragraph in Fig.1

But this tool will extract all the relations among all the words. Most of them are not our targets. So we simplified the CoreNLP tool and only extracted relations that we concern based on identified named entities in last step, as Fig. 6 shows.

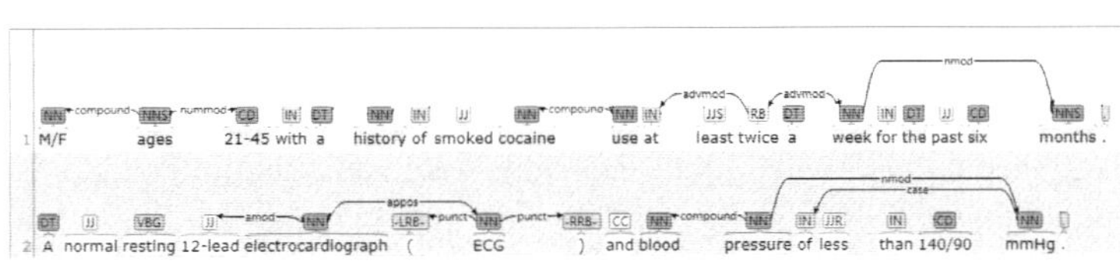

Fig. 6. The simplified word dependency extraction result for the second paragraph in Fig.1

We assume that there is an underlying distribution P over the relations given the parsing results, and then the probability of a relation r whose dependency parsing result is dep could be expressed using the following formula:

$$P(r|dep) = P(e, a|\ dep)$$

Where e is the entity and a is the attribute. Meanwhile, distant supervision is applied on all candidate relations and the probability of a relation r whose distant supervision learning result is *sup* could be expressed as the following formula:

$$P(r|sup) = P(e, a|\ sup)$$

We use Wikipedia and OHDSI as the knowledge base, and model the entity by its value range and unit. For example, the standard written format for blood pressure is" *\d+/\d*", and its unit is "mmHg", so "115/75 mmHg" would have higher probability to be a blood pressure than "11-25". Given the two types of relational probabilities, we could further define the relational assignment probability as:

$$P(r|s)= \theta \cdot P(r|sup) + (1-\theta) \cdot P(r|dep)$$

Where θ is a parameter that balances the two parts and s is the sentence. Next, we select the probability with largest value i.e., the most likely mapping between the entity e and attribute a given a sentence s as context.

After the recognition and extraction of entities and their attributes and identification of the relations between them, the entities were encoded by the standard UMLS terminology. To support downstream large-scale analysis, we standardized the output results in the JSON format. An example output format is illustrated in Figure 2.

4 Experiment

To evaluate the efficiency of our proposed framework, we assess the accuracy and recall of the information extraction in this section. The experimental setup includes a ThinkPad laptop with Intel Core i5 2.50 GHz processor and 10 GB RAM. In our experiment, we use the clinical trial data obtained from ClinicalTrials.gov. 100 clinical trial records were randomly picked and 477 free-text records including eligibility criteria and summary of results and conclusions were acquired. Next, three annotators were asked to label each record with entity, attribute and their relations, and we used the labels agreed to by at least two annotators as the ground truth, with a total of 386 records labeled in this manner. All annotations were completed in Brat [24], a web-based annotation tool. Fig. 7 shows the results.

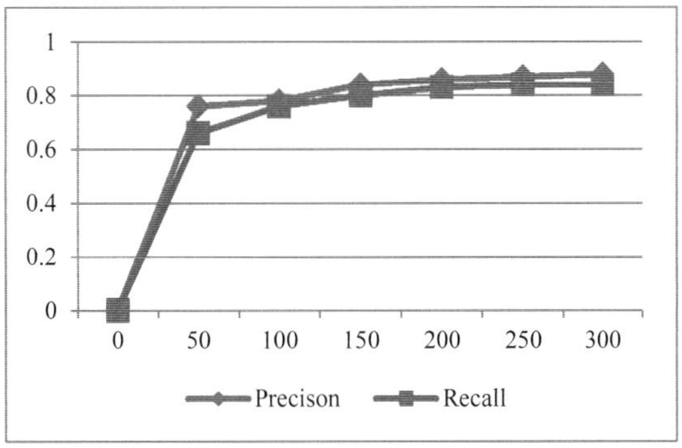

Fig. 7. Learning curves for recognition tasks by different sizes of training sizes.

The results show that when the number of training data is over 200, the performance reaches a stable status, and the average accuracy is 0.83, and the average recall is 0.79 that show relatively high effectiveness. Fig. 8 shows an example of the JSON format output. We do not parse the attribute further because we focus more on the issue of relationship inference. Several tools can be used to separate the attributes into fine-grained parts.


```
{"result": {
  "id": "1",
  "text": " M/F ages 21-45 with a history of smoked cocaine use at least twice a week for the past six months. A normal resting 12-lead electrocardiograph (ECG) and blood pressure of less than 140/90 mmHg.",
  "relation": [
    {"entity": "ages", "attribute": "21-45"},
    {"entity": "cocaine", "attribute": "at least twice a week for the past six months"},
    {"entity": "ECG", "attribute": "12-lead"},
    {"entity": "blood pressure", "attribute": "140/90 mmHg"}
  ]
}}
```


Fig. 8. Example of the JSON format output

5 Discussion And Future Work

Structured clinical trial records can enable more rigorous comparisons of trial populations and better meta-analyses of collective generalizability of related clinical trials and also pave the path to thorough studies of clinical trial participants and their representativeness of the general population. In this paper, we proposed a knowledge - based distant supervision framework to extract information from all types of free text data in clinical trials records. Our experiments demonstrate the effectiveness of our method. In the future, we will explore the active learning methods [18] or reinforcement learning [20, 22] to annotate the criteria eligibility to reduce the annotation cost. Also, we are interested in constructing the query expression for clinical trials records and build the interface to search all kinds of clinical trial records.

Acknowledgment

This work was supported by the Ohio Department of Higher Education, the Ohio Federal Research Network and the Wright State Applied Research Corporation under award WSARC-16-00530 (C4ISR: Human-Centered Big Data).

References

1. Miotto, R., Jiang, S., Weng, C.: eTACTS: a method for dynamically filtering clinical trial search results. Journal of biomedical informatics 46(6), 1060-1067 (2013).
2. Tu, S., Peleg, M., Carini, S., Rubin, D., Sim, I.: Ergo: A template based expression language for encoding eligibility criteria. Technical report (2009).
3. Tu, S.W., Peleg, M., Carini, S., Bobak, M., Ross, J., Rubin, D., Sim, I.: A practical method for transforming free-text eligibility criteria into computable criteria. Journal of biomedical informatics 44(2), 239-250 (2011).
4. Bhattacharya, S., Cantor, M.N.: Analysis of eligibility criteria representation in industry-standard clinical trial protocols. Journal of Biomedical Informatics 46(5), 805-813 (2013).
5. Weng, C., Wu, X., Luo, Z., Boland, M.R., Theodoratos, D., Johnson, S.B.: EliXR: an approach to eligibility criteria extraction and representation. Journal of the American Medical Informatics Association 18(Supplement_1), 116-124 (2011).
6. Boland, M.R., Tu, S.W., Carini, S., Sim, I., Weng, C.: EliXR-TIME: a temporal knowledge representation for clinical research eligibility criteria. In: AMIA summits on translational science proceedings, p.71, (2012).
7. Hao, T., Liu, H. and Weng, C.: Valx: a system for extracting and structuring numeric lab test comparison statements from text. Methods of information in medicine, 55(03), 266-275 (2016).
8. Nguyen, T.V.T. and Moschitti, A.: Joint distant and direct supervision for relation extraction. In: Proceedings of 5th International Joint Conference on Natural Language Processing, pp. 732-740 (2011).
9. Angeli, G., Tibshirani, J., Wu, J., Manning, C.D.: Combining distant and partial supervision for relation extraction. In: Proceedings of the 2014 conference on empirical methods in natural language processing (EMNLP), pp. 1556-1567 (2014).
10. Purver, M., Battersby, S.: Experimenting with distant supervision for emotion classification. In: Proceedings of the 13th Conference of the European Chapter of the Association for Computational Linguistics, pp. 482-491. Association for Computational Linguistics (2012).
11. Wallace, B.C., Kuiper, J., Sharma, A., Zhu, M., Marshall, I.J.: Extracting PICO sentences from clinical trial reports using supervised distant supervision. The Journal of Machine Learning Research 17(1), 4572–4596 (2016).
12. Yuan, C., Ryan, P.B., Ta, C., Guo, Y., Li, Z., Hardin, J., Makadia, R., Jin, P., Shang, N., Kang, T., Weng, C.: Criteria2Query: a natural language interface to clinical databases for

cohort definition. Journal of the American Medical Informatics Association 26(4), 294-305 (2019).
13. Sun, Y., Li, Q.: The research situation and prospect analysis of meta-search engines. In: 2nd International Conference on Uncertainty Reasoning and Knowledge Engineering, pp. 224-229. IEEE, Jalarta, Indonesia (2012).
14. Li, Q., Zou, Y., Sun, Y.: Ontology based user personalization mechanism in meta search engine. In: 2nd International Conference on Uncertainty Reasoning and Knowledge Engineering, pp. 230-234. IEEE, Jalarta, Indonesia (2012).
15. Li, Q., Sun, Y., Xue, B.: Complex query recognition based on dynamic learning mechanism. Journal of Computational Information Systems 8(20), 8333-8340 (2012).
16. Li, Q., Zou, Y., Sun, Y.: User Personalization Mechanism in Agent-based Meta Search Engine. Journal of Computational Information Systems 8(20), 1-8 (2012).
17. Li, Q., Sun, Y.: An agent based intelligent meta search engine. In: International Conference on Web Information Systems and Mining, pp. 572-579. Springer, Berlin, Heidelberg (2012).
18. Sun, Y., Loparo, K.: Context Aware Image Annotation in Active Learning with Batch Mode. In: 43rd Annual Computer Software and Applications Conference (COMPSAC), vol. 1, pp. 952-953. IEEE (2019).
19. Sun, Y., Loparo, K.: A Clicked-URL Feature for Transactional Query Identification. In 2019 IEEE 43rd Annual Computer Software and Applications Conference (COMPSAC) , vol. 1, pp. 950-951. IEEE (2019).
20. Sun, Y., Loparo, K.: Topic Shift Detection in Online Discussions using Structural Context. In 2019 IEEE 43rd Annual Computer Software and Applications Conference (COMPSAC) , vol. 1, pp. 948-949. IEEE (2019).
21. Sun, Y., Loparo, K.: Information Extraction from Free Text in Clinical Trials with Knowledge-Based Distant Supervision. In: IEEE 43rd Annual Computer Software and Applications Conference (COMPSAC), vol. 1, pp. 954-955. IEEE (2019).
22. Sun, Y., Loparo, K.: Learning - based Adaptation Framework for Elastic Software Systems. In: Proceedings of 31st International Conference on Software Engineering & Knowledge Engineering, pp. 281-286. IEEE, Lisbon, Portugal (2019).
23. Tang B, Cao H, Wu Y, Jiang M, Xu H. Recognizing clinical entities in hospital discharge summaries using Structural Support Vector Machines with word representation features. BMC Med Inform Decis Mak. 2013;13(Suppl 1):S1.
24. Brat Rapid Annotation Tool. http://brat.nlplab.org

Authors Index

Announcement

World Congress DSA 2020

The Frontiers in Intelligent Data and Signal Analysis
July 12 - 23, 2020, New York, USA

www.worldcongressdsa.com

We are inviting you to our fourth World congress on the Frontiers of Signal and Image Analysis DSA 2020 to New York, Germany.

This congress will feature three events:

- the 16th International Conference on Machine Learning and Data Mining MLDM (www.mldm.de),
- the 20th Industrial Conference on Data Mining ICDM (www.data-mining-forum.de),
- and the 15th International Conference on Mass Data Analysis of Signals and Images in Artificial Intelligence&Pattern Recognition MDA-AI&PR (www.mda-signals.de).

Workshops and Tutorial will also be given.

Come to join us to the most exciting event on Intelligent Data and Signal Analysis.

Sincerely your,
Prof. Dr. Petra Perner

MLDM icdm mda

www.mldm.de www.data-mining-forum.de www.mda-signals.de

Journals by ibai-publishing

The journals are free on-line journals but having in parallel hardcopies of the journals. The free on-line access to the content of the paper should ensure fast and easy access to new research developments for researchers all over the world. The hardcopy of the journal can be purchased by individuals, companies, and libraries.

Transactions on Machine Learning and Data Mining
(ISSN: 1865-6781)

The International Journal "Transactions on Machine Learning and Data Mining" is a periodical appearing twice a year. The journal focuses on novel theoretical work for particular topics in Data Mining and applications on Data Mining.

Net Price (per issue): EURO 100
Germany (per issue): EURO 107 (incl. 7% VAT)

Submission for the journal should be send to:
info@ibai-publishing.org

For more information visited: www.ibai-publishing.org/journal/mldm/about.html

Transactions on Case-Based Reasoning
(ISSN:1867-366X)

The International Journal "Transactions on Case-Based Reasoning" is a periodical appearing once a year.

Net Price (per issue): EURO 100
Germany (per issue): EURO 107 (incl. 7% VAT)

Submission for the journal should be send to:
info@ibai-publishing.org

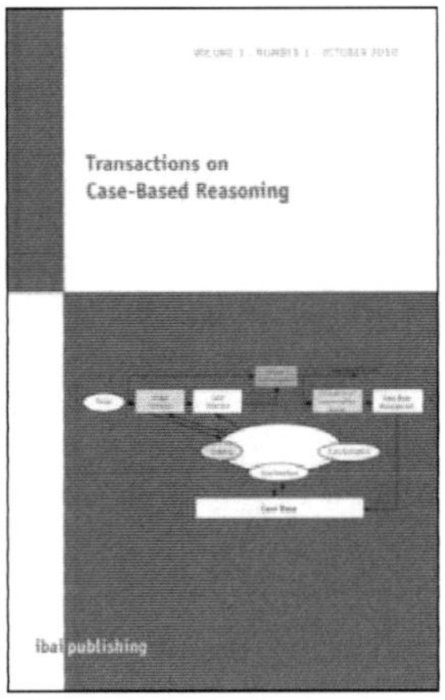

For more information visited: www.ibai-publishing.org/journal/cbr/about.html